TO BE A
WOMAN

· · · · · · ·

TO BE A WOMAN: THE BIRTH OF THE CONSCIOUS FEMININE

. . . .

EDITED BY

CONNIE ZWEIG

JEREMY P. TARCHER, INC.
Los Angeles

Someday there will be girls and women whose name will no longer signify merely an opposite of the masculine, but something in itself, something that makes one think not of any complement and limit, but only of life and existence: the feminine human being.

—RAINER MARIA RILKE
Letters to a Young Poet

Library of Congress Cataloging-in-Publication Data

To be a woman : the birth of the conscious feminine / edited by Connie Zweig.
    p.   cm.
  Includes bibliographical references.
  ISBN 0-87477-561-2
    1. Women—Psychology.   2. Femininity (Psychology)   I. Zweig, Connie.
  HQ1206.T55   1990   89-49506
  155.6'33—dc20   CIP

Jeremy P. Tarcher, Inc.
5858 Wilshire Blvd., Suite 200
Los Angeles, CA 90036

Distributed by St. Martin's Press, New York

Design by Tanya Maiboroda

Manufactured in the United States of America
10 9 8 7 6 5 4 3 2 1
First Edition

CONTENTS

. . . .

Prologue   I

PART 1
Retracing Our Common Evolution:
The Search for the Abandoned Feminine

1. Sukie Colegrave
   The Unfolding Feminine Principle in Human Consciousness   19

2. Riane Eisler
   *Social Transformation and the Feminine: From Domination
   to Partnership*   27

3. Robert M. Stein
   From the Liberation of Women to the Liberation of the Feminine   38

PART 2
Re-Mothering Ourselves:
Healing Our Relationships with Women and the Feminine

4. Emily Hancock
   The Girl Within: Touchstone for Women's Identity   55

5. Nan Hunt
   In the Laps of the Mothers   64

6. Lynda W. Schmidt
   How the Father's Daughter Found Her Mother   76

7. Naomi Ruth Lowinsky
   *Mother of Mothers: The Power of the Grandmother
   in the Female Psyche*   86

8. Marion Woodman
   Conscious Femininity: Mother, Virgin, Crone   98

9. Kathleen Riordan Speeth
   The Madonna   III

PART 3

Re-Fathering Ourselves:
Healing Our Relationships with Men and the Masculine

10. Linda Schierse Leonard
    Redeeming the Father and Finding Feminine Spirit   125

11. Manisha Roy
    *Developing the Animus as a Step Toward the New Feminine
    Consciousness*   137

12. Jane Wheelwright
    The Breakdown of Animus Identification in Finding the Feminine   150

13. Polly Young-Eisendrath
    Rethinking Feminism, the Animus, and the Feminine   158

PART 4

Resacralizing the Female Body:
Healing Our Relationships with Rhythms, Instincts,
and Desires

14. Betty De Shong Meador
    Thesmophoria: A Women's Fertility Ritual   173

15. Deena Metzger
    Re-Vamping the World: On the Return of the Holy Prostitute   181

16. Elizabeth S. Strahan
    Beyond Blood: Women of That Certain Age   188

PART 5

Reawakening the Divine Feminine:
Healing Our Relationships with the Goddess Archetypes

17. Merlin Stone
    The Gifts from Reclaiming Goddess History   203

18. Jean Shinoda Bolen
    *Athena, Artemis, Aphrodite, and Initiation into the Conscious
    Feminine*   217

19. June Singer
    Finding the Lost Feminine in the Judeo-Christian Tradition   222

20. Sylvia Brinton Perera
    Descent to the Dark Goddess   234

PART 6
Renewing the World:
The Feminine and the Future

21. Genia Pauli Haddon
    The Personal and Cultural Emergence of Yang-Femininity   245

22. Edward C. Whitmont
    The Future of the Feminine   258

23. Robert A. Johnson
    Femininity Regained   268

Epilogue   271

Notes   275

ACKNOWLEDGMENTS

. . . .

My acknowledgments to:

The contributors to this volume: for your colorful tiles in the mosaic that portrays the abandoned Feminine and her reemergence as the Conscious Feminine in our lives.

The women in my motherline: my maternal grandmother, for the legacy of woundedness that drives the search for healing; my mother, for her steadfast commitment to her own search and to me, whom she reads like an open book; and my sister, for holding the opposite pole as a mirror reflection.

My friends and *sorors mysticas*: Marilyn Ferguson, for the precious gift of the written word and for her fierce loyalty to the search; Marian Rose —whose ideas permeate this book from beginning to end—for the truth and for our love; and Belinda Berman-Real, for lifelong sisterhood.

Suzanne Wagner, for holding my hand through the labyrinth; Jeremiah Abrams, for his sweet, patient friendship, thoughtful comments, and fruitful collaborations; Jeremy Tarcher, who stretched the rules to permit me to compile this book and who supports my creative efforts always; Steve Wolf, whose friendship has been a bottomless well of love.

And, finally, my father, whose rare combination of intelligence and spirit captured me. No matter how far I travel, I will always be your loving daughter.

PROLOGUE

· · · · · · ·

Like many creative efforts, this book was inspired by a dream:

I'm in my mother's dressing room. The wallpaper, a soft shade of olive, is covered with pink flower blossoms. Atop the marble bureau sits an ornate pink marble jewel box, a vase of dried pink roses, a framed photo—the twinkly, wide-eyed smile of me as a baby.

My mother approaches, wearing a long, black swinging skirt and tall, black leather boots. She's walking toward me, something on her mind. She sets down a green bowl of ripe apricots, motioning for me to help myself. As I bite into the sweetness, chewing all around the pit, I gaze out the window at the dark blue mountains in the background. I feel a longing for places far away from my mother's dressing room, places exotic, filled with the smell of strange spices and the lure of strange men.

My mother's voice jars me back to the small green room. "Let's do your hair for tonight." I sit on an embroidered stool before the mirror and she proceeds to tease my hair to three times its former size. She's looking pleased with herself, as the size of my head expands. Then she sets down the comb, takes both hands and begins to smooth down the edges, until a bubblelike shape forms. Then she lifts the hairspray and fills the air with the sticky mist. She folds her arms and looks satisfied.

I get up and begin to walk toward my bedroom, stopping off in the bathroom. My father's bloody head is in the bathroom sink.

Unlike many of my dreams, this one did not fade quickly into oblivion. It remained clear and all-of-a-piece in my mind, as if insisting on being recognized. It haunted me with questions: Why did I chop off my father's head? Why did I feel no remorse at this horrible act? Why did I let my mother redesign me? Why did her efforts feel so contrived, so incomplete?

In my hunger to understand these issues in my own development, I entered Jungian analysis. I had undergone several other forms of psycho-therapy, but I had not worked with the unconscious through my dreams. As I began to unravel the coded messages of this and other dreams, I also began to uncover some of the key steps in the dance of the developing Feminine principle within all women.

From this dream I learned that my alignment with my father—and, through him, with the male-dominant or patriarchal bias of society—had to be sacrificed. To be a woman—to fully, consciously own my female identity—I needed to sever the connection with the logical masculine mind that had run my life like the captain of a tight ship.

My father, a highly educated, generous, verbal, dominant personality, had eclipsed my mother in our household. Many of her gifts remained hidden to me. In the dream, I am beginning to let her shape me, to realign with her feminine influence. However, her efforts at this point are inadequate; she leaves me feeling only superficially touched and attractive only as a social stereotype. Her real gifts—as an artist of extraordinary talent and a perceptive student of human nature—are not yet available to me.

Before beginning the research that grew into this book, I had been a meditation teacher for many years. I was well versed in Hindu and Buddhist theories about the development of human consciousness. I understood that, like biological evolution, the evolution of consciousness proceeds in stages that unfold with specific experiences within the psyche. However, unlike biological evolution, psychological growth is a self-conscious process; it takes effort and intention to move ahead. This growth process can be sped up with certain practices that enhance our internal experiences, such as meditation and psychotherapy or analysis, as well as with the practical knowledge of how to integrate these experiences into conscious life.

As I began to read widely in Jungian depth psychology and women's spirituality and to speak with other women about their own psychological and spiritual development, I came to realize that my spiritual patriarchs had offered little insight to me *as a woman*. Eastern philosophies, rooted in monastic traditions, tend either to ignore gender differences or to assume women's lower spiritual status. (A few even propose that a person cannot attain the higher stages of evolution in a female body; she must await rebirth as a male.) Not one attends to the specific needs and gifts of women.

As I began to turn away from these hierarchical groups and their "sky gods" and to divest myself of their male-centered philosophical baggage, I began to look to my own experience, and to that of other women, to re-create my understanding of women's spiritual development. I began to ask pointed questions:

- What does it mean to be a woman in a man's world for those of us who do not wish to stay home and "become like our mothers" or to strive aggressively and "become like men"?

- Why do many women in conventional marriages, pinched into confining shapes and forced to carry the weight of feeling for two human beings, suddenly feel so angry that they are initiating divorces in droves?

- Why do some women express deep disappointment with the reality of career success and with the promises of feminism, so that they now say that in some essential way they have forgotten how to be a woman?

- Why are so many women rushing to have babies relatively late in life, in an attempt to ensure that they do not miss this quintessentially female experience?

- Why is interest in feminine spirituality and the Goddess so widespread? What is painfully absent for women in our culturally ordained religions, and what is present in this emerging one?

The answers can be found in a woman's longing to be authentically "feminine," to experience herself fully as a woman and, at the same time, to be a strong, independent individual whose power and authority are rooted within her. It is the search to meet this deeply felt need that has fueled these diverse cultural trends.

However, our society is so structured that it leaves this longing unmet. As Polly Young-Eisendrath and Florence Wiedemann point out in their profound book *Female Authority*, a woman cannot be both a healthy adult and an ideal woman. If she adopts a vocal, capable attitude, she is deemed too "masculine" and therefore becomes unattractive to men. On the other hand, if she chooses a style of femininity that is defined by men and a male-dominated culture, she is left dependent, powerless, and without choices. Either way, many women today report feeling deeply dissatisfied *as women*.

Slowly but surely, as I let myself steep in these troubling waters, there emerged a particular pattern of women's development that fits into the larger picture of human evolution and that appears to have direction and purpose, unfolding in an orderly way. It was almost as if I could see, in my mind's eye, one of those films of a flower unfolding through time-lapse photography, except this was an image of Woman.

Moreover, I observed a parallel development in my own life and in the larger culture. This Evolutionary Vision, described below, is a crucial link, which many had seen before me: Evolution moves through the individual and the collective on a parallel track. In fact, individual psychological development recapitulates the entire development of the species. In this way we are intimately connected to all human beings in any stage of evolution.

Also, for this reason, those few individuals who develop advanced modes of awareness can serve as beacons pointing the way for the rest. This principle may hold true not only for saints and sages who appear to be leagues ahead of us; it also may mean that those people who are doing the difficult incremental work of psychological differentiation hold the keys to our future as well.

THE EVOLUTIONARY VISION

Stage 1: Matriarchal Consciousness. Everyone is born of Woman. We develop initially in relation to a personal mother, in a contained instinctual world of feelings and sensations. In this closed universe, which is frequently called *participation mystique*, we have as yet no boundaries around the self, no division between "I" and "not-I," "self" and "other."

Like individuals, cultures also take root in what can be called the Great Mother archetype. People live in small tribes or clans close to the earth, their identities contained within the group. Some archaeologists and historians believe that such early agricultural peoples worshipped a female deity and had little penchant for war.

This early, undifferentiated stage of both individual and collective human development personifies the instinctual, *unconscious* Feminine principle. We can observe it in contemporary native cultures in which the group remains more important than the individual, and in which the people's relationship to nature is tied to their relationship to the divine. The mythic quality of these cultures lies in a sense of unity with the natural world. Some investigators have suggested that our myths of Eden and other paradises may stem from this little-known era of prehistory, or from this state of matriarchal consciousness.

Stage 2: Patriarchal Consciousness. Inevitably, individuals break away from the all-containing group and the unconscious Mother archetype. They begin to develop a budding sense of individual identity. When this happens, an entirely new social structure arises, with its attendant beliefs and customs. A new thinking style also arises in which people focus on differentiating self from other, subject from object, part from whole. The transition is made from *participation mystique* to *analytical objectivity*.

We know little about the details of how this transition from matriarchy to patriarchy in societies at large takes place; but we do know the outcome—patriarchy, a form of social organization in which the father or eldest male is recognized as the head of the family or tribe, and descent and kinship are traced through the male line.

This particular social and political way of life, which has peaked in the West today, is characterized by "rugged individualism," the hero who strives for dominance and personal gain even to the detriment of the community, and a widespread belief that men (and the Masculine principle) outrank and outvalue women (and the Feminine principle).

This cultural shift into patriarchal consciousness is reflected in individual development as a person begins to separate from the unconscious bond with the mother in order to gain a sense of autonomy and ego boundaries. Jungian analyst Marion Woodman explains patriarchy in psychological terms as the hero's journey out of the unconscious: the dragon slayer on the way to finding personal power.

Typically, the father breaks this primary unity with and dependence upon the mother. Eminent Jungian analyst Erich Neumann wrote that matriarchal consciousness is attuned to unconscious processes, while patriarchal consciousness separates itself from the unconscious into a discrete "head ego." He suggested that this stage begins at the end of the first year of life and resembles a "second birth."

Like patriarchal cultures, individuals in the patriarchal stage are governed by the Father archetype and characterized by action, will, analysis, striving, and competition. This stage becomes the general process of growing up, leaving our parents behind and learning to care for ourselves, gaining the appearance of independence in every sphere of life.

But psychologically, deep within, many of us do not fully separate from one or both of our parents or from the stereotyped expectations of society. We have learned from psychoanalysts (such as Freud and Alice

Miller), from developmental psychologists (such as Jean Piaget, Erik Erikson, and Lawrence Kohlberg), and more recently from proponents of the Alcoholics Anonymous twelve-step recovery model that most people do not develop fully balanced egos or a sense of real individuality in our society; we remain dysfunctional in some essential ways. We continue to carry mother and father within us, not only following in their footsteps but often actually walking in their shoes. We re-create our parents' patterns, becoming second-generation alcoholics, abusive parents, or compulsive high achievers. Or we rebel against them, believing ourselves to have broken the patterns, but actually remaining unconsciously trapped within them.

For women, whose source of ego identity is our mothers, this developmental process unfolds in one way. We identify with our mothers as our origin, both biologically and psychologically. So, to be a woman, we need to face the paradox of breaking the personal identification yet remaining grounded in the Feminine.

For men, whose source of ego identity is their fathers, the need to struggle to be free of their mothers is key. Men's development involves becoming consciously grounded in the Masculine, so their developmental process unfolds in another way.

But, sadly, for almost everyone, childhood wounds are left unhealed; deeply felt needs are left unmet. Eventually, we bring these into our intimate adult relationships, expecting our own unfinished business to be completed by our loved ones. I believe this happens partially because we are not taught that this patriarchal stage of evolution—the psychological development of a separate, healthy ego—takes conscious effort on our parts. Without intense personal work with a psychotherapist, guide, or mentor who assists us to heal our wounds and who points out the pitfalls along the way, the ego does not fully develop on its own; it remains to some extent in a childhood state.

Stage 3: Emerging Consciousness. For a long time, Western philosophers and psychologists with a developmental perspective believed this emergence of a separate ego to be the peak of human evolution, just as they saw patriarchal society as the peak of cultural evolution. Today, however, many people point to the winding down of patriarchy and the tentative beginnings of a new era, just as they point to the ever-increasing destructiveness of egocentric values and the life-enhancing potential for more transpersonal ones.

Two phenomena in particular have helped to catalyze the cultural transition out of a rigid patriarchy: feminism and the study of early goddess cultures. These two lenses on our cultural surrounds are crucial because we have lived for thousands of years like fish in the waters of patriarchy, blindly assuming that it's the way of nature.

Feminists have made a rigorous reanalysis of gender stereotypes. Their gift has been a wake-up call to the widespread oppression of women in this form of society. Despite their obvious political failures, nothing has gone untouched: parity in the workplace, equality in our intimate relationships, a non–gender-based education for our children have become widespread goals.

In addition, feminism created sisterhood—a realignment of women with women. This has enabled women to make men and the Masculine less of a personal priority, and for some of us less of an obsession, in our lives. Sisterhood has taught us about the equal value of women's relationships with women, a revelation for those of us raised with the goal of finding and winning a man above all else, in competition with other women.

Feminism also has brought a rising awareness of the need for women's power of definition, our own language, and a means to affect institutional change. This has resulted in a lineage of women scholars who are rewriting large chunks of history and revealing gender bias in language, religion, and many other areas. At this time, the substantial scholarly and sociopolitical work that has been done by thousands of women has moved feminism from its initial reactive phase, which was characterized by efforts to gain equal power within the patriarchy, to a more mature vision, leading, hopefully, to a deeper individuality.

The second lens on patriarchy has been the discovery of female-based, pre-patriarchal cultures. The findings of female investigators and theorists such as Marija Gimbutas, Merlin Stone, and Riane Eisler have overturned our assumptions about values and lifestyles in ancient "matriarchal" cultures. We have discovered that much that we take for granted today (such as the nuclear family with a male head of household, or a monotheistic religion with a male god) has not always been the rule of thumb. As a result, we can begin to imagine rich alternatives to our patriarchal patterns.

The costs of the one-sidedness of a patriarchal rule have been great. Many have linked it to the global ecological disaster we now confront, because it wrenched us away from a direct connection with the earth. With this primal split, several others followed: Women, previously linked to nature's ways, lost their instinctual powers and became subservient to men. The divine, previously linked to nature and the human body, was banished to the heavenly realms, leaving profane much that had been experienced as sacred.

Today, it is common among certain groups to lament this social and political development. Many people are fascinated with native peoples and what they can teach us about living softly on the earth and honoring her ways. However, we have come too far to return to the earth and to adopt regressive modes of life, whether they appear to be more natural, more matriarchal, or more spiritual. Certainly, we can seek and find great value there; however, we need to renew our relationship to the earth and to the divine in a conscious way, carrying with us the gifts of full development in a patriarchal society: our well-defined individuality and our inquiring minds, upon which the Western world was built.

Returning again to the individual, many of us have come to learn that ego development is a stage in a larger maturation process. Because of the groundbreaking work of people like humanistic psychologist Abraham

Maslow and transpersonal philosopher Ken Wilber, the ceiling upon human growth rises to new heights. We have been inspired to practice spiritual disciplines in an effort to break through the willful, single-focused rule of the patriarchal ego. And, for the first time in history, during the past twenty years transcendent, ecstatic experiences have become democratized, available to many thousands of people.

I believe this is a sign of what Carl Jung called *enantiodromia*, which means that sooner or later the pendulum swings and everything turns into its opposite. Jung identified this as a principle that governs cycles of natural life. In the psyche, if an extreme, one-sided tendency dominates conscious life, in time its opposite will build up energy and eventually attempt to break through the dominant pattern. Jungian lecturer and storyteller Robert A. Johnson explains the counterculture revolution of the 1960s in this way: The rigid rule of the thinking function resulted in a massive swing toward the feeling function.

Today the old forms of masculine rule die, as it becomes increasingly clear that our patriarchal attitudes and their institutions cannot support life on earth. In the same moment, the strength of feminine values grows, in an effort to bring balance to the larger system. The breakthrough of the Feminine requires the breakdown of the Masculine and, as a consequence, a time of crisis while the center of power shifts. At the individual level, the Feminine archetype, also known as the Goddess, ushers in the ego's awareness of the fact that it is no longer the sole dominant factor.

Many therapists, working with people's dreams, have reported this transition and have tried to explain it in a number of ways. In her book *The Search for the Beloved*, Jean Houston says:

> Many of us in research and clinical psychology have recently witnessed in our research subjects and clients a remarkable activation of images of female principles, archetypes and goddesses. The recent proliferation of books, articles, and conferences on the "rise of the Goddess" is a phenomenon that has great implications for culture and consciousness.
>
> The women's movement may be the outward manifestation of what is happening on depth levels in essential, mythic and archetypal space-time. Whether the movement has evolved because the crisis of the external world is calling for the rise of the Goddess to restore the balance of nature, or because the release of women into full partnership demands a similar release of its archetypal principle, or even because, in the cosmic cycle of things, the time of the Goddess has come round, we cannot say. But all the evidence indicates that the Feminine archetype is returning.

Culturally, this means that we need to stop devaluing the Feminine and permit her once again to take her rightful place in the scheme of things. Psychologically, this means that to be a woman we need to become reestablished in our Feminine ground, to throw off our identification with the Masculine principle and our male-dominated society. Our first step is to begin to understand the nature of the Feminine principle and our development toward the Conscious Feminine.

WHAT IS THE FEMININE?

"Feminine" is an adjective derived from *femina*, Latin for woman. It describes something that is "of women or girls; having qualities characteristic of or suitable to women: gentle, delicate, etc." At times in this book, I used "feminine" as an adjective in this conventional way; it is spelled then with a lower-case *f.*

However, when I refer to "the Feminine" as a noun, I denote an innate universal pattern in the human psyche, which Jung called an archetype and which is not restricted to one gender but is present in both women and men. In men, this Feminine element in Jungian psychology is called the anima. In this context, also, "the Masculine" is not restricted to men but is an attribute of every human being. In women, this Masculine element is known as the animus. When referring to the Feminine principle, or archetype, I spell it with a capital *F.* Likewise, when referring to the Masculine, I spell it with a capital *M.*

The Feminine and the Masculine, then, are not about our sex organs; they are about the structure of our consciousness. They are two ways of seeing and reacting to our experience that are distinct from each other, expressed in different images, behaviors, and emotional responses.

For example, the Feminine aspect of ourselves might react to an illness by contemplating it for symbolic meanings and nurturing it slowly back to health; the Masculine might respond by moving quickly with an invasive procedure to remove the symptoms. Both approaches hold value and are called for under different circumstances.

In psychospiritual traditions the world over, the Feminine and the Masculine are root metaphors for the built-in polarity of opposites that exists in the natural and symbolic worlds, much like the well-known Chinese qualities *yin* and *yang*, which lie embedded within one another inside of a larger whole. As Jung said of the Feminine and Masculine, "This primordial pair of opposites symbolizes every conceivable pair of opposites that may occur: hot and cold, light and dark, north and south, dry and damp, good and bad, conscious and unconscious."

Jungian analyst Marion Woodman has pointed out that these opposite traits function like the poles of a magnet. Opposites attract; likes repel. Psychologically, if a person remains unconscious of one pole, then he or she gives up the ownership of this trait and loses its gifts by projecting it outside, such as a woman projecting the Masculine onto a man. The woman becomes dependent on that outer person to carry the Masculine principle.

When this particular projection occurs with large numbers of people, as happened in our society, then men are burdened with carrying all of the qualities of the Masculine, such as analytic thinking, independence, and goal-orientation. The women are denied these qualities and charged with carrying Feminine traits such as feeling, interdependence, and process-orientation. The men, in turn, are denied these qualities.

On the other hand, if a person is aware of both the Masculine and Feminine poles, then there is a harmonious dynamic within the psyche. As a result, a fuller development of a wide range of capacities becomes possible.

In addition, the relationship between these two elements is reciprocal: as the Feminine in a woman is brought to consciousness and clarified, it permits the growth of a stronger Masculine principle, which in turn supports a more clearly defined Feminine. Each is finely attuned to the other, and the unity of the person's whole psyche is determined by the sovereignty of each element.

Historically, the qualities associated with the Feminine archetype have been drawn from mostly male observations of women's bodies (their receiving, containing, and birthing abilities) and of women's roles (nurturing, caretaking, and sustaining others). Today, however, women are defined less and less by biology, and are also growing less constrained by the idealized projections of men. Also, the research findings of people in many fields have helped to flesh out our definition of the Feminine, freeing her from culture-bound meanings and giving her a wealth of other values. Therefore, for the first time, the Feminine can become *conscious* in women—not male-identified, not in reaction to something other, not compensating for something missing.

For this reason, we are forced to question the archetypal definitions that have endured for so long; we are called to reimagine the Feminine in her emerging mode. Marion Woodman begins this process by suggesting a few characteristics of feminine energy:

- The Feminine prefers process to product, meandering and enjoying the pleasure of the journey, rather than, like the Masculine style, determining a goal and moving directly toward it in a straight line.

- This process-orientation involves presence in the body—in this moment—a full emotional and sensory acuity, a permission to follow one's bodily experience, rather than to listen to thinking alone.

- The Feminine also involves receptivity, while the Masculine is quick to act. Today, Woodman notes, our sensory and psychic receivers are closed down to defend against widespread brutality. We have become afraid and untrusting and cannot surrender to receive love. But the Feminine receives—from the cry of the planet to the cry of the soul.

In the earlier transition from matriarchal consciousness into patriarchal consciousness (which is recapitulated in the evolution of each individual woman), the Feminine is sacrificed and abandoned. In both men and women, she is banished from consciousness and goes underground, becoming part of the shadow world. From the vantage point of the world of light, she appears powerless and dependent; while up in the world of light, the one-sided reign of the Masculine concentrates power in technology and threatens collective destruction.

Today, with the coming end of the patriarchy, the Feminine is like a root shooting up through the cracked concrete surface of the culture. The evidence for her reappearance is apparent in our growing concerns with deep ecology, the Goddess, even the newly forming men's movement. Therefore, the Conscious Feminine is the next image to pull us forward on the human journey.

As our own feminine nature evolves within the collective imagination and manifests in us and in society at large, the Feminine principle is trans-formed. The archetype breathes new life, takes on a new countenance, and offers us new meanings.

While the unconscious Feminine emerged through instinct, the Conscious Feminine unfolds through imagination. That means, this stage in human development is intentional. Evolution calls on us to focus on Her, to begin now, in this moment, to imagine an embodied, fulfilled Feminine principle. For in so doing, we will reinvigorate the forces of life; we will serve as midwives to ourselves and to each other.

MY PERSONAL STORY

I would like to tell a bit of my own story to illustrate the parallel with the collective one because, like any woman's story, it is in some ways the story of all women. And through my personal tale you will be introduced to the main themes of this book.

The first daughter of two, I was very intimate early on with my mother, who was devoted and attentive. I have met very few women who have felt with their mothers the kind of loving bond we have shared.

However, she had sacrificed her life as an artist to be a full-time wife and mother. (She has only now, forty years later, returned to her passion of painting.) In addition, my mother was deeply troubled, scarred from her own early life events, and she was frequently depressed while I was young. My father, a more extroverted personality, competed for my attentions.

In our house, we made a game of dividing the family into "teams," pairs of family members who shared similar tastes and appeared to be more alike than the others. I was teamed with my mother, my sister with my father, because we physically resembled one another, respectively, and we seemed to share more sensibilities in common.

However, at some unknown crossroad, my father's impressions on my plastic young psyche seemed to take more deeply. I can recall feeling in early adolescence that being a girl seemed somehow irrelevant to my identity (a shocking idea in retrospect). My father would tell me that with my abilities I could do anything, implying anything that a man could do. And I believed him.

Throughout my childhood, in fascinating, wide-ranging, combative dinner-table discussions, my father groomed my mind to be, like his, a ruthless sword, to discriminate fact from fiction, feelings from hard reality. And my mother's feeling world became increasingly remote and unattractive, appearing chaotic and out of control. The desire of other girls I knew to marry and make babies seemed to me the death of possibilities; I remember intuitively understanding early on the use of the same word "nuclear" to describe the family and an unwinnable war.

As I watched my girlfriends adorn themselves to be attractive to boys and to play increasingly sophisticated games of flirtation, I felt mystified. There were so many more important things to be done! I wondered why they bothered.

Today this pattern has come to be called "a father's daughter," which refers to a woman who, at some stage, begins to unconsciously identify more with her father and with the Masculine element within (the animus) than with her mother and the Feminine principle. Fathers' daughters tend to be adept in the Father World of society, competent and confident— except, perhaps, about our own femininity, which is not expressed in stereotypically attractive ways. This was essentially my experience during my high school and college days.

Because our culture, too, is structured around the Masculine principle, many people find little value in conventional feminine qualities. For men, this means a rejection of those parts of themselves that might be nurturing, receptive, and caretaking, and a corresponding overdevelopment of those parts deemed masculine. In addition, it means that most men seek those buried qualities outside themselves in women, while at the same time unconsciously devaluing them.

For women, this second-class status of the Feminine principle makes it difficult to identify with our very natures, what Jane Wheelwright calls the female biological ego. As a result, we unknowingly adopt a certain set of characteristics to survive "in a man's world" which, like makeup, cover another set of qualities or instincts that may be less suited to survival. One lovely woman friend told me that, in order to deflect the constant seductive pressures of men beginning in her early teens, she intentionally "neutered" her appearance and learned to act gruffly, like "one of the guys." Her experience, which mirrored my own, eventually leads to an internal conflict between feeling powerful in the world and feeling attractive as a woman.

In Jungian circles, women like my friend and myself are referred to as having a strong animus-complex, which means we are run by our unconscious inner male component rather than by our ego, which is feminine. However, since some women have learned the lessons of feminism, this idea has been thrown into question, as we reevaluate whether any qualities such as "nurturing and receptive" or "opinionated and aggressive" can be appropriately assigned to either gender.

In any case, women with a highly developed animus stand in contradistinction to anima-women, who, knowingly or unknowingly, take on the culture's stereotypical image of beauty and femininity in order to please men and maintain conventional relationships. Rather than shape themselves to become like men, anima-women shape themselves to stay connected with men.

When I reached college age my father suggested that I attend the University of California at Berkeley, and I agreed. Even in his "all-knowing ways," he could not have foreseen the ripple effects of this seemingly innocent decision, though in later years he wished many times that he had. I entered the university a virgin, a supporter of the Vietnam War, a student eager to live the life of the mind and follow a course of study that would lead to a productive life.

After one year and a long series of initiations, I had opened many locked gates. If my dream, cited earlier, were taken apart like a puzzle, I suppose I could have dreamt even then about decapitating my father. But it would take another twenty years before the first part of the dream—the realignment with my mother—could emerge from my psyche.

The contents of my life story for the two decades that followed are less important for our purposes than the general process of raising consciousness. As I began to approach my fortieth birthday, I felt a tidal wave of change breaking on the shores: my life of the mind as a voracious reader, science writer, journalist, and editor still held riches, but it left me somehow empty *as a woman.*

I began to have fantasies of tossing it all aside and becoming a midwife, to be engrossed in the life of the female body and its wonders. For the first time, I began to feel empathy (even envy!) for the many women who set aside careers to have children, a phenomenon that had been a total mystery to me. Still unmarried and fully enjoying the single life only a few years before, I began to seriously seek out men who wanted commitment. And I made my own home, a beautiful mountain retreat, even as I found myself still whispering with the disdain of a former tenants' organizer, "Me! a Los Angeles homeowner!"

Of course, all of these symptoms could have been chalked up to midlife, that inescapable fork in the road that is marked by the sign: No U-turn. But my inner life was telling me that more was going on than the passage of time. As one thing was dying, another was being born: I have come to call it the Conscious Feminine. This is the subject of this volume: the emergence of an individuated and fulfilled style of femininity.

Our collective description of the journey is far from complete. We can begin to see signs on the horizon of the Conscious Feminine emerging in the collective: a rising respect for the values of relatedness, community, ecology, consensus, and healing. As these values become more contagious, they bring balance to the patriarchal institutions under which we have lived for so long.

Like the evolution of human consciousness as a whole, our individual evolution is an unending story, with countless detours and difficulties. However, I have come to see that for all women on the journey of awakening there are certain gateways through which we pass, each with its own trials and rewards.

GATEWAYS TO THE CONSCIOUS FEMININE

This book is structured around those key experiences that hold the potential to provide entry to the new level of consciousness—gateways to the Conscious Feminine. I had not been aware of this organizing principle when I first spoke with the contributors about their themes. But as the material was delivered, it became increasingly clear that each author was describing a way of healing a certain important relationship or a certain domain of life, and that this healing opened a gateway or entry point to the Conscious Feminine.

Eventually, I came to see the birth of the Conscious Feminine as a kind of glue, a context that holds together the many disparate themes contained here, which have been explored during the past decade in women's literature but which have not been framed in a developmental context until now.

Part 1, Retracing Our Common Evolution, opens with the big picture to provide a historical overview of the three main eras in human development: matriarchal, patriarchal, and emerging. The authors describe each era's predominance of the Feminine or Masculine principle, focusing on how the split between the archetypes creates a rift in the collective reality. The abandonment of the Feminine principle by society then leads to social, political, and spiritual crises, as well as deep personal and interpersonal problems.

Part 2, Re-mothering Ourselves, explores the roots of the mother-daughter wound. Every girl's essential feelings about herself, her body, and her relations with others are rooted in her bond with her mother. She is our source, and she is our model of how to be a woman.

Because most mother-daughter relationships are sorely lacking in intimacy and/or independence, we find ourselves longing for the mother who never was—and who never could be. This section is essentially about re-mothering ourselves by finding, through a range of options, a means to awaken within ourselves those mothering qualities that we seek from outside.

These options include reconnecting with "the girl within," nurturing and mentoring by a surrogate mother such as a therapist or friend, revitalizing the relationship with one's own mother, experiencing conscious motherhood, witnessing childbirth, or receiving the gifts of a grandmother or crone.

Part 3, Re-fathering Ourselves, explores the wounded relationship between a woman and her personal father, the patriarchal culture, significant other men, and the internal Masculine (or animus). All of these influences work together to form our images and expectations of men and the Masculine domain.

Like our bond to the Mother World, this formative link to the Father World also is imperfect. We are called upon to heal our relationships and, ultimately, to re-father ourselves by making conscious the father within, in his dark and light aspects, and the animus and its hold on our identities. This section also explores feminism and its role in awakening women to the nature of the Father World.

Part 4, Resacralizing the Female Body, is composed of three pieces of creative imagination that call upon us to ritually heal our relationships with our rhythms, instincts, and desires. Renewed interest in ritual of all kinds signifies a renewed connection between the natural and symbolic worlds.

In her book *An Image Darkly Forming*, Jungian analyst Bani Shorter describes her clients' use of rituals in psychotherapy to awaken and embody a conscious femininity. Although traditional rituals can be learned and adopted today, many women are finding that they can imagine and invent new rituals for female empowerment that meet their deeper needs. These three pieces on menstruation, sexuality, and menopause point the way.

Part 5, Reawakening the Divine Feminine, describes the banishment of the Feminine from the spiritual realm by a masculine God. As girls and women in a society that offers no female face of God, we have been bereft. Therefore, we have turned in large numbers to other times and places for a vital alternative to our "white-bearded old man in the sky."

Seeking to heal our relationship to the Goddess archetypes, we have uncovered a legacy richer than we dreamed. This section explores the Divine Feminine in ancient goddesses of pre-patriarchal times, in the Greek pantheon, and in the Gnostic goddess of wisdom, Sophia. There is also a piece on Inanna and her underworld sister, Ereshkigal, which explores the dark, depressed aspect of the Divine Feminine.

Part 6, Renewing the World, explores the impact of the changing archetype of the Feminine as we move into the emerging era. The contributors envision a shift from our current value system—based on "phallic masculinity," the search for objectivity and perfection, and the need for analysis and control—toward the more feminine values of relatedness, inclusiveness, feeling, flow, ambiguity, and introspection. A final legend from King Arthur's court reveals clues about how the lost Feminine can be regained.

This book, then, brings the collective imagination to bear on the theme of the birth of the Conscious Feminine. I hope that you will find the dialogue both inspiring and useful, a rich resource for your own development in becoming a more fully conscious human being.

PART 1

· · · · · · ·

RETRACING
OUR COMMON
EVOLUTION:
THE SEARCH
FOR THE
ABANDONED
FEMININE

But in fact we were always like this,
rootless, dismembered: knowing it makes
   the difference.
Birth stripped our birthright from us,
tore us from a woman, from women, from
   ourselves so early on
and the whole chorus throbbing at our
   ears
like midges, told us nothing, nothing
of origins, nothing we needed
to know, nothing that could re-member
   us . . .

Homesick for myself, for her. . . .

ADRIENNE RICH
"Transcendental Etude"

In the novel *1984*, George Orwell foresaw a future in which a "Ministry of Truth" would rewrite society's books and refashion its ideas so that they would fit the requirements of the men in power. According to Riane Eisler and other contributors to this volume, this eerie phenomenon already happened long ago, when the rule of the Masculine principle became entrenched in a patriarchal society, when the laws of human nature were rewritten—and the Feminine principle was banished.

In this opening section, the authors draw the big picture of human development—from a Matriarchal Age to a Patriarchal Age to the Emerging Age. Sukie Colegrave and Riane Eisler retrace the large cycles of our personal and social transformation in order to provide a framework within which to view today's transition—the end of patriarchy and the reentry of the Feminine to center stage.

Colegrave and Eisler view the cycles of history through the lenses of mythology, anthropology, and feminism. Robert M. Stein tracks the same split of the Feminine and Masculine archetypes, but he focuses on the psychological domain and the effect of the split on our relationships. Each author concludes that when the balance of power shifts between the Masculine and Feminine, distinct developmental phases can be detected that reveal distinct jumps in the levels of human consciousness.

In the collective, each era has its own mythology, its own story about the creation of human life on this planet, including a paradise and a "rise" or "fall" out of it. In addition, each era has its own panoply of gods and goddesses, who reveal characteristic relationships between the two essential archetypes.

All three essays explore the changing dance of these archetypes on a grand scale: What is life like within the arms of the Great Mother? What are the costs and benefits of sacrificing the Feminine to gain ego development and a society based on the ways of power? Why do feminine values find no home in the patriarchy? Why is the devaluation of the Feminine principle throughout history tied to the devaluation and oppression of women?

In her opening essay, Sukie Colegrave weaves together the strands of individual and collective evolution. She describes the universality of movement from the undifferentiated, unconscious Feminine principle, through the more focused, active Masculine principle, to a more differentiated, transpersonal Feminine awareness. Ultimately, the rebirth she sees is a spiritual one, the result of the symbolic death of the ego and its transitory values, and the rise of the Self, whose values are eternal.

Riane Eisler views history (and prehistory) through a social and political lens. She looks for the meaning of "feminine" in early cultures that did not devalue it, and she finds clues there for our struggles today.

Eisler makes a contribution to reframing our language and thus to revising our view of history. Matriarchy, she says, is not the opposite of patriarchy; matriarchy is not characterized by the domination of one group over another. Instead, she proposes the terms "dominator" society versus "partnership" society; the first is organized around the ranking of people over one another, the latter around linking. When she reviews cultures via this new classification, history takes on a different shape.

While Eisler emphasizes the splitting off of the Feminine in the social and political domains, Stein focuses on the split in the psychological and interpersonal domains. He links the painful limitations of contemporary stereotyped roles to the limitations we have placed on the Feminine archetype within both women and men.

A knowledge of our evolutionary and psychological history (where we've been) can open a doorway on the future (where we're going). It can reveal previously unseen human capacities, values, and lifestyles. And it can offer inspiration to those who lose sight of our progress.

However, we have to be careful not to try to predict the future from the past. After all, consciousness does not evolve in a straight line. And, although the direction in which we are heading is becoming visible, the destination is not yet determined.

1 · THE UNFOLDING FEMININE PRINCIPLE IN HUMAN CONSCIOUSNESS

· · · · · · · ·

SUKIE COLEGRAVE

With broad brushstrokes, New Mexico therapist and author Sukie Colegrave paints a picture of the evolution of human consciousness on two levels at once: individual and collective.

We begin, both as persons and as a species, in a preconscious state of unity, in the womb of the Great Mother—safe, all-containing, and nondual. As differentiation begins to take place and individual egos start to emerge out of this wholeness, the all-encompassing Mother becomes smothering; the inevitable need to separate stems from our natural need for independence and autonomy.

The result of this emergence out of wholeness is an individual ego with the capacity to identify and control the Other; socially, the result is the patriarchy, the collective identification with the Masculine principle—the rule of objectivity, duality, and domination.

Evolution out of one stage and into the next always calls for a sacrifice. With this step, unity with nature and other living beings is lost; the Feminine is cast off from the social, psychological, and spiritual realms.

This reigning imbalance of the Masculine principle leads inexorably to its opposite: the Feminine is reemerging, and with it the values of relatedness, receptivity, love, and reverence are gaining renewed respect. In the individual, a fully developed ego, which can face the Other in its separateness yet deeply experience their bond, is a new stage in human consciousness, which permits the growth of transpersonal values. In the collective, Gaia, the Great Earth Mother, is becoming conscious of herself.

Sukie Colegrave studied Jungian psychology in London and Boston, and Chinese language and history at London University. She is the author of Uniting Heaven and Earth: A Jungian and Taoist Exploration of the Masculine and Feminine in Human Consciousness *and* By Way of Pain: A Passage into Self. *She currently works as a psychotherapist and writer in Santa Fe, New Mexico.*

Chuang Tzu wrote:

> In the Golden Age good men [and women] were not appreciated; ability was not conspicuous. Rulers were mere beacons, while the people were free as the wild deer. They were upright without being conscious of duty to their neighbors. They loved one another without being conscious of charity. They were true without being conscious of good faith. They acted freely in all things without recognizing obligations to anyone. Thus their deeds left no trace; their affairs were not handed down to posterity.
>
> And so in the days when natural instincts prevailed, men [and women] moved quietly and gazed steadily. At that time there were no roads over mountains, or boats, or bridges over water. All things were produced, each for its own proper sphere. Birds and beasts multiplied; trees and shrubs grew up. The former might be led by the hand; you could climb up and peep into the raven's nest. For then man [and woman] dwelt with birds and beasts, and all creation was one. There were no distinctions of good and bad [human beings]. Being all equally without knowledge, their virtue could not go astray. Being all equally without evil desires, they were in a state of natural integrity, the perfection of human existence.

Was such a Golden Age, a Garden of Eden, ever enjoyed by human beings? The answer awaits the emergence of more refined methods of historical research. But as images of the condition that precedes the birth of consciousness, these words of the Chinese sage, like the biblical descriptions of the Garden of Eden, convey a flavor of the tranquil, harmonious unity that characterizes the timeless, undifferentiated preconscious matrix of the human soul in its condition before the separation into conscious and unconscious, I and you, we and them. Chuang Tzu's images remind us of the organic, spontaneous integrity that underlies and embraces the distinctions between human and animal, matter and spirit, life and death; the seamless whole that creates and informs the different parts and passages of existence. They also remind us of the ignorance and unknowing that characterize this psychological condition—the absence of choice and individual freedom, the lack of opportunity for conscious creativity and love.

How or why this peaceful, preconscious state of being began to differentiate into the world of opposites, thereby initiating the process of history and the emergence of human consciousness, remains as mysterious as how or why the infant sacrifices its embryonic oneness with the mother to claim its individual "I." But as this separation occurs, both at the dawn of human history and at a certain moment in each individual life, the preconscious Golden Age of the soul begins to dissolve and differentiate into an experience of conscious and unconscious. And humanity's preconscious oneness with the cosmos transforms into a sense of being contained within the world, embraced by the arms of the Great Mother of heaven and earth.

For as long as collective and individual consciousness feel nourished, contained, and inseparable from the womb of the Great Mother, they imagine her as an essentially benevolent, omnipotent, and all-embracing being.

Whether she is worshipped as the Lady of heaven and earth, the Lady of the beginning and end of all creation, or the Lady of plants and animals, she is conceived as the spirit of earth and the forms of spirit, both virginal and bisexual. In Egypt she was called Isis, "Mother of all, being of both male and female nature." In Babylonia she was Ishtar, goddess of the moon, addressed as "O my God and my Goddess." In ancient China she was the spirit of the valley that never dies, the mysterious female that is called the root of heaven and earth.

The Great Mother's capacity for virgin birth is attributed to her wholeness. For in her the Masculine and Feminine archetypes or energies, still unseparated from each other, rest in unconscious embrace. Her virgin bisexuality expresses an unconscious psychological wholeness, which can and does for certain periods of psychological life coexist with the physical differentiation of male and female. It reflects a level of psychological being in which the individual or the group lives without any conscious experience of the psychological differences between the Masculine and Feminine archetypes, and without any conscious individuality. They exist instead as psychological infants embraced within the arms of the Great Mother, to a greater or lesser extent dependent on her for their identity and psychological well-being, whether she is experienced as cosmic Goddess or projected onto individual mother or wife.

The benevolence of the Great Mother rule of human consciousness continues for as long as it serves the psychological needs of the unfolding individual or group. But when a soul is ready to begin to experience its freedom and individuality, its capacity for awareness and understanding, and its potential for relationship and human love, the powerful embrace of the Great Mother's unconscious wholeness ceases to feel like a warm, safe womb and begins, from the perspective of the emerging I-consciousness, to feel devouring, claustrophobic, and threatening. At this time images of her munificence are eclipsed in mythology and dreams, those collective and individual mirrors of psychological unfolding, by images of her demonic nature. In ancient China she became the Great Mother of the West, a fearful creature with a human face, tiger's teeth, and a leopard's tail, dwelling in a mountain cave and ruling over plague and pestilence. In Assyro-Babylonian mythology, Tiamat, who first gave birth to the world, is also the image of blind primitive chaos "against which the intelligent and organizing Gods struggle." And in Hindu mythology Kali, the divine mother, has another face as the Terrible Spider Woman, the all-devouring maw of the abyss.

The struggle of the newly emerging consciousness to differentiate itself from and overthrow the rule of the Great Mother assumes a variety of mythological forms, but all share an essential characteristic: They reflect the masculine energy, either individually or collectively, striving to separate from its unconscious embrace with the Great Mother, so that it may claim and assert its independent authority and power. This birth into consciousness of the Masculine archetype and its consequent victory over the Great

Mother archetype, both historically and individually, inaugurate the era of psychological patriarchy.

Today, at a time of the reluctant and overdue dying of the reign of the Great Father in our collective psychology and culture, it is easy to forget that, like the Great Mother era, the patriarchal epoch served an essential and creative purpose in human unfolding. Its psychological orientation was—and continues to be, during certain passages from childhood to adulthood for both men and women—a precondition of the birth of conscious femininity and the unfolding of individual wholeness. The heroic masculine energy that succeeds in differentiating itself from the dark unconscious embrace of the Great Mother ruptures the psychic world in such a way as to allow an experience of the differences between I and you, matter and spirit, male and female. It thereby inaugurates a revolution in human experience, perception, and understanding. By way of its energy and power, the individual and the collective consciousness succeed in wresting from the unconscious the experience of discrimination, individuality, and otherness. They thereby develop the capacity for choice and freedom as well as, at least to some extent and on certain levels, the ability to understand and thereby control many of the hitherto unpredictable happenings of material and psychological life. Moreover, the hegemony of the Great Father enables us sufficiently to simplify the mechanics of physical survival and comfort so as to provide us with space and time to listen to and explore other dimensions of ourselves.

The considerable and well-documented abuse of women and the earth, the denial and devaluation of the Feminine, and the physical and instinctual devastation caused by political and economic wars precipitated by the ego-oriented power of the Great Father are more a reflection of individual and collective subservience to his competitive, separative, and hierarchical rule than an inevitable consequence of his presence. Without the emergence and maturation of the masculine energy we might not today have unfolded a sufficient sense of our own individuality to be able, within ourselves and within our social, political, and economic spheres, to invite and receive the Feminine into consciousness. Without his archetypal energy we might be unable to listen for and follow the threads that enliven and connect the worlds of opposites, which the masculine discriminating power helped to reveal and, in part, to create.

As the ancient sages intuited, the soul unfolds by way of relationship to and attraction of opposites—in particular, matter and spirit, and the two arms of Divinity, the Masculine and Feminine. The patriarchal revolution in human consciousness together with its cultural, social, and political reflections enable us to recognize and unfold one arm of this divine being. The psychological imbalance created by the Masculine hegemony invites into consciousness the other—the Feminine complement.

While men tended to be the initiators of the patriarchal revolution, the emergence of the Conscious Feminine from the unconscious embrace of the Great Mother has tended to be conceived and gestated by women. Not those who, angry with the oppression of their gender under patriarchy, have attempted to become patriarchs in female bodies, nor those who attempt to turn back the psychological path out of a nostalgia for the sexually undifferentiated rule of the Great Mother—but those who, hand in hand with acknowledging and honoring the Masculine within men *and* women, have begun to hear and welcome into consciousness the emerging seeds of the Feminine. Such women do not imitate patriarchal patterns by seeking to co-opt the Feminine into the service of personal ego or to identify it with the female body. For, whereas it is the nature of the hierarchical and separatist Masculine archetype to create a world in its own one-sided and divisive likeness, it is the nature of the Feminine to recognize, experience, receive, and nurture the whole. As the Masculine differentiates the opposites, the Feminine fosters relationship between them as they live and manifest at each level of being—as sexual communication; as the complementary energies within each human soul; as the two modes of thinking, the analytical and the connective; and as the two poles of the universe, matter and spirit.

While the Masculine separates, discriminates, controls, conquers, endures, overcomes, strives, and creates, the Feminine receives, allows, yields, absorbs, dissolves, unites, connects, and gestates. So, whereas the Masculine and the patriarchal revolution enabled the individual "I" to emerge into consciousness from out of the unconscious underworld depths of the Great Mother womb, the unfolding of the Feminine within the soul allows this individual "I" to begin to return to and connect with its greater being—its body, soul, and universal spirit; to recognize its relationship to the larger community of earthly and cosmic life, the divine unity that breathes the separate parts, peoples, nations, planets, and stars into existence. The Feminine allows our experience of ourselves and the world to move from an I-It perspective to an I-Thou, and eventually to an I-am and an I-that-is-We perspective.

Without losing the valuable powers and insights of the analytical, Newtonian masculine perspective, which has revealed many of the different parts of our earthly, psychological, and cosmic nature, the Feminine enables us to dissolve the redundant conceptual and perceptual divisions that sever these parts from each other and the organic whole. It allows us to recognize that body, soul, and spirit, for example, are not only different and separate levels of being but are simultaneously intimately connected, involved in a continuous dance with each other, reflecting and communicating their respective well-being as well as their dis-ease. The Feminine enables us to realize that any useful method of therapy, education, or social organization needs, therefore, to attend to and honor each level of existence as well as the mobile, sensitive relationship between them.

The patient, uncritical receptivity of the Feminine allows the repressed, denied, dissociated, and unconscious parts of the soul to rise into consciousness. It invites us to relinquish the patriarchal vision of body and matter as instruments to be manipulated and exploited in the interests of knowledge and ego autonomy, or feared as the quagmire of unconscious and instinctual suffering, mystery, and darkness. Instead, the Feminine enables us to welcome, honor, and enjoy them as the instinctual reflection and correspondence of soul and spirit, the clothes of our divinity. It sensitizes us to the different images of soul so that we can feel and receive into consciousness our emotional wounds and hungers—which, buried for decades, even lifetimes, obstruct the free flow of energy and inhibit our capacity to understand, relate, and love.

The weaving, nature being of the Feminine enables us to appreciate and experience the holistic nature of the world, which complements the disjointed Masculine perspective. It allows us, for example, to sense the presence of the earth tree, to feel and unite with its individual life-force, as well as with the archetypal tree that lives in the soul as image and on earth as trunk, root, and branches. In helping us to merge with the different qualities and energies of soul and earth, the Feminine leads us into an awareness of them as inseparable attributes and limbs of our being, of Being itself, without our betraying our soul by identification with any part alone.

By inviting us to experience all earth things as integral aspects of our whole, the Feminine contributes to the awakening of our sense of responsibility toward this planet—to our realization that we are not here to abuse but to care for it. We are enabled to understand and experience ourselves not as earth's rulers but as its custodians, beneficiaries, and ultimately its co-creators.

Through unfolding within us the threads of relationship between the opposites of spirit and earth, male and female, life and death, conscious and unconscious, the Feminine gives birth to individuals and human communities capable of reflecting and embodying their source of being and becoming—the Self. The Feminine gently expands our souls by dissolving superfluous and illusory parameters, useful though these are at other moments of our becoming. It teaches us to hear and follow the spontaneous rhythms of our unfolding; to recognize and feel the sacred will of body and soul, the "Thy will" we may once have attempted to dominate and control. The Feminine unfolds a path of becoming characterized by relaxing rather than striving.

Through dissolving the rigid delineations and unnecessary compartmentalizations that prevent our relationship to and experience of the organic whole, the one Self, which underlies ego and individuality, the Feminine helps us to sacrifice the lesser identity for the greater. She invites us to relinquish the goal-oriented, striving approach to individual becoming, our attachment to ego-autonomy, our wish to possess and control, and finally even our desire to identify with our ephemeral personality and being. In so doing, the Feminine awakens in us the capacity to understand Chuang Tzu when he said that he was not sure whether he dreamed he was a butterfly or whether he was a butterfly that dreamed it was Chuang Tzu. And we can understand C. G. Jung's boyhood question of whether he was the boy sitting on the stone or the stone on which the boy was sitting.

As we risk entering this place of shifting and dissolving questions about our own identity, the Feminine impulse to allow rather than to possess, to experience life as process rather than as static parts, can take us deeper into the dying that is the precondition of our becoming. It can help us to let go, to sacrifice personal attachment to the reservoirs of wisdom, power, and love that the birth into consciousness of our divine nature—the Self—has made accessible to us. As we do this, the individual "I" sheds its identity with the personal, ephemeral, and time-space reflection of its being. It reconnects, or perhaps connects consciously for the first time, with its cosmic and immortal I-ness—the "I" that is you and I, earth and universe; the "I" that is choosing to express part of its nature through the individual physical form and personality with which we once identified. With this sacrifice of outgrown identities we become capable of moving freely along the whole spectrum of consciousness, connecting our universal and temporal being. We become able to appreciate and enjoy our material *and* spiritual natures, as well as the creative freedom of choice that is ours once we have experienced our unity with the source of creation.

By way of this death and new birth, our capacities for feeling and for more refined emotions such as love, reverence, and serenity, intensify. At the same time, our coarser emotions begin to wither and transform as there are progressively fewer ego desires, fears, or aversions to disturb the tranquility of our hearts. In becoming able to reflect, however palely and obscurely, the unconditional love and wisdom of Self, our souls are constantly fulfilled and our interests inseparable from the interests of Self.

With this shift of identity from the ephemeral ego and personality to the universal or Higher Self, we return to the beginning. We enter the psychological virgin wholeness of the Great Mother and know her for the first time. For as Philo of Alexander said, "The congress of men for the procreation of children makes virgins women. But when God begins to associate with the soul, He brings it to pass that she who was formerly woman becomes virgin again." In our androgynous virginity, capable of relating to the masculine and feminine energies in their different manifestations and at their different levels of being, but identifying with neither, we become unobstructed channels for the flow of spiritual energy into body and earth, as well as for the corresponding flow and transformation of earthly energy into spirit.

In those moments when we choose to experience the cosmos that is our being, we leave behind the archetypal energies of male and female and experience the one source that gives birth to their polarity. As Jesus said in the Gospel of Saint Thomas, "When you make the inner as the outer, and the outer as the inner and the upper as the lower, and when you make male and female into a single one, so that the male shall not be male and the female [shall not] be female, then shall you enter [the Kingdom]."

This kingdom of the soul is characterized, among other things, by love. This is not just the love that serves the other as oneself and cares for the earth as the embodiment of our divinity; nor merely the love of physical and psychological devotion, or the unconditional love that cannot be shaken by the other's response, attitude, or action; nor solely the transcendent, objectless love that is the life-force and essence of soul, accessible as an illimitable source whenever we choose to turn within and drink. Including and beyond all these, this love is love as bliss: love as wisdom and ecstasy. It is comparable perhaps, though in a small way, to the ephemeral ecstasy that alights upon us when, before the inner marriage of body, soul, and spirit, we project onto another our unrealized inner partner and glimpse the one Self by falling into love.

2 · SOCIAL TRANSFORMATION AND THE FEMININE: FROM DOMINATION TO PARTNERSHIP

. . . .

RIANE EISLER

In her highly successful book The Chalice and the Blade *(1987), Riane Eisler traces the unseen forces that shape human culture, from prehistory through recorded history and into the future. She reconstructs an early world of partnership between men and women, which lasted about 20,000 years, then veered off on a "bloody 5,000-year detour" of male domination. Later, at a certain historical turning point, Eisler says, the men in power deliberately buried the truth about the egalitarian nature of past society so that it would seem to people (as it does to us today) that men were always in charge—as fathers, politicians, priests, or God.*

In her article, written for this book, Eisler draws on a rich mix of anthropology, literature, politics, and myth to explore the relationship between culture and the Feminine. Using a systems approach, she sees a historical pattern of power: male control is tied to domination of others, hierarchical ranking, war, and a transcendent god. However, she says, there were times, which are lost to historical record, when human groups were more egalitarian, connected by linking, and not war-like. They also worshipped an immanent female deity. Eisler's conclusion is that the oppression of women is tied to the repression of feminine values.

If this is the case, men's fear that the end of male domination will lead inevitably to female domination is baseless. Eisler envisions instead a partnership society in which neither gender is associated with inferiority or superiority, and more so-called feminine values can be shared by everyone.

Eisler contends that we now face a crossroad similar to the one we faced when the shift from a matrifocal to a patrifocal society took hold. Signs of change toward an emerging era of partnership can be seen in grass-roots groups that seek to create equal relationships, harmony with the environment, and peaceful societies. The psychological work needed to consciously integrate the Feminine principle will speed the coming of a partnership society.

Riane Eisler is the author of The Chalice and the Blade: Our History, Our Future *and co-founder of the Center for Partnership Studies. She has taught at the University of California and Immaculate Heart College.*

Like many other women, during the 1960s I felt a powerful stirring within me, an awakening for which I did not yet have a name. As time went by, I realized this was the awakening of the awareness of my identity as a woman, the reawakening of something long suppressed yet integral to my very being: a conscious femininity.

As the years passed, this awareness strengthened and expanded. I began to understand how profoundly my own life was shaped by, first, the suppression and distortion, and later, the implosive and explosive power of my evolving feminine consciousness. What was at first no more than a yearning became an intensive search, a journey that has taken me to realms of thinking and feeling that have given new content, purpose, and, above all, integration to my work and my life.

Over the past two decades, my research coalesced into a systematic reexamination of our cultural past, present, and future. My findings, which are in part detailed in my book *The Chalice and the Blade: Our History, Our Future*, indicate that the reintegration of women and so-called feminine values such as compassion, nonviolence, and caring into all areas of life is one of the most important developments of our time—a central component in the urgently needed shift from what I have called a dominator system of social organization to a partnership system.

My work also verifies something which, once articulated, seems obvious, but which has been effectively obscured because of the suppression of feminine consciousness: The way a society structures the most fundamental of all relations—the relations between the female and male halves of humanity and between the values stereotypically associated with femininity and masculinity—affects the entire social system, its institutions and its values.

Specifically—and of central importance for our time of nuclear bombs and environmental pollution—whether women and the Feminine are valued and integrated into social governance or looked down on and suppressed directly affects whether our daily lives as individuals are generally harmonious or are enmeshed in what has aptly been called the war between the sexes; it also directly relates to whether a society is peaceful or warlike, democratic or authoritarian, ecologically balanced or imbalanced. In effect, this key dynamic can determine to a great extent our quality of life.

As I look back now, I marvel at how far I have had to come in my inner and outer journey and at how much farther I still have to go. Sometimes I wonder how I could ever have been so unaware, so unconscious not only of the central importance of the Feminine in how we construct our society and our world, but of what is now my most profound and indispensable sense of self as a woman and a person. But most of the time I am simply grateful for having been born into this exciting time of awakening consciousness, a time that will be remembered in years to come as a major turning point in the evolution of our planet and our culture: the time when the Conscious Feminine broke through age-old fetters, not only in the minds and hearts of women but also in men.

RECLAIMING OUR FEMININE HERITAGE: OLD CLUES AND NEW FINDINGS

Has this much-talked-about emerging feminine consciousness suddenly sprung forth full-blown during the second half of the twentieth century, like Athena was said to have leapt out of the head of Zeus? Or does it have antecedents, psychic and spiritual roots that we are only now beginning to reclaim?

What does "feminine" really mean? What is its role in the evolution of human culture? How does it relate to the female half of humanity? Above all, what are its implications for the future of all of us, both women and men?

These are some of the questions for which I have tried to find answers as, drawing from many disciplines, I have worked to reconstruct a gender-holistic picture of our past and present and bring together a new vision or blueprint for a future when so-called feminine values are restored to social governance. Part of the confusion has been that these qualities have been exiled to one gender. As a result, the oppression of women and of the so-called "Feminine" have gone hand in hand.

I say so-called Feminine because, clearly, men are also capable of caring, nonviolence, and compassion, and women can be just as identified with so-called masculine values like conquest and domination as men have been taught to be. And I say restored to social governance because, largely thanks to what British archaeologist James Mellaart calls a "veritable revolution in archaeology," we are now learning that for many thousands of years in our prehistory women and "feminine" values were *not* subordinate to men and "masculine" values.

This is not to say that these were ideal societies. But they appear to have been societies in which masculine identity was not equated with domination and conquest—whether of women, other men, other nations, or nature—and in which softer, more feminine values, such as nonviolence and nurturance, were not considered fit only for women and "effeminate" men.

A good entry point into this picture of our cultural evolution is through a fresh look at the many familiar legends about an earlier, more harmonious and peaceful age. The Judeo-Christian Bible tells of a garden where woman and man lived in harmony with each other and with nature—a time before a male God decreed that woman henceforth be subservient to man. The

Chinese Tao Te Ching describes a time when the yin, or Feminine principle, was not yet ruled by the yang, or Masculine principle, a more harmonious time when the wisdom of the Mother was still honored and humanity lived in peace. The ancient writings of the Greek poet Hesiod tell of a "golden race" who tilled the soil in "peaceful ease" before a "lesser race" brought in Ares, the god of war.

While for many people these stories are merely religious or poetic allegories, there is general agreement among scholars that in many respects they are based on prehistoric events. However, until now, one key component—the allusion to a time when women and men lived in partnership and men did not hold feminine values in contempt—has generally been viewed as no more than fantasy.

Just as archaeology, in its infancy, helped to establish the reality of Homer's legendary Troy with the excavations of Heinrich and Sophia Schliemann, so today archaeological excavations indicate that stories of a time when women were not dominated by men also are based on earlier realities. For example, Mesopotamian and later biblical stories about a garden where woman and man lived in harmony with each other and with nature in part derive from folk memories of the first agrarian (or Neolithic) societies, which planted the first gardens. Similarly, the legend of how the glorious civilization of Atlantis sank into the sea may be a garbled recollection of the matrifocal Minoan civilization—a remarkably peaceful and uniquely creative culture where women and "the Feminine" played leading roles—which is now believed to have ended when Crete and other Mediterranean islands were massively damaged by earthquakes and enormous tidal waves.

These new archaeological discoveries (coupled with reinterpretations of older digs using more scientific methods such as radiocarbon dating, which put prehistoric time scales back thousands of years) reveal that civilization is much older than was previously believed. They also reveal a hitherto neglected but critically important earlier phase in our cultural evolution: millennia of general peace and prosperity when all the basic technologies on which our civilization is built were developed in societies that were *not* male dominant, violent, and hierarchic.

In other words, they provide us with a far different view of our cultural antecedents than the long-accepted notion of prehistory as a linear upward progression of stages, from savagery to civilization. And they directly contradict the view that warfare, male dominance, and the conquest of nature are divinely or genetically ordained or, alternately, are prerequisites for "higher civilization."

As Mellaart reports from his excavations of Catal Huyuk, an early cradle of civilization going back many thousands of years before Sumer, the characteristic social structure of these early civilizations appears to have been generally egalitarian. According to Mellaart, the comparative size of houses, the nature of their contents, and the funerary gifts found in graves show that there were no extreme differences in status and wealth.

Data from Catal Huyuk and other Neolithic sites also indicate that in these societies, where women were priestesses and craftspeople, the female was *not* subordinate to the male. Indeed, in sharp contrast to most present-day religions, the supreme deity was female rather than male: a goddess rather than god.

Moreover, dispelling the notion that war is either "natural" or the inevitable price we pay for civilization, these appear to have been civilizations where warfare was not the norm. There is a general absence of fortifications. The extensive and considerably advanced art lacks scenes of "noble warriors" killing one another in battles, of gods and men raping women, of "glorious conquerors" dragging back prisoners in chains, which are so ubiquitous in later art.

Even more fascinating—and relevant to our time—this type of more peaceful and "feminine" social organization seems to have continued well into the Bronze Age, culminating in the "high" civilization of Minoan Crete.

Nikolas Platon, the former director of the Acropolis Museum and superintendent of antiquities in Crete (who excavated that island for more than fifty years) reports that this technologically developed civilization, with its viaducts, paved roads (the first in Europe), and advanced civic amenities, had a generally high standard of living. Even though there were differences in status and wealth, and probably a monarchic type of government, there is evidence of a large emphasis on public welfare—very unusual in comparison with other "high" civilizations of the time.

Here, as in the earlier Neolithic, the subordination of women does not appear to have been the norm. Cretan art shows women as priestesses, as figures being paid homage, and even as captains of ships. As Platon writes, in Minoan Crete "the important part played by women is discernible in every sphere."

Equally important, and integrally related, the influence of feminine sensitivity is ubiquitous in Minoan art and life (as it is also in the earlier Neolithic, where images of female deities are common). Indeed, the influence of the Feminine is so powerful in this uniquely peaceful and creative last-known matrifocal society that Platon reports that the "whole of life was pervaded by an ardent faith in the goddess Nature, the source of all creation and harmony." This, he says, "led to a love of peace, a horror of tyranny, and a respect for the law."

HUMAN POSSIBILITIES:
A GENDER-HOLISTIC VIEW

To some people, the idea of a society in which women and "feminine" values play leading roles immediately elicits the picture of a world where men, rather than women, are subordinate. Indeed, when the first evidence of prehistoric societies that were not male dominant began to be unearthed in the nineteenth century, most of the scholars of that day automatically concluded that since they were not patriarchies, they must have been matriarchies. But matriarchy is not the opposite of patriarchy. It is, rather, the flip side of a *dominator* model of society—a way of structuring human relations in which the primary principle of social organization is ranking, beginning with the ranking of one half of humanity over the other.

The real alternative to a patriarchal or male-dominant society is not a matriarchy but a *partnership* model of social organization, in which the primary principle of social organization is *linking* rather than ranking. Here—beginning with the most fundamental difference in our species, that between male and female—diversity is not equated with either inferiority or superiority, and more "feminine" values such as caring, nonviolence, and compassion can be given operational priority.

This new system of classification makes it possible to see how and why some of the most creative and progressive periods throughout recorded history have been times when women and "feminine" values have been on the ascendancy. For instance, although this is rarely noted by most religious scholars, in many of the early Christian communities women took the same leadership roles as men. Moreover, in many of these early Christian communities, which both preached and practiced nonviolence and equality, the deity was seen as female and male: both holy Mother and Father.

Similarly, the troubadours and troubatrixes, who flourished in the courts of Eleanore of Aquitaine and her daughters Alix and Marie, elevated woman and the Feminine from their subservient and despised status, asserting that the Feminine principle was integral to both women and men and that masculinity should be a gentle thing—as in the term *gentleman*. Not coincidentally, it was the troubadours who introduced what the church called Mariology, the worship of Mary as a Divine Mother, in essence a reinstitution of the ancient goddess worship.

Perhaps most important, this gender-holistic picture of our cultural evolution shows that we as a species have choices, and that one of these choices is a way of living in which "feminine" values *and* women play a central role in both our psychic and social structures. For if we reexamine our cultural history from a perspective that takes into account the whole of humanity (both women and men) and the whole of history (including prehistory), we begin to see that underneath the great surface diversity of human social organization lie certain patterns that are otherwise not visible.

For example, at first glance, Hitler's Germany, Khomeini's Iran, the Japan of the Samurai, and the Mesoamerica of the Aztecs would seem to represent completely different cultures. But once we look at the whole picture, including the status of women and so-called feminine values in these societies, we are able to identify their dominator social configuration. We then see that these otherwise widely divergent societies have striking commonalities characteristic of the dominator model. They are rigidly male dominant, with a basic contempt for women and "soft" or "feminine" values. They have a generally hierarchic and authoritarian social structure. And they are characterized by a high degree of social violence, ranging from child- and wife-beating within the family to aggressive warfare on the larger tribal or national level.

Conversely, we also can see striking similarities between otherwise extremely diverse societies that are more sexually egalitarian and in which "feminine" values are correspondingly higher in the scale of operational social values. Such societies tend to be not only more peaceful but also less hierarchic and authoritarian. This pattern is illustrated by anthropological data (e.g., the BaMbuti and !Kung), by contemporary studies of trends in more sexually egalitarian modern societies (e.g., Scandinavian nations such as Sweden), and by the prehistoric data that have been briefly presented in the previous section.

WOMEN, THE CONSCIOUS FEMININE, AND THE FUTURE

Why are these patterns only becoming visible today, at the same time that we are reclaiming our ancient feminine heritage and experiencing the emergence of an international feminist movement, and with it a more conscious, intentional feminine awareness?

I believe this concurrence is not coincidental. "Feminist consciousness" is a phrase that began to gain currency in the 1960s. On a personal level, it refers to a new way of looking at ourselves and at the world in which conventional dogmas about women's divinely or naturally ordained subordination are no longer accepted. On the social level, it refers to the result of a special group process: a coming together of women not only to ask new questions about the nature of reality, but to support and nurture one another in a new social sisterhood. On the cultural level, it refers to the mounting recognition that the subordination of women and of "feminine" values like caring and compassion lies at the core of an aberrated—and increasingly suicidal—social system.

In the sense that they are contemporary responses to the potentially lethal danger that the dominator system poses to our planet in our high-technology age, the massive changes in consciousness reflected in the contemporary women's movement are new and radical. But, as we have seen, the emerging feminist consciousness also has very ancient roots.

Indeed, the roots of feminism as a social protest movement probably go all the way back to that cataclysmic time in our prehistory when the dominator system was first imposed—when both women and the Chalice (as the symbol of "feminine" values) were subordinated. This was the time when, as UCLA archaeologist Marija Gimbutas writes, the goddess-worshipping societies now being documented by the archaeological spade were overrun by invaders from the arid fringes of the globe. The invaders, quite literally, worshipped the lethal power of the Blade, and brought with them their contempt for women and everything associated with "soft" or "feminine" values.

Even from the much later writings of ancient Greece, there is compelling evidence that, despite their severe oppression, Athenian women protested against both male dominance and war. For example, in his famous play Lysistrata, Aristophanes tells how the women of the warring Greek city-states got together and successfully plotted to make their husbands stop fighting by refusing to have sex with them until they did so. And in Eva Keuls's brilliant The Reign of the Phallus, a strong case is made for explaining, as an organized act of feminist protest against the Peloponnesian War, the breaking of the penises on hundreds of statues of the god Hermes in Athens around 415 B.C.E. (This was a time when, as Keuls writes, the phallus had become a symbol not of sexual love but of male domination and conquest.)

Moreover, the intuitive recognition of the pivotal importance of the Feminine in human affairs is certainly not new. Even during recorded (or dominator) history, many volumes have been written about the Feminine —ironically mostly by men, since during this time women were by and large effectively barred from writing and publishing.

It is, however, revealing that in most of these writings—exemplified by the works of clergymen such as Heinrich Kramer and James Sprenger, poets like William Blake, philosophers like Herbert Marcuse, and psychologists like Carl Jung—the Feminine has been alternately romanticized and vilified. As Sophia or Hokhmah, the Feminine has been exalted as man's conscience, as his symbol of wisdom. As man's muse, the Feminine has been depicted as his inspiration, his guiding light. On the other hand, darkness, weakness, evil, and deceit also have been equated with the Feminine—as in the archetypal myths of Pandora and Eve—providing more than ample fuel to the argument that the Feminine must be suppressed at all costs. The opposite argument—that the restoration of the Feminine to social governance is essential, particularly in our age of technological dehumanization—also has been made by a number of men, such as cultural historians Henry Adams and Lewis Mumford. But, curiously, the seemingly obvious relationship of the Feminine to flesh-and-blood women has been almost entirely ignored.

Only rarely, as in Christine de Pizan's extraordinary twelfth-century Cite de Dames (City of Women), have the voices of women themselves been heard. De Pizan's proto-feminist work was an impassioned defense of the contribution of both the Feminine and women to our world.

Similarly, in Mary Wollstonecraft's groundbreaking eighteenth-century In Vindication of the Rights of Women, and in Elizabeth Cady Stanton's historic nineteenth-century Seneca Falls address, we find a more integrated approach. Wollstonecraft's impassioned response to "rights of man" philosophers like Rousseau (who extolled the Feminine while at the same time vociferously relegating women to their "proper" or subordinate place) is a cry of the heart. Stanton, one of the great leaders of the first phase of the

American women's movement, powerfully appeals to both our hearts and minds. And in the second phase of the modern feminist movement—the great upsurge of political and social action, writings, and personal and social transformation generated by the twentieth-century women's liberation movement—a third and fundamental theme has been brought to the fore: that of the spirit. The eco-feminist writings of women such as Susan Griffin, Mara Keller, Gloria Orenstein, and Charlene Spretnak make the specific and essential point that a spirituality that honors both women and nature is central to a sustainable future.

However, while the twentieth-century women's movement—and with it, the global spread of feminist consciousness—is unprecedented in its depth and strength, until now it has been in large part reactive, in the form of intellectual reassessment and social protest. The conscious reexamination of the existing social structure and the identification of dominator elements that need to be changed has been an essential first step. But the most exciting aspect of this powerful movement is its more creative aspect: the conscious creation by women, and increasingly by men, of more "feminine" personal and social partnership images and realities.

Ours is a species that quite literally lives by stories and images, by the myths—be they religious or secular—that tell us what is "sacred," "natural," and "true." And for a long time our conscious minds have been fettered by stories and images that serve to maintain a dominator system.

For example, the all too familiar archetype of the hero as killer (all the way from Odysseus to Rambo) inculcates the minds of both men and women (beginning when we are little children) with the notion that domination and conquest—whether of women, other men, other nations, or nature—is what makes a man truly masculine. The powerful archetype of woman as evil seductress (from Circe in the *Odyssey* to Glenn Close's role in *Fatal Attraction*) serves to further justify men's domination over women and the Feminine. And fairy tales in which Sleeping Beauty passively waits for Prince Charming to wake her not only condition both little girls and little boys to associate passivity and powerlessness with women; their intrinsic message is that there is no such thing as a "Conscious Feminine"— that without a man to wake her, a woman has no consciousness at all.

It is not easy to leave behind these hallowed stories and images about "real" women, "real" men, and how the two should "naturally" relate. These sexual stereotypes have been our cultural staples, the stuff out of which we have constructed how we think and feel, even what we dream. This is why the contemporary questioning of what it really means to be a man or a woman—and with this, what "masculine" and "feminine" might mean in a partnership rather than a dominator society—is so important.

But in this process of consciously unraveling and reweaving the conventional myths and images of masculinity and femininity, we have to be aware of the danger of again finding ourselves unconsciously ensnared in the web of dominator gender archetypes—and unwittingly again weaving a tapestry of both dominator myths and realities. For example, in the still prevailing yin/yang and anima/animus mythology, we find the Masculine associated with the "higher" powers: the sun and the sky. By contrast, the Feminine is described as the "dark" and "earthly." So powerful are these associations that most of us find it difficult to imagine anything else—even though many are familiar with the biblical passages where Jeremiah rails against the people of Israel for "backsliding" to the worship of the Queen of Heaven, and with the fact that in Japan the emperor claims his right to rule as a descendant of the Sun Goddess.

Clearly, these ancient images of the Feminine as associated with the heavens and the sun directly contradict the idea of male as active, light, and rational, and female as dark and irrational. But just as clearly, the association of the Masculine with what is above and the Feminine with what is below serves to maintain a dominator mentality by unconsciously reinforcing the idea that the rule of men and masculinity over women and femininity is simply "the way it is."

There is enormous dominator resistance to the contemporary partner-ship movement, both within us and from the culture at large. In religion, we see today the resurgence of mysoginist dogmas and practices in both Moslem and Christian fundamentalism. In education, we still find the rel-egation of anything associated with women or the Feminine to the ghetto of women's studies. In politics, we see not only the re-idealization of "strong-man" rule; we even find the co-option of some women in positions of leadership to adopt the stereotypically "male" or hard stance that ultimately serves to maintain the male-dominated system in which they have risen as "exceptions" to the rule.

But there is also enormous forward movement—such as the growing awareness that we cannot graft a peaceful and ecologically balanced global system onto social structures founded on the force-backed domination of one half of humanity over the other. Most important is that more and more people see that there is no way to build a world guided by "feminine" values and at the same time preserve institutions and belief systems that maintain women's subordination to men.

It is an exciting time—a time of crisis and opportunity, a time that systems theorists call a period of disequilibrium and hence of potential systems transformation. But the possibilities of a fundamental breakthrough rather than breakdown in our cultural evolution are not just of theoretical interest; they are of intense personal and planetary interest in a time when the Blade—the ancient symbol of a system based on force or the threat of force—is the nuclear bomb, and when "man's conquest of nature" threatens the very ecology on which all life on this planet depends.

When I look back and see how radically my own consciousness has changed in a little over two decades—and with it my life—I find experiential proof that fundamental change is possible. When I look around me—at all the men who are redefining fathering to incorporate "feminine" behaviors that only a short time ago were exclusively associated with mothering; at all the women who are bringing what sociologist Jessie Bernard calls a

RIANE EISLER   37

"female ethos" into the "man's world" of politics, economics, and science; at all the families that are recognizing once unquestioned dogmas like "spare the rod and spoil the child" as child abuse—I see objective proof that the transformation from a dominator to a partnership society is already well on its way. Observations like these reaffirm my Conscious Feminity and strengthen my belief that, despite the obstacles, we *can* create a future governed by the Chalice—the ancient symbol of the power to give and illuminate life.

3 · FROM THE LIBERATION OF WOMEN TO THE LIBERATION OF THE FEMININE

· · · · · · · ·

ROBERT M. STEIN

The Feminine principle has been split off not only in the mythological, social, and political realms, but also in the inner life of individuals, where it could have the power to provide eros, relatedness, nurturance, and a kind of authority that comes from soul. For this reason, the Feminine is often missing in our interpersonal lives as well, in the sacred space between us and those we love.

In this fascinating exploration of the consequences of the split archetypes, Los Angeles Jungian analyst Robert Stein asks some basic questions: What is the Feminine principle? How is it linked to and distinct from women? Why have women been captured in the constraints of mothering or the trap of playing sex object? What is the Masculine principle? How has it contributed to keeping women constrained? What is the root of dissatisfaction in traditional male-female relationships, which are now breaking apart in epidemic numbers?

Stein distinguishes between what is instinctual or archetypal for us as women and men, and what is acquired, imposed on us by a culture that prizes certain values over others. He explains that many qualities we consider to be "feminine," such as maternal feelings, and others we consider to be "masculine," such as phallic power, do not apply to gender (women and men) but apply to archetype (Feminine and Masculine), which exists in both sexes. This confusion results in psychological splits within both men and women, resulting in the tremendous difficulties we suffer in relation to one another.

Drawing on the gods and goddesses of Greek culture, he attempts to outline characteristics of the Feminine and to show how they have been undervalued in our culture, which is ruled by the spirit of the Masculine principle. Ultimately, Stein says, to be a woman one must become aware of the play of the Feminine within, yet not be captured by her in any singular form.

Robert M. Stein, M.D., is a Jungian analyst in private practice in Los Angeles. The author of many published papers, he is best known for his seminal study of the incest mystery, Incest and Human Love *(1984).*

For many women, marriage seems to have become more of an oppressive prison than a sanctuary. And no longer is the education of little girls solely for the purpose of teaching them the arts of pleasing and winning a man, homemaking, and motherhood. However, mating, nesting, and family-making are still deeply rooted instinctual needs that cannot simply be tossed aside. The archetypal roles that both women and men have lived out in our culture are not only due to education and conditioning; these are ancient roles that have instinctual parallels among many other species.

Feminism has been primarily concerned with freeing women from these roles and with attaining equal rights and status for women. It has asked in what way these roles are oppressive. How have they developed? Are they oppressive only to women, or are men equally oppressed by them? Are men responsible for forcing women into these roles? Have women perhaps had a need to assume these roles, and have men had a need to assume their corresponding roles?

Depth psychology has taught us that cultural patterns, even though they may become oppressive to the human spirit, have their origins in deep archetypal or instinctual roots. If these archetypal Feminine and Masculine roles have emerged in order to satisfy certain basic needs, then we might do well to explore the nature of these needs and how they may be affected by change. Whenever changes threaten basic needs, human nature will resist them. So, we might better effect the necessary changes if we know more about the resistance. In addition, just as our scientific and cultural progress has had detrimental effects on the balance of nature, so too must we be careful about the consequences of changing these archetypal patterns in the male-female relationship. We must attempt to find the most creative way of effecting these necessary changes so that they do not backfire, as have our technological advances.

C. G. Jung is responsible for introducing the ancient concept of the archetype into modern psychology. I use the term *archetype* to express the presence of a divine force within the human soul that manifests itself in all the typically human patterns of thought, feeling, imagery, and behavior. This implies that the directing energy and intelligence within the soul comes from a divine source, and that human instincts are one of its manifestations. So, when we say women are stuck in archetypal feminine roles, we must recognize that these roles are not simply human creations but that they also express an aspect of the divine.

Every culture, every religion has attempted to express the archetypal Masculine and Feminine in their gods and heroes. The ancient Greeks were particularly gifted in their ability to describe divine activity—every state and every capacity, every mood, thought, act, and experience was mirrored in a deity. In our attempt to explore the archetypal roles in which modern women are caught, we shall take advantage of this Greek perceptiveness.

The most obvious role that women have had to accept is that of *mother*. Every religion has had mother goddesses. What are the divine qualities contained in the image of mother? Mother is soft, warm, loving, gentle, sensitive, receptive, nourishing, and supportive. She is all-accepting and always there to respond to the needs of the child. She has no life of her own apart from her child. She lives only to give birth to children and to nurture them until they are ready to be on their own. Surely women are the natural carriers of this maternal function, especially because men are unable to give birth to children.

But the maternal involves much more than giving birth to actual children. Giving birth, for example, is as much a psychic or spiritual phenomenon as it is a literal act—such as giving birth to an idea, a vision, or any creative work. The maternal is a powerful force that expresses itself through a wide range of human attitudes, emotions, and behavior. The qualities just listed are certainly not exclusive to women. A man too must develop these qualities or he is not quite human. Unfortunately, in our culture women have been burdened with the responsibility of being the sole carriers of these essential maternal qualities.

Woman also has had to carry the almost equally heavy burden of *love goddess*. As a consequence, she has had to put an enormous amount of energy into attending to her physical appearance and developing her capacity to stimulate erotic desires in men. This too has instinctual parallels among many other animal species. Is it not the scent of the female in heat that arouses the sexual desire in the male?

While the maternal capacity and the need to evoke erotic desires in the male through her physical charm and beauty are certainly instinctual dominants in women, to be forced to identify with these roles prevents a woman from developing her individuality. Furthermore, a creative, evolving male-female relationship is impossible as long as women remain in these archetypal roles and men in their corresponding "macho" (physical or intellectual) roles.

This reality—that women have largely identified with these roles and that men have generally remained on a similar primitive level, relating to women only as maternal or erotic archetypes—has contributed much to the sterility of modern marriages. The traditional patriarchal marriage was a viable institution as long as it was contained in a larger community and the couple found their meaning in raising children and perpetuating the life of the community. But since the breakdown of community, since marriages have become isolated city-states cut off from the meaningful, renewing rituals of communal life, couples have become more and more dependent on each other for intimacy, companionship, and spiritual renewal. Furthermore, after the children are grown and leave to form their own isolated units, marriage for the older couple no longer has any meaningful function as an essential nucleus for family life.

For a woman identified with the roles of mother and love goddess, this can be catastrophic. Her function as mother begins to lose its central importance, and her aging body makes it difficult for her to maintain her confidence in the powers of her erotic charm. What then is to hold the marriage together once motherhood is no longer so important and her youthful body has aged? Once a woman is stripped of the power of these archetypal roles, she has only herself to offer in a relationship, and if she has left herself undeveloped as she has played out her roles over the years, she feels empty and worthless. This is why feminism became such a vital force.

The tendency in the women's movement to place the blame for the oppression on men is, I believe, a great mistake. Clearly, basic instinctual needs have been fulfilled for both men and women as they have lived out their respective roles. And in the past these roles have not necessarily been any more oppressive than are the instinctual patterns governing animal relationships. Historically, men and women not only have been biologically dependent on each other, they also have been dependent on each other for psychological completion—men have carried the so-called masculine qualities and women the feminine. I believe the breakdown in traditional marriage, family, and community relationships is part of an evolutionary process leading toward higher levels of psychological integration and wholeness.

The inherent differences between male and female tend to become obliterated when women view their oppression mainly in terms of the male's need to dominate, to keep women in an inferior and servile position. What madness to denigrate the instinctual attraction that every woman feels for a physically or mentally strong and courageous male! And how can we simply dismiss the male's attraction to a warm, receptive, loving, and/or sexually seductive female as merely a product of cultural conditioning?

Even though most women appreciate the receptivity and nurturing of sensitive men, many complain that they miss the feeling of their own femininity that a more purely masculine male evokes. Many men also complain about the modern woman being too aggressive and castrating.

Paradoxically, the more a woman identifies with the archetypal feminine qualities of her nature, the more dependent she becomes on a man to make her feel whole and feminine. The same applies to the "macho" male who, as we all know, needs to be able to rescue the pure, soft, innocent, helpless maiden to complete and confirm his image. For both women and men, the way out of this type of dependency is for the ego not to identify with either the Feminine or the Masculine. What I mean by this is that both Feminine and Masculine, like yin and yang, are universal qualities of the soul to which we must have access in order to feel and to express our totality. The ego that identifies solely with either one loses this capacity.

We are all still struggling against cultural images that identify womanliness with the Feminine principle and manliness with the Masculine principle. For the modern woman striving for autonomy and independence, a good connection to the phallic aspects of her nature is essential. Unfortunately, out of fear of becoming too masculine, many women continue to hold onto their old patterns of relating to men even though they have learned to employ many of the same assertive tactics that men use to accomplish their professional goals. Consequently, after a hard day's work, many professional women feel possessed by this foreign masculine spirit and totally cut off from their femininity. This is particularly true for women who identify mainly with their feminine nature.

To identify with a particular aspect of our nature is to narrow and limit our personality. Such identifications as we have been discussing also lead to a polarization and split between the Masculine and Feminine. So the woman who must be assertive on her job feels very unfeminine when she has to be forceful, "like a man." But for the woman who realizes that she does not have to behave like a man in order to assume responsibilities that were once the province of men, a door is opened to tap into the roots of her own phallic or yang power, which is as basic to her as are the more womblike, yin qualities of her nature.

The main reason women feel so unwomanly in their newly won professional positions is that they have feared trusting their own phallic capacities to penetrate and generate. The more "feminine" a woman is, the more unconscious she will be of her own masculine qualities and the more she will experience them as foreign to her nature. Instead of feeling nourished by the spontaneous expressions of her own yang energy, she will feel threatened and overwhelmed. It feels much safer for her to learn to play the game according to the rules that men have developed, which tend to exclude her own forceful yang powers that arise from the depths of her being, like the enormous power that enables the womb to push the newborn child through the birth canal.[1]

Let us now attempt to explore the nature of the oppressive force that has not allowed women the freedom to realize their full potential and to develop psychologically. If not men, then who or what is responsible for the inferior economic and social status of women? And who is responsible for the prevailing attitudes that women are intellectually inferior to men, that they are irrational, guided more by emotions than reason, and therefore unstable, weak, childish, and morally inferior to men?

Depth psychology has established that both masculine and feminine qualities are contained within the souls of everyone. In our Western culture there has been an overdevelopment of the masculine perspective, which has resulted in a glorification of reason, objectivity, detachment, and noninvolvement and a denigration of all the subjective feelings and life-involving emotions. This powerful masculine force or spirit is primarily responsible for the oppression of women. But this distorted masculine perspective is deeply embedded within the psyches of both men and women. All the social, economic, and political changes will be worthless if this spirit that has been so oppressive to the Feminine continues to dominate. Having made this necessary shift to the psychological arena, our main concern becomes the oppression of the *Feminine*, not of women.

Let us briefly explore the nature of this spirit, this masculine deity that has finally provoked the wrath of so many women. One god in particular comes to mind: the ancient Greek god Apollo, who is still very much alive and kicking—at least for the modern physician, who on his graduation day must recite the Hippocratic oath, which begins, "I swear by Apollo. . . ." Apollo is a god who views the universe from afar, from a position of complete detachment and impersonality. His main concern is with clarity, order, and moderation. From his remote Olympian heights he is a dispassionate observer as we poor mortals struggle with our individual fates. Spiritual loftiness is a key part of his essence, and he is oblivious to the eternal worth of the human individual and the single soul. His concern is rather with what transcends the personal, with the unchangeable, with the eternal forms. This Apollonian deity, which I believe dominates our Western consciousness, has no concern for the needs of the individual human soul. The soul's needs for involvement, entanglement, proximity, melting, merging, exuberance, excess, and ecstasy are obliterated by the brilliant beam of this hypertrophied Apollonian perspective.

Apollo personifies a particular tendency toward detachment and impersonality in the masculine spirit. In his world the clarity and the breadth of the mind hold sway.

The feminine spirit, on the other hand, tends to move with the Dionysian thrust of life as it involves and entangles us with all living things. Dionysus, by the way, was a bisexual god, who was worshipped mainly by women in ancient Greece. His world is the life and mystery of the sap, and of the powers of the earth. He personifies proximity and union, in contrast to Apollo's distance and detachment. While Apollo's distance and clarity emphasize cognition, Dionysus plunges us into immediate contact with others and with the quick of life.

Apollo and Dionysus need each other. Without Dionysus, Apollo leads to the neglect and abuse of basic human needs, to the destructive manipulation of nature, and to a severe alienation from the earthy, maternal life-source of our own natures. Dionysus without Apollo leads ultimately to the obliteration of reason and culture. The Greeks knew that these two gods belonged together, and they were both equally honored in Delphi. Theological speculation even identified the one with the other.[2]

One of the most important consequences of our modern Apollonian distortion of life is that our world has become de-souled. Only the rational mind has been left with a bit of soul. The body, feelings, emotions, instincts, earth, nature, matter, living creatures, have become mere mechanisms totally devoid of any directing intelligence.[3] This final lofty Olympian elevation of the mind is the product of the Enlightenment and of Cartesian philosophy: "*Cogito, ergo sum*" (I think, therefore I am). For Descartes, the body, with its animal-sensual nature, is viewed as a substance distinct from the mind and subject only to mechanical laws; the body is passive while the mind is active and capable of free will. The rational mind is superior to the emotional-bodily roots of human nature because it can control and overcome the animal passions. The mind, says Descartes, is moved by soul, while the body is moved only by animal spirits. Only the mind has soul. And the prime mover is God, whose directing intelligence is continually manifesting itself in the rational mind. God has implanted motion in the human body and all other matter, but then he has abandoned all matter. "Mechanical laws govern the material world—man obeys the same laws since he is nothing but a more complex form of organization of the same processes that dominate other aspects of nature."[4]

These metaphysical assumptions have had an enormous influence on the development of Western science, and they still underlie most of modern Western thought. Any woman who buys this Apollonian distortion automatically devalues and mistrusts her so-called irrational feelings and intuitions, as well as the mysterious intelligence of the emotional-bodily roots of her nature. Of course, the Cartesian split between mind and body, and soul and body, is equally damaging to men who, in projecting the irrational and vulnerable aspect of their own nature onto women, have suffered from an even greater loss of soul.

One can hardly talk about the Apollonian oppression of women without recognizing that men have been at least equally oppressed by this ruling spirit of our times. The Feminine in both men and women is suffering. The liberation of the Feminine, rather than of women, is really what is needed. While the economic, educational, and social advantages that men have had over women are obvious and need to be corrected, I don't believe this is the main issue. As long as our culture and its institutions are ruled by a depersonalizing, dehumanizing spirit, the Feminine will continue to be abused and devalued no matter how many gains women make toward equality.

One of the main tasks of my profession, psychotherapy, is to help liberate, redeem, and heal the oppressed and rejected Feminine within the individual soul. It is no accident that modern psychotherapy originated out of Sigmund Freud's attempt to cure hysterical women. Certainly in those days women were still attempting to live up to some Victorian image of the proper lady, which was a terrible violation to the feminine soul. The Feminine cannot be confined to one-dimensional images. Let us further explore some of the attributes of the Feminine so that we might better understand the nature of the psychological task.

We already have discussed some of the qualities of the Mother archetype, but we have only touched upon the nature of the love goddess. Behind the current image of the "playgirl" ideal, which is so clearly a perverse masculine distortion of the Feminine, there must exist an important essence of the goddess. Of course, these plastic, sexless models of the "golden" goddess are a far cry from the enchanting beauty, the smiling charm, that radiates from Aphrodite and enraptures the senses. The cool detachment, the unmovable, untouchable distance that the playgirl maintains, has no connection at all to the Greek goddess. Quite the contrary. The great appeal of Aphrodite is her eagerness to surrender, to voluntarily bend toward the love-stricken with an undisguised yearning that is itself irresistible.

Aphrodite symbolizes a divine gift that does not belong only to women but belongs to all of life. Walter Otto offers us a larger, richer image of the world that she inspires with her spirit:

> From her comes not so much the ecstasy of desire as the charm which kindles and propels it. She is the enchantment that radiates from things and beings and enraptures the senses with its smile. Not only men and beasts but plants, inanimate images and appearances, even thoughts and words, derive their winning, moving, overwhelming sweetness from her.[5]

Thus, the world loses its sweet, yielding, enrapturing beauty when this Divine Feminine quality, which the Greeks called Aphrodite, is so denigrated that it becomes the bitter, sterile, hollow plastic husk of the "playgirl."

When I think about the Feminine, my initial images are of softness, gentleness, sensitivity, receptivity, warmth, moisture, responsiveness, containment, nurturing. Nothing sharp, probing, pushing, abrasive, phallic in any of these images. Rather, water; receptive, fertile earth; the womb. This certainly does not exhaust my images of the Feminine, but these all-accepting, all-embracing and nourishing, maternal, womblike aspects are basic. The exciting, bewitching, erotic charm of Aphrodite is certainly not unfamiliar to me.

I also have experienced a very direct, quick, clear, pragmatic type of logic that focuses sharply on attending to an immediate situation involving someone's welfare. I believe this usage of the intellect is feminine, in contrast to the impersonality and total disregard for the individual of the Apollonian intellect. Let us once again turn to the Greeks for support and elaboration of this view.

Pallas Athene, the goddess who never had a mother but was born from the head of Zeus, is such a clear-sighted goddess as I have described. Although she is equal to Apollo in her clarity and capacity to reason, unlike him she is a goddess of nearness. "She inspires man to boldness, a will to victory, courage, but always with directing reason and illuminating clarity."[6] She is always near and involved with the person: sharing, advising, helping, encouraging, and rejoicing in success. In comparing her to Apollo, Otto gives us an insightful view of her world:

> In Apollo we recognize the wholly masculine man. The aristocratic aloofness, the superiority of cognition, the sense of proportion, these and other related traits in a man, even music in the broadest sense of the word, are, in the last analysis, alien to a woman. Apollo is all these things. But perfection in the living present, untrammeled and victorious action, not in the service of some remote and infinite idea but for the mastery over the moment—that is the triumph which has always delighted woman in a man, to which she inspires him, and whose high satisfaction he can learn from her. The divine precision of the well-planned deed, the readiness to be forceful and merciless, the unflagging will to victory—this, paradoxical as it may sound, is woman's gift to man, *who by nature is indifferent to the momentary and strives for the infinite.*[7]

Athena is oblivious to what we call tenderheartedness. "Neither wisdom nor vision, neither devotion nor pleasure is her will. Consummation, the immediate present, action here and now—that is Athena."[8]

Another important aspect of the Feminine is related to a free, wild, independent, youthful, unspoiled nature spirit that has no interest in merging with a man. For the Greeks this aspect was reflected in the virgin goddess Artemis. Many young women today tend to identify with her. The need to return to the pristine beauty and wonder of nature also belongs to her world:

> Here everything is mobile and withdrawn and pure. The lucidity of the goddess hovers over meadows and lakes; her bright spirit is wafted in the solitude of forest, in the lonely lights of mountains; she causes the mysterious magic of solitude in nature and its breathless tremor, its playful tenderness and the sternness into which it can suddenly transform itself. To her belong the beasts of field and forest, which she protects maternally in their need, and harries to death as game with reckless pleasure. But man too belongs to her realm. Her manifestation is the tart sweetness of the young body and the young soul, the loveliness that shrinks at the fervor of the lover and turns cruel if he approaches too near. Inspirited by her is lightness of foot, which can only run or dance: hers is the morning freshness with its shimmer and clarity, in which, as in a dewdrop, the colorful fire of the heavenly rays glint and gleam.[9]

While we have only touched upon a few of the basic qualities of the Feminine—the maternal; the erotic; the bold, pragmatic reason; and the elusive spirit of the wood—what they all share in common are closeness to the earth and involvement with living things; the need to nurture, to promote growth; the need for closeness, for union with another or with nature. For the most part, the Feminine seems to move most comfortably and freely when it is close to the earth and nature. In contrast, the Masculine tends to seek distance from the earth, to find freedom in pure spirit, in the realm of abstract ideas and universal principles. Once again, let me stress that Masculine and Feminine are qualities that belong to both men and women. Anyone who identifies with only one of these opposites cannot really develop psychologically.

As symbols, Masculine and Feminine are the root metaphors, par excellence, for the fundamental affinity and polarity of all opposites. As I have written elsewhere, the most important function of the incest taboo is to promote the formation and internalization of images in the human psyche of the sacred union between the divine couple.[10] This internalization of the archetypal image of the harmonious union between the Masculine/Feminine opposites is essential for internal balance and wholeness and for the experience of intimacy with others.

The incest wound describes the wounding developmental splits between the Masculine/Feminine opposites, love/sex, mind/body, spirit/matter, inner/outer. One of the consequences of the incest wound is the prevalent internal split in our Western culture between the maternal-spiritual and the erotic-sensual aspects of the Feminine—between the Virgin Mary and Aphrodite. As a consequence of such wounds, a man then tends to associate purity, softness, comfort, and tender, loving sentiments with wife-mother; and erotic aggression, sensual abandonment, excitement, and passion with the promiscuous hussy or the "other woman." This same split occurs in women as a consequence of the incest wound, so that they too suffer from this fragmented perspective.

Hand in hand with the split Feminine goes a similar split within the Masculine; that is, between the understanding, protective, paternal aspects and the aggressive, phallic, sensual, dynamic aspects. The healing of these splits has much to do with the redemption of the Feminine. In contrast to the Masculine, the Feminine cannot tolerate being stuck in a fragmented, compartmentalized state.

Let us return to the psychological task of the redemption of the Feminine. An appreciation of the basic feminine attitude of acceptance of and harmony with nature is absolutely essential. The Feminine always respects and honors nature's mysteries. Unlike the Masculine, the Feminine seldom attempts to go against nature or to penetrate and dissect the mysteries in order to gain control over nature so that it can manipulate it to its own advantage. In this sense the Feminine is submissive to nature and unable to alter or change the course of natural events. But it is just this apparent submissiveness and helplessness, this complete acceptance of *what is*, that has not been respected by the masculine spirit in our culture. Above all, we must confront that inner masculine voice that continually makes us feel ashamed and inadequate about those aspects of ourselves that appear weak, helpless, dependent, and impotent when viewed from some perverse masculine perspective of strength, intelligence, and potency. While the Feminine may not have the power or inclination to alter the course of nature, its relationship to nature gives it a strength that the Masculine lacks. The spirit that enables a woman to flow with the rhythm of her monthly moon cycle, to patiently and joyfully endure the nine months it takes to give birth to a child, is something a man must develop or all his best-laid plans and creative efforts will be constantly aborted. Without a feminine respect for nature's ways, the ingenuity of the masculine spirit soon becomes destructive to life.

Openness, receptivity, responsiveness to life's forces are characteristic of all aspects of the Feminine. While the capacity to initiate action is contained in the Feminine, the generative life-force is essentially phallic. Understanding the reciprocal relationship between the masculine and feminine aspects of the soul is important to the psychological process of feminine liberation. If we neglect and denigrate the soft, open, receptive feminine aspects of ourselves, our lives become progressively more rigid, empty, sterile, inert, and filled with meaningless action.

By the same token, if we fear opening up to the sudden, spontaneous, irrational influx of our phallic energies, nothing moves, nothing changes, and our lives become stagnant. A positive relationship to the phallic root of the masculine spirit is absolutely essential for creative development, for the liberation of the Feminine, and for the liberation of women.[11] As long as a woman is afraid, angry, and rejecting of the Masculine within herself, as long as she continues to fight the battle mainly "out there" instead of inside her own soul, she will never really become free of her oppressive dependency on men, because she has essentially cut herself off from the phallic source of her own power and potency. Furthermore, she will continually provoke men to incarnate and act out the very thing she fears, which, of course, only intensifies her conviction that men are self-centered, dominating, and untrustworthy.

Above all, the Feminine places the highest value on relationship. Consistent with the Masculine's fascination with the infinite is its tendency to view relationship in terms of purpose and accomplishment. In contrast, relationship is an end in itself for the Feminine spirit, and it feels violated when a relationship is being used primarily for any other purpose, even a worthy one.

We have touched upon some of the psychological factors involved in feminism, on the nature of the Feminine, and on the need to differentiate more clearly between the Feminine and woman. As long as a woman does not distinguish and differentiate herself from the Feminine, she will continue to experience men as saviors or oppressors. In either case, she remains dependent on a man to connect her to her own phallic nature and unconscious of the psychic dimensions of her oppression, which are far more important and in more urgent need of attention.

. . . .

PART 2

Re-Mothering Ourselves: Healing Our Relationships with Women and the Feminine

Every mother contains her daughter in herself and every daughter her mother.

C. G. JUNG

We must be willing to *suffer* our mothers within us, to see to the roots of their behavior within us, and to forgive and transform it in ourselves. We also may be able to see through to our common lot as women, finding in our inner mothers responses to powerlessness, perversions of spirit, or distorted potentials. Becoming conscious of the negative effects of our mothers on our lives is not enough; it is as if we must take our mothers *in* and carry them psychologically as they once carried us physically.

KATHIE CARLSON
In Her Image

The Mother World is that realm of life that contains women and the Feminine. For women, this includes our personal mothers, daughters, and sisters, and perhaps today we might add our collective sense of sisterhood with all women. At another level, this realm contains the Mother archetype, in her positive (nurturing, sustaining, loving) aspect and her negative (seductive, devouring, destroying) aspect. The Great Mother archetype also appears as our bodily source, the earth, and as our spiritual source, the Divine Goddess.

(For men, the Mother World also includes wives and the anima, or the unconscious feminine element in the male psyche, sometimes referred to as soul.)

For women, the Mother World is the world of origin, the source of knowledge about our identities, our bodies, our futures. In an earlier era of depth psychology, Erich Neumann wrote that all egos were masculine by nature, while the unconscious was considered feminine. Today it is widely accepted that women's egos are feminine, a legacy of our mothers.

For this reason, sorting through our relationships with our mothers (both the living person and the images we have gathered up over the years) is a primary step toward creating our own distinct and independent identities as women. We can begin by trying to make conscious those aspects of ourselves that we have absorbed unknowingly from our mothers. These may include creative and useful traits, such as an artistic sense or a love of business, wilderness, or children. They may also include our mother's "shadow" qualities, excess baggage we would be better off without, such as dependence on men, substance addiction, or a deep sense of insecurity. We need to become aware of those disliked and rejected qualities in her that we have struggled to disown, which may have entered us unconsciously, because they probably continue to influence us below the boundaries of awareness.

These are the first steps in *re-mothering* ourselves, separating out our own identities as distinct from our mothers and from the archetype. Only then can we provide ourselves as adults with those essential qualities, which we may have missed as children, that will nourish and sustain our growth. In this way we can learn to honor the legacies of the Mother World, choosing those we wish to inherit. Kathie Carlson puts it this way in her book *In Her Image*:

> By turning toward our inner mothers instead of trying to rid ourselves of their unwanted tenancy within us, it is as if we put our mothers into a different context, into the wholeness of ourselves. In this way, we become their matrix, in a sense, we become pregnant with our mothers and carry the possibility of their transformation and rebirth within ourselves.

There are as many ways of re-mothering as there are individual women. No formula fits all. We can try to find a nurturing and creative relationship with a surrogate mother, such as a friend, mentor, grandmother, or psychotherapist; we can join groups of women initiating and guiding other women in awakening the Conscious Feminine; and we can use writing, painting, and active imagination to express the latent parts of ourselves, to speak in the voices that ordinarily are silenced.

Some of us can develop a more conscious, revitalized relationship with our real mothers. This has the greatest chance of taking place after a certain amount of inner work has been accomplished, after strong feelings of anger and blame have been released.

I also believe that our current widespread fascination with deep ecology, and our efforts to reconnect with the earth and our roots in the natural world, are a reflection of a need to realign with the Mother archetype. For some of us, working with the Goddess archetypes also serves this purpose by providing a feminine source that is so much larger than our personal mothers.

In the essays in this section, you will find a rich array of inspiring ideas and practical guidance. As Riane Eisler asked when world culture was detoured from a female-centered one to a male-centered one, Emily Hancock asks when this detour occurs in the identities of individual girls. She proposes that we can reclaim the young girl within us, as she was before she took on the expectations and projections of others, as a way to complete our unfinished business with the past. By nurturing and strengthening that part of the female self, we can mother her back to wholeness.

Nan Hunt explores the nature of the mother/daughter wound in a mutual rejection of each other's essence. She tells stories about how the inherited female bonds of body and instinct are broken. Like Lynda Schmidt and Marion Woodman later in this section, she hints at the complicated relationship between the Mother archetype and the personal mother. And she offers concrete ways of re-mothering ourselves via mentoring with a female friend or therapist.

Lynda W. Schmidt explores her own realignment with her mother after a long stint in the Father World. She introduces us to the useful term *father's daughter*, which refers to those women who deeply identify with their fathers and lose touch with their female identities. Schmidt also wonders what conscious mothering would be like and how it might grow out of instinctual mothering. Like Nan Hunt, she describes losing her female instincts and turning to male experts to help raise her babies.

Naomi Ruth Lowinsky points to our grandmothers as potentially positive sources of feminine modeling. The grandmother has a role in the family as well as a role in the internal world of a woman's psyche. Lowinsky suggests that we need to sort out her influences upon us and upon our mothers in order to uncover the source of our "motherline," the feminine lineage or family tree. Like Linda Schierse Leonard, who suggests in Part 3 of this book that we need to redeem our fathers by appreciating what is valuable in them and separating out what is not, Lowinsky suggests that we need to get realistic images of our mothers and grandmothers, to value their gifts and yet develop the Feminine in our own separate ways.

Marion Woodman's overarching description of the archetypes of mother, virgin, and crone sums up our vision of the Mother World within. For her, re-mothering is a consequence of the difficult work of psychological differentiation and a spiritual awakening that brings wisdom to the soul. She explains how unconscious mothering can give rise to conscious mothering, which awakens the virgin, the symbol of spiritual wholeness that Woodman perceives in people's dreams these days. The birth of the conscious crone follows, the wise one who comes about as a result of a life fully lived and who offers love without strings attached.

Kathleen Riordan Speeth, with painterly words, depicts the Madonna and child, the mother and virgin in a physical and spiritual union. She closes this section with an image that is both awesome and inspiring.

4 · THE GIRL WITHIN: TOUCHSTONE FOR WOMEN'S IDENTITY

· · · · · · ·

EMILY HANCOCK

Emily Hancock asks a key question: When does the invisible influence of the male-centered culture begin to impress itself on a young girl, deterring her natural feminine development? Hancock, a Berkeley psychotherapist, has found that a young girl between the ages of eight and ten is still innocent and playful yet fast becoming self-contained and responsible. Although she may become a tomboy, at this age she is not yet behaving in reaction to boys or men.

In her book The Girl Within, *Hancock describes in detail the process by which the girl's female sense of mastery becomes derailed. Typically at puberty her mother joins the official culture to teach her to be a "lady." If this happens in conjunction with her father stepping out of the picture at adolescence, her natural ways are cut short, and she is forced into the cultural mold.*

Hancock proposes that by recapturing early memories of the girl within, we can regain the sense of self we had before others' projections and expectations took hold. This more natural or essential self exists within us independent of relationship to others; it has its own style, sensibilities, joys, and fears. Like the inner child discussed widely in psychology circles today, the girl within offers us a source of renewal, a way for women to offer re-mothering to the young girl who still lives within each of us.

Emily Hancock, Ed.D., author of The Girl Within, *began her research on women's development at Harvard University, where she earned her doctorate in human development in 1981. She teaches adult development at the Center for Psychological Studies in Albany, California, and has a private practice in Berkeley.*

Now that women's roles are up for grabs, we are finally beginning to ask who and what a woman might be if defined according to her inner sense of self instead of by the rules of the patriarchy. With our growing awareness that womanly strengths have been bent to the needs and ends of others, we have turned at last toward delineating, affirming, and expressing the self. But the culture has been hard-pressed to spell out how these goals, new to women, can be won on women's own terms. These days a man can still follow in his father's footsteps to exercise time-worn "male" pre-rogatives, but the "new woman" can hardly count on her mother's ways to carry her through. Caught in a peculiar historical moment, she turns away from a seemingly useless past to traverse unfamiliar territory with neither a map from her forebears nor the counsel of elders to guide her.

On the face of it, contemporary culture appears to support her goals, opening the world of achievement to the new woman's challenge. But underneath this apparent liberation a variety of forces threaten to undercut her femininity and defeat the very self-realization she seeks. Freedom from the restrictive roles of the past—and from the psychological confines those roles imposed—has opened the gate to female consciousness. But the rules of the patriarchy, insidious because they are disguised as equal freedom, still operate to shape a woman's development. Many women who seek to break out of the confines of domestic roles, for instance, forfeit their quest for a natural, female existence that encompasses both purpose and care by being forced to conform to a male model. That model demands that she push womanly concerns to the sidelines, strip down to her competence, and outfit herself in corporate drag. Too much cultural change in the name of feminism has led us to applaud the "male" qualities she displays, sup-porting a woman's endeavors to be like a man. Virtually obliged to take up residence in the "real world," the new woman unwittingly casts her lot with the patriarchy in the name of escaping it.

The new woman thus lives in a man's world where she is turned against womanly strengths that lie at the heart of her identity. Little does she suspect that the plethora of choices now offered to females constitutes an illusion. Duped by the promise that she can have it all, she is compelled instead to *do* it all by a culture that offers its members only a single way to count. Captivated by the patriarchy's masquerade, she becomes less conscious of the split between who she "really" is and what she appears to be. This disconnection from her primary identity sends her veering around a dan-gerous curve when it comes to the development of the authentic female self.

How might such an unwitting daughter of the patriarchy pursue her quest for individuation? Absent a female blueprint for identity, how is a woman to realize her true self?

The answers to these questions lie, according to a study I made of women's ego development,[1] in "the girl within," the spirited, playful, self-contained girl of eight, nine, or ten years of age that a female carries in memory as a touchstone for the woman she can become. In generations fpast, restrictive experiences that bound us to the feminine ideal caused us to lose our grip on this girl. Now the opposite rendering—woman as man—threatens to derail her. Despite such destructive pulls, however, some women rediscover this primary childhood identity. Those who circle back to her find in the forgotten girl a key to unlocking the essential female self.

Who is this "girl within"? What deep truth does she possess? Poised between the make-believe of preschool and the thrall of adolescence, a girl this age occupies an intermediate zone of childhood, an interim space between fantasy and reality that fosters creative self-ownership.[2] Playful yet purposeful, she has opened the gate to the age of reason. Practically an old hand at school, she is already reading and calculating, playing group games, acquiring athletic skills, and absorbing the rules of her young society. When she has the good fortune to grow up in a family that encourages independence and celebrates achievements, a girl this age meets the world on her own terms. A soaring imagination combines with competence and adventurous longing to take her far from home, both in imagination and reality. The rapid development of the girl's mind, the acceleration of her know-how, the shift in the way she thinks[3] are acknowledged by cultures around the world. Nature and society conspire to allow a girl this age to flourish; harmony and integrity abound as she enjoys a wholeness of self, a unity with the cosmos, a natural radiance.

In the midst of a marital crisis, Megan, a thirty-one-year-old woman in my study, recalled such a girl. Jolted by her husband's affair just after the birth of their first baby, Megan realized suddenly that she had no identity of her own. She had counted on marriage itself to provide her a sense of self. Frightened when she found that such an assumption had led her to abandon her own quest, she faced the difficult task of building an identity. This she did by making choices, decisions that sprang from a newfound sense of who and what she was. Defining herself through this process reminded her of a critical experience she'd had at the age of nine, when her family had moved from New York City to the suburbs, interrupting Megan's confirmation studies. Without the aid of her parents, she arranged with her teachers to send her lessons through the mail so she could complete them by herself.

This act of independence was lodged in Megan's image of herself: "At nine, I can remember walking on a fence, all around a park, thinking I really liked being nine years old and I wouldn't mind being nine forever," she recollected. "I was finding out about the world, not doing anything particularly momentous, just thinking those thoughts to myself as I walked along the fence. I remember having a real sense of joy, of confidence about negotiating the world on my own. The image I have is of a child with a long string to hold onto, one she can move freely around. I felt secure and self-contained. I had a sense that 'I can get by in the world, even if it means I am alone. There's a way for me to negotiate it. I can do it.' "

Vulnerable in her new motherhood and distressed by the marital crisis, Megan hearkened back to this self-possessed child and recaptured the sense of purpose she had embodied as a girl. She rediscovered the forgotten autonomy and initiative she needed for adult independence. The nine-year-old had carried those materials in memory even as they became unfamiliar to Megan in the process of growing up. Now that girl served as a touchstone for the woman she would become. Retracing her steps and finding within herself a child she could rely on led Megan to the feminine roots of her womanly strength.

What waylays the girl within? How is her self-ownership negated? What becomes of her élan?

Although there is no single experience of girlhood, the scores of women I have talked with give a surprisingly uniform account of growing up and losing the girl within. They recall this girl as one who makes the world her own. Liberated from the confines of the family, she is proud of her newfound ability to order and direct her life. Suddenly "in business for herself,"[4] her competence at home and school grows in one long upward sweep. Applauded for being both smart and strong, she is mistress of excellence.

Even if her circumstances are limited, a girl this age can aspire to far-reaching objectives in her imagination—a new and private inner realm that no one else is privy to. There, if nowhere else, the sky is her limit, her ambitions are boundless; anything is possible. Contradictions do not deter her: future archaeologist and lawyer, she will practice law during the winter and go on digs when summer comes. Would-be oceanographer, astronaut, governor, neurosurgeon, symphony conductor, bank president, or judge, she is, ideally, supported by others in her future vision of herself. Her goals are rarely subject to criticism; her choices do not yet include losses; only later will one choice preclude another. Her girlhood experience encompasses male and female, work and play, independence and dependence—without subordinating either to the other. Unfettered by feminine conventions, she can think, she can plan, she can do!

A tomboy at heart, this is the time in a female's life when, paradoxically, she is most often allied with her father and yet *least defined by the patriarchy*. The culture provides her a hiatus between the ruffled panties and Mary Janes of her earlier years and the comely decorum it will demand as she grows older, permitting her a brief respite from its construction of the female. At the center of a universe in perfect harmony, she is master of her destiny, captain of her soul. She is the subject of her own experience.

But suddenly, well before puberty, along comes the culture with the pruning shears, ruthlessly trimming back her spirit. Adults who had left her to her own devices now anticipate her blossoming femininity and nip her expansion in the bud. As the culture draws the line between little and big, play and work, female and male, its agents feel obliged to intervene. Old templates of female as nurturer persist, making a girl's initiative threatening. Too often, the teacher who had encouraged the ambitious archaeologist now warns that archaeology requires five languages. The little rancher who had been given a lasso for her birthday is informed, in the gentlest way perhaps, that only men are cowboys. The anatomy books that affirmed her interest in medicine are subtly replaced with a nurse's watch suitable for taking a pulse. Once tolerated as inconsequential, an older girl's visions of her adult self grow subject to scrutiny. Her elders deflate her "grandiose" ideas, deem them unrealistic. Myriad ways are found to pinch her back and shape her.

Conformity marks the era of the older girl, in spite of changing times. Seldom permitted to be a tomboy once her features start to mature, she is expected to "behave like a young lady." Taken out of the treehouse of her earlier days, the girl is brought back into the human environment and expected to cultivate social graces. The feminine mandate to care for others persists beneath the modern whitewash, stifling her impulse to climb, to run, to scale a ridge—and to otherwise follow her active pursuits. Where her girlhood competence knew no bounds, her feminine effectiveness is channeled into the interpersonal realm as she approaches puberty. While her brother is encouraged to expand his initiative and exercise his independence, she is turned to feminine compliance. Previously abroad in the world of nature, the older girl must come inside.

As she trades her blue jeans for a skirt, her father, just yesterday her staunch supporter, pushes her out of his lap and draws back to let her mother take over again. Even these days, her mother may subtly shape her activities to fit feminine stereotypes, training her in the same roles that have defined *her* as wife and mother. The official culture—a patriarchal culture that places its lock on her mother, aunts, cousins, teachers, *and* her father —defines her as "female" instead of as "person" when she is returned to the women's world. The link between who she is and what she does, no longer direct, is broken. She gives up "doing" in favor of "being" a good girl. Instead of suiting herself, she tries to please those around her. Impressed with the importance of others' opinions, she molds herself to what she thinks others want her to be.

An exuberant athlete at nine, many a girl is a careful young lady at eleven as female appendages begin to intrude on pure physical prowess: unwieldy breasts, broadening hips, softening contours clutter the taut streamlined body of her androgynous youth. No matter how proud she may be of "becoming a woman," physical changes hamper a girl's freedom and weaken the confidence she earlier placed in her physical skills. With a girl's puberty comes a lag in growth; with the boy's comes an increase in mass. As he catches up to and surpasses her in height, weight, and muscular force, the boy, for the first time, is bigger and stronger than the girl. As he gets stronger, smarter, louder, she feels weaker and less certain. Her body softens while his hardens. Sexual dichotomies divide a girl against herself by labeling her strengths and interests as unfeminine. The abilities that assured her place among peers now jeopardize her popularity; a sinewy body, impressive height, and forceful strength belong to the boys. While the boy's adolescent changes portend increased dominance, the girl's imply, recurrently, the mandate to nurture and the need for restraint. His experience of adolescence is one of increased power; hers is one of increased risk. His freedoms are dramatically expanded while hers are curtailed. He is encouraged to explore; she, cautioned about her feminine vulnerability, is expected to stay close by. He is urged on while she is coerced: diminutive in comparison to her male age-mate, she can no longer fend off an attack. For him, new lands are filled with conquest; for her, safety resides at home. The world is his oyster; it holds dangers for her. The girl-world of eight or nine thus yields, long before adolescence, to a world divided by sex.

The older girl succumbs to the culture's image of the female, object to the male subject. Her childhood displays give way to hiding—skills, excellence, aspirations, parts of the self—first from others in order to please, eventually also from herself. No longer free to project herself into the future with the egocentrism natural to her age, she works to curb her competence. Competition intensifies the conquests of her brother; in her it yields to compromise.[5] Competence enhances the male; it still desexes the female.[6] The unity of her activities falls away as a girl's own goals are cast against a "womanly" life. Female roles impinge; stereotypes take over. She cannot help but feel caught by contradictory imperatives: even as she dons her soccer uniform, ads for a deodorant implore, "Never let them see you sweat." Self-confidence is subverted by self-consciousness as a girl judges herself as others judge her—against an impossible feminine ideal. To match that ideal, she must stash away a great many parts of herself. She gives up being childlike in order to be ladylike. She loses her position as self; she senses that she is now "other."

In the grand scheme of things, a girl, even today, has little choice but to take her place as a member of the Second Sex, as Simone De Beauvoir named it nearly forty years ago. Ironically, what De Beauvoir wrote still stands: Despite the latest wave of the feminist movement, females of all ages are objectified and devalued. Advertising has multiplied the legion invitations to exploit a woman's sensuality, whether by eating yogurt, drinking a fine liquor, or flying away to vacation on an island beach. Yuppie watering holes to which a woman may repair after work offer up dazzling concoctions with such names as Silk Panties. In fact, females are increasingly sexualized—at a shockingly young age. Alongside vampish women in black lace bras and French-cut bikinis, department-store catalogs feature seven-year-old girls modeling satiny tap-pants and camisoles, their little faces oddly provocative when made up with cherry rouge and lipstick. These girl sirens are impelled to develop into *femmes fatales*. Contained, adapted, and sexualized long before adolescence, they are cowed and tamed as their natural spontaneity gives way to patriarchal constructions of the female. In donning the masks provided by the culture, a girl easily loses sight of who and what she is beneath the feminine facade she adopts in youth.

How can women repossess the essential femininity that the girl of eight or nine embodies, given the social forces that disconnect her from her natural authority? Women in my study who reclaimed an authentic female sense of self did so by delving into the inner realm of memory and imagination where the girl within is harbored. They detailed the experiences that divided them against themselves, driving the essential girl into that realm where she remained hidden—even from herself. They described their pursuit of the authentic self and showed how the female experience had robbed them of it. They described the cultural press that negated their feminine identities in youth, and they conveyed their shock when they discovered, long after making adult commitments that tied them to the destinies of others, that the identities they had assumed since girlhood were bolted to a man-made foundation that was not of their own making. Most important, they unearthed the girl from beneath the rubble she had been buried in by the patriarchy, and reconstructed a womanly identity from the natural materials she had preserved over time. When women probed their inner experience, when they worked their way back to the nascent identity they'd had before they were deflected from it by the culture's exaltation of the Masculine and its denigration of the Feminine, when they reinhabited the inner realm that harbored the girl within, they reclaimed the authentic girl and retrieved her feminine strengths.

Women in the study who tapped that inner realm embedded their images of self in a fertile landscape. In the domain of image and imagination where they were free from patriarchal constructions of the female, they found metaphors for their development that sprang spontaneously from a natural, organic source. Anita, a dance therapist in her early fifties, said, for instance, "My development reminds me of a leaf floating on a pond. At the surface there is quiet: no ripples, nothing happening, just gray, gray water. And then there is a geyser. A great geyser shoots up from a spring and the little leaf on top gets lifted way up high!" For Anita, the long decades that separated childhood from her early forties were static, "latent, dormant years." The sixties' wave of feminism finally provided the habitat for her germination: "And then I read *The Feminine Mystique* and got swept up in the movement. When the climate started warming up, I started to grow like a seed that had been encased in ice." Shackled by a long, unhappy marriage, she was helped to "shake off a tangle of chains" by the rebirth fostered by the movement.

Katherine, a pediatrician in her middle thirties, captured a feminine, generative essence when she compared her children to a garden to be tended and directed her attention to cultivating their potential: "It's like a garden. You've got flowers and you've got weeds," she said. "What I see as my job as a parent is trying to get the flowers to grow in the child's personality. And you want to nourish and make beautiful the potential you find there."

Miriam, a consultant in her middle fifties, likened her development to "a bud blooming and unfolding." She singled out an important feature of the flower: "There are some flowers, like begonias and camellias, whose layers of petals open slowly. It's the petals that are the most important— the unfolding of the petals. Whole layers of petals unfolding like a spiral." The synchronized unfolding was stimulated in Miriam's life by the human potential movement and by reckoning her relationship with her daughter.

Liz provided another flowering image, one that reflected her feminine triumph over forces that nearly put her under. She grew up with a mother who was enmired by domestic misery. Liz had a baby before she married and continued to live at home. Convinced that her failure as a daughter had caused her mother's despair, Liz fell into a depressed mood herself. She finally extricated herself from the "cave of womanly doings" that had de-feated her mother by befriending a woman who was utterly different from her mother—a light-hearted, optimistic woman who loved mothering and female domesticity. This pivotal woman-to-woman relationship helped Liz avert her mother's stifling ways and led to "an awakening and a flowering." Once her identification with the friend had put her at a safe distance from the depressive pull that coerced her mother, Liz married and had three children. Having defeated female pessimism, she felt that she was "bursting into bloom." She added to her metaphorical self-description, "A garden is imminent!"

Perhaps most striking among the women's images—striking for its deep statement as to how a woman must reconcile and forge, moment by moment, the organic stuff of her life by relying on inner initiative, responsiveness, and self-determination—was thirty-year-old Rosabeth's metaphor for her development: "A coastline represents some balancing, some forming that I've done throughout," she said as she took a blank piece of paper and inked out a line with her gold fountain pen. A constantly shifting landform created by the ever-moving sea against the "hard edges" of her nature, it began to look like the coast of Maine as she drew it down the page. "It's rocky. I see it with the blue water and green land meeting. The ocean is a beautiful blue and the land is made of browny-green mountains and rocks—and the land falls up and down. The line is jaggedy. That represents all sorts of experiences that have been upsetting, or exhilarating, or deflating, or instances that made me proud."

The line depicted a juncture of self and life experience rather than representing their division. An abstraction that stood for a meeting of elements, almost like the fence that Megan walked along, the line represented Rosabeth's continually evolving self. "What you have here is a meeting of forces. And my life has been the path between them," she said.

Rosabeth's coastline metaphor borrows on the purposeful autonomy of the inner girl. In that girl's ability to balance the known with the unknown, ocean and rock, competence and care, conscious and unconscious, masculine and feminine, in her willing engagement of the dynamic tension between attachment and autonomy, male and female, work and love, lies the reconciliation of the dichotomies that divide us against ourselves.

Excavated from the inner realm, the girl has much to teach the woman about how to seize the subjective stance that lies at the heart of generative power. She naturally synthesizes the dualities of male and female in her androgyny, fuses work and play in her purposeful activity, reconciles love and hate in her lack of contradiction. She utilizes dependence and independence in the tenacious pursuit of her own interests. She embodies both sides of competence, encompassing social and relational mastery as well as concrete skill. Separate and yet connected, she is autonomous and yet attached. Competitive in the proper spirit, she is driven by mastery—not to dominate and seize power over others but to grasp the mysteries and challenges of the world herself. Brimming with initiative, the girl unifies the basic values of cooperation, care, and competence without distorting them. Like Rosabeth's coastline, she reconciles elements of human nature instead of splitting them apart.

Women's organic images speak to the critical shift we need to restore the natural balance of those values: the shift from object to subject. By reclaiming the girl's sense of self as subject, by countering woman's position as object, by reaching back to catch hold of the girl who embodies a primary feminine identity, women can stay true to the potential of the fertile feminine world that survives apart from the sterility of patriarchal values.

Women have long tended the gardens of others. While providing the context for others' development, they have historically neglected their own. When a woman carries the virginal girl across the threshold into woman-hood, when she speaks in her own idiom as naturally as she mouths the language of the patriarchy, when she hits on the deepest truth about who she is and tells her story of becoming whole, she gains access to a world that is as fertile and abundant as the most verdant gardens. Only when we wed girlhood autonomy to womanly fecundity and recognize the connection between germ and soil will we restore our generativity as a culture and thrive and flower.

In the alliance between the girl who possesses initiative and the woman who knows her generativity lies the creative force we need to become fully ourselves and to make of this culture what it so desperately needs. The fullness of human development depends on circling back to the girl within and carrying her into womanhood.

5 · IN THE LAPS OF
THE MOTHERS

· · · · · · ·

NAN HUNT

In this piece on mothers and daughters, Los Angeles poet and writing teacher Nan Hunt weaves together many themes that appear elsewhere in this book. She explores the widespread damage to the mother/daughter bond, which results in the devaluation of the Feminine by members of the younger generation, their internal identification with masculine ways, and their consequential loss of connection to the "motherline."

One further result of this process is the loss of instinctual mothering, with women turning to male "experts" for guidance in childbearing and rearing. This fact, Hunt implies, reveals the falsity of the myth that women are all-powerful in the home. For even in motherhood, our powerful instincts are often denied and turned over to men.

In exploring the link between the Mother archetype and the personal mother, Hunt proposes that both are endangered today: the Great Mother, our earth, abused and taken sorely for granted, and the mothers of our children, overworked and undervalued, are severely at risk.

I believe that this damage to the Mother has led to an epidemic of inappropriate overmothering, which has come to be called co-dependence. In effect, we try to mother each other in our intimate relationships because the Mother archetype is so severely repressed.

Hunt is calling for re-mothering ourselves at all levels, individually and collectively. She suggests several strategies: We can find a female mentor or surrogate mother, as she did, who embodies a full feminine self and supports our development as women. We can use writing and active imagination to awaken and express latent parts of ourselves. And we can join groups of women initiating and guiding other women in awakening the Conscious Feminine.

Nan Hunt is a lecturer in poetry and creative writing for the UCLA Extension Writing Program. Her courses incorporate depth-psychology approaches to writing. She is president of the C. G. Jung Analytical Psychology Club in Los Angeles. Besides the achievements of motherhood, she has had articles and poetry published in more than forty literary magazines. Her volume of poems, My Self in Another Skin, *came out in 1981.*

We are losing the archetype of the Good Mother. Images of a personal mother and the racial memory of a goddess-like, archetypal Mother continue to appear in our dreams but lack a nurturing emotional energy for many women. Not only have we lost the Good Mother in dreams; we have lost her in actuality. The mother-daughter wound is epidemic.

This is because of an accumulation of effects from poor mothering in the past by women seriously damaged in self-esteem and in their ability to celebrate female qualities. (In fact, many showed marked preference for their sons.) The devaluing of the Feminine has been a legacy carried over from one generation to the next. Until mid-twentieth century, women had to live in societies that denied them political and economic participation, robbing them of personal power. Women whose personalities were formed in environments that suppressed and belittled the full range of female attributes became warped and hurt beyond their ability to repair themselves. The ancient Feminine principle that is instinctively connected to the earth and to matter, the archetype that is the Great Mother of life *and* death and all possibilities, also has been without love and honor in Western societies for at least two thousand years.

Where love is lacking, a negative power fills the vacuum. "Civilized" mothers seemed to lose their instincts for fiercely protecting their young or for a confident maternal wisdom. They surrendered their positive power to outside authority. Shallow relationships, child abuse and neglect, and egocentric control or passive indifference have resulted. To be deprived of an emotionally supportive, enabling mother—one who has strengths that a daughter can emulate—is traumatic and has serious lifelong effects on a daughter's emotional development and relationships.

Every archetype has two sides, positive and negative. For many women of my generation, over age forty-five, and of the generation of my two daughters, ages twenty to forty, an intimate and loving mother-daughter connection has been unfamiliar or unwelcome. For women and men alike, the negative side of the Mother archetype holds the most power. As Marion Woodman, author and Jungian analyst, points out, we are living in a mother-bound patriarchy. Although masculine (father) values still predominate in our culture, most men are as wounded and psychically vulnerable as women because of love-hate ambivalences beginning very early in relationship to psychologically wounded mothers.[1] Both men and women are arrested in a negative mother complex. They do not realize how they are influenced by past clusters of emotions around the idea of mother, which were repressed and submerged into the unconscious mind.

It has been my experience during years of teaching college women that many openly express dislike, even hatred, for their mothers or, at best, describe an uneasy truce with them. Therapists find that this is a current problem for most women clients, many of whom feel that their mothers tried to exercise the control of a petty tyrant. The attempted control over their children's lives communicates much about the desperation of women who felt unable to validate their roles in any other way. Although they were emotional bullies, these mothers lacked self-definition and, therefore, clear and autonomous values to pass on to their daughters. A common image of mother has been an individual with disgruntled powerlessness rather than effective grace.

This is true for Ricki, my thirty-three-year-old student, who has purposely developed a strong and muscular body. She is employed as a machinist in an all-male environment, which she finds quite comfortable. She says, "My mother put up with my step-dad's drinking and running around; she was so passive and dependent. She might cry and complain, but was afraid to leave him or tell him to get out, in spite of her having a good job. I couldn't stand to stay home and see her weakness."

Even the shape and texture of the mother's body often carries the onus of weakness. Monica, a young friend of mine, tells how she was repulsed by the sight of her mother's bulbous breasts and belly, as though she couldn't bear the image of female destiny. Also, her mother's distracted busyness felt like callous indifference to her. As a result, Monica expresses disinterest in conventional marriage and motherly pursuits such as bearing children, even though a very feminine self acts in her dreams and in her maternal solicitude toward her woman partner.

I am another one of those women who did not see anything to emulate in their mothers. I saw my mother plunge into prolonged hysteria and depression because of being rejected by my father for another woman when I was fifteen. My odd reaction was to ignore my burgeoning womanhood because that meant being too vulnerable. At sixteen I was swaggering around an airfield in a man's oversized flight jacket, trying to learn what enabled men to pursue their own interests regardless of consequences, what made them so inured to emotion that they could perform daringly in planes—or anywhere. I had joined the Civil Air Patrol and learned to be a pilot.

Neither parents, school, friends, nor any institution allowed me to experience self-empowerment the way flying did then. I was growing up during the era when girls spent their free afternoons playing Frank Sinatra and Doris Day records at "Coke" parties, while boys practiced sports or studied to get scholarships. My hormones were giving me messages of female sensuality and receptiveness. Some messages I paid attention to, others I tried to ignore. Nevertheless, I gained competence in a world of action and risk and established a base of self-esteem out of which I could later accept my softer qualities, my impulse to nurture and my feeling values.

However, for years, even as a young mother, I thought that men had far and away the most interesting lives, the most control, and the most fun. Male professors were my models of achievement. Part of my legacy to my daughters is that they experienced a mother involved in both family and career, along with artistic pursuits. They also observed how I valued learning and economic independence.

I'm not sure how all this impressed them when they were little; my oldest said later, "To tell you the truth, Mom, I'd rather that you had been home handing out cookies in the afternoon." The problem was that they often saw a harried and distracted mother trying to be and to do too many things at once. I had no real choice during my first daughter's childhood because, being divorced, I had a serious economic struggle to support the two of us. After my second daughter was born I enjoyed marital and economic security but worried that I was not developing my mind. I was afraid to give up the habit of striving for achievement in the world, even temporarily. When I wasn't employed outside the home, I went back to the university to earn my graduate degree.

The upshot of having been a masculine-identified mother was that my two daughters probably absorbed some of that style from me. They may be overly goal-oriented and also may struggle to bring their intrinsic feminine nature to awareness and manifestation. And they will need to deal with the dark but natural side of the mother-aspect: her need to seduce and control those whom she also sustains and cherishes. Whatever they do, I hope they recognize their very individual feelings and values, despite political slogans or popular ideas about womanhood.

It is no wonder that women often act as enemies of our feminine nature, which is inherited through the rejected mother, and that male mentors or masculine values become our gods. Jean Shinoda Bolen types these women as living out the Athena goddess energy, born of identification with the father. Athena, never acknowledging her mother, Metis, stated at the trial of Orestes, "I am always for the male and strongly for my father." Athena women tend to be influenced by masculine ways of being and styles of power. Bolen says:

> To live "as Athena" means to live in one's head and to act purposefully in the world . . . a one-sided existence—she lives for her work. . . . Exclusive identification with rational Athena cuts a woman off from the full range and intensity of human emotion . . . the Athena woman misses the experience of being fully in her body.[2]

The key phrase here is "exclusive identification." A woman who has a more developed sensibility is perfectly capable of shifting from one facet of herself to another in response to different situations.

Carl Jung pointed out that it is psychologically disastrous for the inner Feminine to continue to fight against the mother, because it means a deadening or distortion of instincts inherent to a woman's gender. "The woman who fights against her father still has the possibility of leading an instinctive, feminine existence, because she rejects only what is alien to her." However, resistance to her mother (and to qualities inherent in a mother image) might have serious consequences for a daughter. Jung said further:

> The motto of this type is: Anything so long as it is not like Mother! . . . This kind of daughter knows what she does *not* want, but is usually completely at sea as to what she would choose as her own fate. All her instincts are concentrated on the mother in the negative form of resistance . . . all instinctive processes meet with unexpected difficulties; either sexuality does not function properly, or the children are unwanted, or maternal duties seem unbearable.[3]

However, given a bit more development of consciousness by the daughter, some resistance to the mother is not all bad. It can result in a spontaneous development of intellect for the purpose of creating a sphere of interest in which the mother has no place. I guess that is what I was doing in becoming a pilot, for my mother took absolutely no interest in my flying.

The lure of achievement at the desks of reason and power could become such that a woman would repudiate the darkly obscure female mysteries in which human conception takes place. She might altogether ignore her unconscious when it shows her, by way of dreams and fantasies, the images of her true feelings. It is not my purpose to argue against intellect and achievement in women but to emphasize that the ambitions of the body should also be listened to. I'm urging more of a balance: cherishing the personal Feminine and giving equal respect to motherhood's achievements.

Although women are beginning to shape culture by the impact of our participation in all fields, we can most profoundly change culture by making effective use of the power and influence inherent in our biological natures. For it is the mothers who are in a position to direct the optimum development of human life at its very inception and through infancy—its most formative stages. Today, there is psychological knowledge available to help us be more open to messages from both the personal and collective unconscious, which went unexamined by our mothers.

My concern is for women as potential mothers. For them, the healing of the internalized girl-child and the rehabilitation of the internalized mother are crucial to becoming confident, nurturing caretakers of new life. Negative feelings about their mothers, not expressed and dealt with, are driven into the unconscious, only to accumulate the kind of energy experienced in nightmares or other bad dreams. This kind of hidden negative energy is capable of undermining the ability to love. It blocks relatedness and constructive action. It can cause secret stress and overt physical illnesses.

I think, for instance, of another young woman, Dana, who is joyfully and carefully preparing for the birth of her first child four months from the time of this writing. She has dreams of a threatening, ugly witch trying to forcibly break in through her door. The images and energies of such dreams are frightening to Dana, who does not yet realize they represent some hidden attitude in herself. The witch is a kind of perverted mother image, perhaps connected to Dana's own bad mothering. For one thing, her mother failed to rescue Dana from being physically abused by her father. Dana's dream witch is not the actual mother but an image bearing disturbed emotions clustered around the idea of mother. Now this once-abused daughter is to become a mother; yet the child she was still has not been adequately nourished. However, Dana's work at developing consciousness will strengthen her. By setting aside time each day to mirror her feelings, dreams, and contemplations in her journal, she nourishes herself. She interacts on paper with the good and bad images that dreams bring up from her unconscious.

Jung and the contemporary Swiss psychoanalyst Alice Miller both concluded from empirical evidence that when a marked change takes place in an individual's state of conscious awareness, a change also will occur in the attributes of the unconscious. Adults can transform themselves through *acting* upon self-knowledge.

For women to experience a more conscious, positive motherhood, the fully empowered Feminine aspect also needs to be supported in society. Motherhood is the foundation of all societies. Yet, ever since the hero-warrior tribes overpowered the goddess-priestess cultures, women in Western societies have not moved from motherhood's status to be the makers and sayers of culture. Besides that, most of what has been recorded about motherhood throughout most of *written* history relegates it either to sanctification or damnation.[4] Both extremes are sentimental and undifferentiating and keep women trapped in the polarity between divine madonna and single woman victim. Until we freely have our say and correct the distortions, we forfeit much potential consciousness for everyone.

There have been images of tender mothering in art, particularly work from the humanistic Renaissance, when artists seemed to value the symbiotic dynamics between mother and child. Raphael, Titian, and Rembrandt were among the greater artists who painted mothers not as icons but with realistic and voluptuous anatomies. In these portraits, mothers fondly nursed and cuddled their children.

Of all the madonnas and enigmatic maidens painted by Leonardo da Vinci, the work that impresses me the most is a black-and-white unfinished line drawing, "Cartoon for Saint Anne." I first saw it reproduced in Marion Woodman's book, *Addiction to Perfection*,[5] which discusses the sacrifice of the Feminine principle of love by modern women. The picture is a grouping of Mary, infant Jesus, John the Baptist as a boy, and Saint Anne, Mary's mother. A serene Mary sits with one leg over her mother's, halfway on her lap. Jesus actively leans out of his mother's lap toward the child John, who rests one arm on Saint Anne's other sturdy thigh. Saint Anne is a commodious presence embracing them all.

A wealth of symbolic implications, metaphysical and philosophical, resides in the details of this holy family portrait. Yet the figures are as earthy as peasants, with an easy, sensual familiarity that is Italian, not northern European or Anglo-Saxon. I've never seen an adult daughter sitting on her mother's lap that way. The physical intimacy, the harmony of a genuine and affectionate balance between mother, daughter, and their offspring speaks to me. It speaks joyfully but also painfully, because I am reminded of what I missed—a sense of my mother's flesh, her arms enfolding my body cherishingly close to hers, her eyes reflecting my face.

Woodman uses this drawing by Leonardo to illustrate the archetypal, womb-blood connection, generation upon generation. Honoring that connection is necessary to a perception of motherhood beyond history, a perception that is, in fact, primordial, in the sense of the Latin roots of that word: *primus* and *ordiri*, "to begin a web." Think of the mothers spinning progeny out of their own body substance, propelling a line from themselves into unknown futures, doing this with faith in nature and in their own destinies.

In my family, two women's stories about how the inherited female bonds of body and instinct were broken come before mine. Determined to break past mother-to-daughter cycles of dysfunction and misunderstanding, I have tried to distill useful meanings out of these stories.

My grandmother Frances was one of six children and the oldest girl. Her father was a miller in a village outside of Prague. As a girl, Frances was the object of much comment from villagers because of her daring dives off the bridge above the churning millpond. She was also a remarkably strong swimmer at the nearby lake. Those activities ended when, at puberty, she developed full, rounded breasts and hips. Then she was made to "act like a woman."

When she was sixteen, her mother and father told her a huge lie. They said that her second cousin Joseph (of whom she had always been fond) had written from America asking for her hand in marriage. The parents packed up her clothes, bought a third-class steerage ticket with money sent by Joseph, and shipped her off. Arriving at Ellis Island in 1898, she was met by cousins who sent her by train to Chicago, where Joseph greeted her with astonishment and repressed dismay. It was Christie, her younger sister by one year, whom he loved and for whom he had sent.

Frances was the victim of parental control, parental opportunism, and the belief that an oldest daughter should be settled into marriage first, no matter what. Any trust that had existed between mother and daughter was defiled. Frances's mother surrendered to the expediency of custom rather than relating feelingly to her daughter as one female to another.

Frances found herself, at age sixteen, virtually alone in a rowdy, stock-yard city very unlike Prague with its impressive architecture, art, and music. She could not understand the natives and could not find any intimate welcoming in her husband's eyes. Eventually, Frances had four girls and three boys with Joseph. Her body understood nothing. Emma, the firstborn, died of black diphtheria, audibly choking to death in bed beside her sister Mary.

Strong swimmer that she had been, Frances never swam in Lake Michigan, and she never learned the new language with any facility. None of her children ever learned to swim. They did learn English at school and eventually forgot how to speak Bohemian with their mother. Fat grew around her bones in spite of constant labor: preserving fruits and vegetables from her garden, washing clothes on a scrub board, plucking chickens for soup. She rarely left the house. Joseph shopped for the clothes and groceries. One day Frances ran out of the house with her apron still on, disappearing for two days until she was found half-conscious under a tree on the shore of the lake. She was institutionalized for "melancholia." Her children were placed in an orphanage for a year or two. Furloughed periodically, she tended them distractedly, vaguely. Sometimes, when they disobeyed her, she slapped or kicked them.

Eight-year-old Mary became "little mother" to five younger siblings. When she entered the first grade, she had understood not a word the teacher was saying. But her yearning to be accepted as a real American motivated her to learn quickly. At sixteen she left home and high school in Kenosha, Wisconsin, for a secretarial job in Chicago. Mary, my mother, was a flapper at seventeen—and a very successful representation of that 1920s style. Her thick, long chestnut hair was cut into a bob. Her lips were painted bright red. Daring girls smoked, so Mary smoked. She drank bathtub gin after dances. Her slim knees, in pale silk stockings, were exposed from beneath a scandalously short skirt. Although a flapper's legs were on display, her breasts were mashed flat against her torso by silk or gauze binding. The intent was to look boyish and therefore bold. Mary's friends dressed the same and took trendy boys' names: Bobbie, Jackie, Billie. The term *flapper* suggests something hanging loose. A British derivation means a young wild duck not yet able to fly well.

Flappers like my mother looked like they were going to fly away from old boundaries, but most of them never got off the ground. They only won a bit more choice in husbands than their mothers had had. In their hearts, underneath their teddies, they still wanted to be nice girls, with everything nice girls get: a man to take care of them, a pretty house, and well-behaved children. They had free-looking bodies yet retained tradition-bound psyches. Not much thought about new options had been generated while they danced the Charleston or hit the speakeasies downtown.

In an old photograph Mary holds me, a month-old infant, as she stands, body and profile turned sideways to the camera. Her dark, limpid eyes are serious, her contours surprising after childbirth: hips and bosom flat as a platter. However, nature had tricked her. Her small breasts (to her embarrassment) produced an overabundant supply of milk. She was persuaded, against her original intent, to nurse me—and to give her excess milk to a baby in the hospital nursery whose mother was not producing milk.

Perhaps my mother's flapper image misled my father to hope for some wild unconventionality in the bedroom, but what he discovered was an unsensual woman, full of aches and complaints. Inwardly she was tragically fixed in her yearning to be mothered; outwardly she parroted the common, narrow attitudes about sexuality and propriety: "A lady does not give in to a man unless she's married," or, forgetting her Charleston days, "A lady does not flaunt herself" (which I took to mean in body or in opinions). Her efforts to flatten earthy, feminine aspects of herself became quite symbolic.

My mother and many like her sacrificed their individual autonomy to outside authorities. Women acted as if they didn't have faith in the authority of their natural calling—motherhood. Because they had no support for intuitive and instinctual inclinations, they repressed them and relied upon such authorities as the church, which taught the Pauline doctrine that women's voices were not to be heard there or in public. Women abdicated their power to male experts and rule-makers. Consequently, the cherishing and enabling nurturance of new human beings has been sabotaged right up to our era.

One expert to whom my mother and many others in her generation listened was John Broadus Watson, founder of behaviorist psychology. His theories separated human beings from their link to other creatures that have complicated instinctive reactions. In particular, he did not recognize the necessity of the symbiotic bond between mother and child.

"It is a serious question in my mind whether there should be individual homes for children—or even whether children should know their own parents . . . much more scientific ways of bringing up children will mean finer and happier children," stated Watson in "The Dangers of Too Much Mother Love."[6] Besides publishing in many professional journals, Watson wrote for such popular magazines as *Independent Woman* and *Harpers* from 1917 to the early 1930s. His radio broadcasts on molding human character by scientific control reached large audiences in the Midwest, where I was brought up. Other advice from Watson:

> Never hug or kiss [your children], never let them sit on your lap. If you must, kiss them on the forehead when they say good night. Shake hands with them in the morning. . . . Mothers just don't know when they kiss their children and pick them up and rock them, caress them and jiggle them upon their knee, they are slowly building a human being totally *unable* to cope with the world it must later live in.[7]

Watson claimed that a mother's mere presence, subjective and emotional, would corrupt the child. The American Psychological Association evidently agreed with him, awarding Watson their gold medal and citing him as one of the vital determinants of the form and substance of modern psychology. His influence was pervasive—and pernicious.

Since learning about Watson, I've been surveying men and women born in my era, asking if their mothers followed Watson's methods of strict infant feeding schedules and minimum touching. A large majority recall that their mothers (most of them college-educated) believed they were doing the enlightened thing in following Watson's "scientific" child-rearing advice. As a result, we "Watson babies" suffered insufficient maternal bonding. We never developed feelings of close affection for our mothers.

Later, in the 1950s and 1960s, behaviorism enjoyed even more public attention when the work of B. F. Skinner gained renown. He credited Watson's earlier book, *Behaviorism*, with starting his interest in psychology. Besides his much-publicized programming of laboratory animals, Skinner invented the Air-Crib, a germ-free, air-conditioned, soundproof box to serve as a mechanical baby tender, providing an "optimum" environment for the first two years of life.

What were the unconscious motivations of these experts that made them so willing to commit symbolic matricide? They were in pure pursuit of logos—perfect, objective reason. Killing off the mother's power seems necessary to those serving the Masculine principle, Jung explained. In the age of reason and technocracy, nothing has defended nature's Mother Goddess against this onslaught.

Alice Miller has studied past centuries of what she calls "poisonous pedagogy," theories promoting physically and emotionally abusive methods for raising children. Conscientious European mothers and fathers followed these theories promulgated by male authorities. The emphasis was on control and discipline (most often beating) from the parent and obedience from the child. One nineteenth-century theorist insisted that exuberance was to be disciplined out of children because it led to unruliness. Children must be shielded from all influences that might stimulate feelings, pleasant or painful. Fathers take on this task because, as Miller explains, "mothers, who are ordinarily entrusted with their children's education, very rarely know how to deal with unruly behavior successfully."[8] Note the word "entrusted," used as though child-rearing were not a natural consequence of motherhood but a chore granted to mothers from higher personages.

Those who are expected to give a lot need to have a healthy emotional supply out of which to give. Mothering requires much giving, so that those who nurture new life should have a childhood filled with sensitive regard for their emotional health. Because that was not the case for many of us, we have had to learn how to re-mother ourselves. This process resurrects feeling.

People attending co-dependency groups today discover how repressed and unrecognized their feelings of abandonment, fear, helplessness, and rage have been. As adults, they continue to carry many of these feelings hidden in their unconscious minds. Old feelings may be left over from long ago; but whatever is repressed acquires additional energy, the kind of energy nightmares contain. Release and resolution of these stagnating emotions are vital for prospective mothers, because those who were prisoners of repression are not free to enjoy the free-feeling spontaneity of their children.

So, how do we re-parent? One way is to mirror our lives in personal journals or in art, trying to make creative resolutions in stories, poems, or pictures. I worked for many months on a story depicting my distress over my parents' divorce. Each revision helped me gain clearer insight into their personalities and my intense reactions. I began to acquire more intimate knowledge about them and about myself. Those imaginative confrontations on paper brought a release of old tears. Then I could acknowledge some positive influences: my dad's great sense of humor and my mother's tenacity.

Some women have been fortunate to find surrogate mothers in older women who help them re-mother themselves. Such a woman, twice my age, became my friend when I was thirty-six. Miriam (Bunny) Flarsheim dressed and moved with elegant grace, yet had attitudes as earthy as a gypsy's. A delightful and wise conversationalist who prized relatedness, she said, "Nothing I did ever pleased my mother . . . perhaps here lies the reason for my prancing through life mothering gently and subtly all who come into my path—because everybody needs a mother all the time."[9] Her example of emotional honesty and expansive tolerance was one I had rarely noticed previously in a woman. She had lost her oldest daughter to cancer. Gradually, I became a "stand-in" for that daughter. Bunny's generous affection and encouragement healed me. We had met in a Unitarian discussion group, and our lively discussions about love, art, literature, and how to relate to my daughters continued for more than twenty years by voice and by letter.

Nourishing the inner child with tender acceptance enables us to mature psychologically. In behalf of that neglected child, it means enjoying playfulness and body pleasures such as dancing, sports, or drama. That also means taking time to awaken and find significance in childhood memories, perhaps through counseling, or by creating rituals that honor the child self who became the woman self. Thirteen years ago, I was one of seven women who met weekly in order to talk and write about emotionally compelling stages of our lives. Out of that telling, we developed a readers' theater drama entitled *Dark and Bright Fires: Women's Collective Autobiographies.*[10]

By filling up the emotional emptiness we get stronger. Then we can regard our mothers and their lives with compassion. Despite their failings, our foremothers were pioneers who came out of decaying societies carrying old prejudices, taking small excruciating steps toward greater consciousness. Forgiveness is a crucial goal for the well-being of women because it helps to rehabilitate the Good Mother archetype. She begins to transform into the universal, timeless Great Mother who affirms the power of the instinctive Feminine within us. And that is exactly how some women are beginning to see her in dreams.

Our steps involve journeys to mental lands. By using active imagination, we can create dialogues with the many secret aspects of ourselves. We do not abandon the images of our feelings when they appear in dreams, but bring them into integration with our conscious lives.

Nor Hall writes about the "daughters of imagination," as she calls those who choose not to bear children but who create by making rich contributions to society. However, as she emphasizes, "those among us who have borne children or wish to be literal mothers, need to recall our essential role . . . for, if the mothers [imaginative, not literal] who conceive of new forms of language and culture forget their connection to the body, to the real female depth of tissue, to the earth (their Mother), the life they create will be sterile."[11] Our role as biological mothers is not only to conceive but also to bear testimony to what we know and learn as we give ourselves passionately to the fostering of life. One day, we also will be the chroniclers and commentators in a society where feminine perspectives are respected.

It is impossible to discuss the experience of raising children in glowing, endearing terms alone and still be honest. Although sentimentality and exaggeration have shaped stereotypes of motherhood, stark confession is more appropriate. For me, that would become a book, with much of it describing the paradoxes of adoration and irritation in child-rearing.

Motherhood is a status I have enjoyed—and suffered—for many years, but never regretted. My efforts were not always skillful. For instance, discipline was inconsistent because I avoided spanking and tried to reason with my daughters before they were capable of understanding my explanations. At times I was impatient and almost as immature emotionally as they were. My inner child still needed the approval and support my mother had been unable to give me. In retrospect, I regard mothering as the most important thing I've done, and continue to do.

Motherhood was not my only important effort. I wanted to be a flyer, a writer, a wife, a lover, a social worker, a scholar, and a professor. Surprisingly, I have been all of these. What I didn't realize when my daughters were preschool age was that a lot of my energy was wasted yearning for more time and opportunity to do other things, especially writing. I could have invested more creative thinking in what was immediate and just as profound: the mystery of a child's development. If only I had realized then a simple fact: the usual longevity and flexibility of women allow most of us to fulfill several roles. Even being wholly dedicated to children's care as a full-time mother normally occupies a woman for only about a quarter of her life span.

Bunny Flarsheim demonstrated that. Her life was long, full, and never static. While a young wife and mother of five children (two adopted), she gave her wholehearted energy and intelligence to rearing them. That was in the 1920s when most fathers left at breakfast, returned at night to give a few commands, then sent the children to bed. Bunny, however, chose a mate who shared in the children's daily care. Later, when the children were old enough to attend school, Bunny began to study with psychiatrist Karl Menninger. She became a psychotherapist; years later she retired with her husband to live in Tabago. Returning to the States, she became involved with Elisabeth Kübler-Ross, giving seminars about death and dying; then she founded a hospice project. At age eighty-six she began to write for the first time—a newspaper column. From Bunny, I learned that a woman's life can produce several different harvests—each in the appropriate season.

6 · HOW THE FATHER'S DAUGHTER FOUND HER MOTHER

. . . .

LYNDA W. SCHMIDT

Lynda W. Schmidt, a second-generation Jungian analyst, offers a very personal account of her journey to align with the Feminine from two points of view: as the daughter of a mother and as the mother of daughters.

Schmidt spent her childhood on a cattle ranch where she had little personal mothering but a strong relationship to nature, the impersonal Mother archetype. She expresses distaste for the constraints of the Mother World, as do many fathers' daughters. And she notes that at a certain point she found herself "divorced from her own sex."

She offers an interesting insight about herself: because mothering stood so far outside the bounds of awareness for her, she later began to overmother unconsciously in her therapy practice. This, it seems, is one explanation for the widespread, much-discussed phenomenon of co-dependence we see today.

Eventually, after losing her precious contact with nature through living too long in the Father World, Schmidt began to re-create her relationship with her mother. For some of us, this re-mothering process cannot be direct because our mothers have died or are unavailable for a relationship. But, fortunately, for Schmidt and her mother, Jane Wheelwright (author of chapter 12 in this book), this enriched contact has meant creative collaboration and a revitalized family.

This piece was adapted from an earlier version published in the Los Angeles Jungian journal Psychological Perspectives, *volume 14, number 1, 1983.*

Lynda W. Schmidt was born in China and lived in England and Switzerland while her parents, Jane and Joseph Wheelwright, completed their training as Jungian analysts. She is a training analyst of the C. G. Jung Institute in San Francisco. She has published several articles and a book describing a trek in the Himalayas. She now lives with her husband in Maine.

It is no longer enough, in our society, to orient ourselves around the Masculine principle. Since the emergence of the Judeo-Christian era, the development of Western culture has been centered around the control of nature, instincts, biology, the physical world, and the relations between the sexes. Robert Graves, prolific Greek scholar, poet, and novelist, has said, "The political and social confusion of the last 3,000 years has been entirely due to man's revolt against woman as a priestess of the natural magic, and his defeat of wisdom by the use of intellect." I, too, think that the males of our species, after being under the power of the matriarchy for 35,000 years, took command of social development and, in the process, threw out the baby with the bathwater.

Now there is a reckoning. The "baby" turns out to be half the population—women—plus that aspect of men which derives from the fact that they, too, are creatures of nature and instinct.

As one of the women who subscribed to the patriarchy, which means I grew up as a father's daughter, I, too, have had to come to a powerful realization of the matriarchy. What I have come to understand from my expanding circle of women friends and clients, and from a belated experience of the woman who happens to be my mother, concerns far more than "mothers." For this middle-aged father's daughter to "find her mother" is turning out to involve a whole new lease on life, and may be representative of a cultural shift. In the likelihood of this being an increasingly common phenomenon, I would like to share my thoughts and experiences of fathers and mothers and daughters.

First, I would like to define the term *father's daughter* as I am using it here. It is the daughter with a powerful, positive relationship with her father, probably to the exclusion of the mother. Such a young woman will orient herself around men as she grows up and will have a somewhat deprecatory attitude toward women. Fathers' daughters organize their lives around the Masculine principle, either remaining connected to an outer man or being driven from within by a masculine mode. They may find a male mentor or guide, but they may, at the same time, have trouble taking orders from a man or accepting teaching from one.

A woman can get away with this pattern for a long time, given that it coincides with the way our culture is still organized. But it is likely that one day she will realize that she is divorced from her own sex. She may want to reclaim her heritage as a woman. If a father's daughter is lucky, she may be able to work out a new relationship with her own mother, or she may find that she can rediscover herself in relation to her own daughter and/or to women friends.

I grew up in the Artemis mode. Artemis was a goddess whose childhood was spent on the wild island of Delos, without supervision. Her mother, Leto, was left by Zeus, Artemis' father, and Artemis had little relationship with either parent. Zeus was glamorous and all-powerful, while Leto was less visible. Artemis took after Zeus and became powerful, independent, and solitary; she was the goddess of childbirth but was not motherly. It is not surprising, then, that the Artemis type of father's daughter has a difficulty with supervision. She was never supervised, and so she does not want supervision later, nor does she want to exercise it over others.

In my own life, I too sought out men, but deep down, out of consciousness, what mattered to me, I realized eventually, were the wilderness and animal life. As a father's daughter I wanted to please men and, whenever I was near them, that is what I did. When there was no one around, though, I fell into the unconscious and merged with nature in a "participation mystique." So it was not that I had no experience of the Great Mother; it's just that she did not speak English or wear a dress.

There are many other types of fathers' daughters, including those who are initially merged with their mothers and come under the spell of their fathers later on. Perhaps such women could be described as *apparent* fathers' daughters. Also, I believe there are women who were initially fathers' daughters, but through loss of the father—by death, divorce, or prolonged absence, literal or psychic—come under the control of powerful mothers. Such a mother may exert her power over her daughter overtly by overwhelming her with a domineering, possessive attitude, or covertly by subtle manipulation. Either way, this daughter may have begun as a tomboy, or daddy's girl, or companion of the father, only to lose him while still a child or young adolescent. If the mother has a powerful will (and perhaps, consciously or unconsciously, drove the father away), this young girl may fall under her spell and develop as an *apparent* mother's daughter. She has a particularly confusing situation because she is going to feel the masculine energy within but have no channel to pour it into. Yet the Mother World does not quite work for her either, so she may find herself hanging suspended between the two.

My own experience of the Mother World was nearly completely archetypal—that is, impersonal—as was my mother's before me. She and I, in our different eras, grew up on an enormous cattle ranch, more or less unsupervised, free to live or die in the heart of a vast wilderness of ocean, range country, and mountains. Our companions were siblings and cousins of similar age, plus animals of all sorts—from the domestic horses, cattle, and dogs, to the wildest mountain lions, coyotes, and rattlesnakes. We had sublime and lethal adventures, and everything in between. But we had little human mothering. We did get solid fathering from the cowboys, who expected as much from us girls as they did from the boys.

Because of their special vision and drive, my mother and father had business in the world that really could not include rearing children in the conventional way. For me, then, the major resource of my life was the wilderness, nature (which is the Great Mother/Female Self) in an unarticulated form. My principal mother was, therefore, an archetype, an atmosphere, a geography. There was minimal flesh and blood personal mothering; and so, as Artemis ran wild with her twin, Apollo, in the forests, so did I, on a wild cattle ranch with my same-age cousin, Jimmy.

The ranch, as I knew it in the 1940s, was rich in materials. There were treasures everywhere, and I have always collected from nature like a packrat—special stones, odd bits of wood or shells, rattles from snakes, arrowheads, bones, horns, feathers. So many things. It was not until I worked in my analyst's sandtray building imaginary scenes out of all sorts of objects, which would reveal the hidden state of my psyche, and later began to collect objects for my own sandtray, that I began to link up with the materialism of manmade things.

On the ranch we had few toys because we had everything else to play with. Our clothes were always the same: blue jeans, shirt, and tennis shoes or cowboy boots. Our hair stuck out of our heads any which way, knotted like horses' tails. To this day, I comb my hair only once in the morning and again at night.

It makes me nervous to think of a human mother having the power over me that nature did, yet it is my impression that that is what it is like for mothers' daughters. On the ranch we had to keep tuned to everything going on around us, or else we would be in danger for our lives. We had to be alert for booby traps in the ground, such as gopher holes, that would trip us or our horses, breaking legs or heads. We had to swim in the ocean with constant caution against being crushed by great waves or swept away by the undertow. We had to watch for rattlers, scorpions, black-widow spiders, pay heed that we not fall off a suddenly turning cowpony, or be run over by an angry bull, or kicked by a frightened calf. We had to read the minds of animals and cowboys or be humiliated or injured. Is this what it is like to be a mother's daughter?

On the positive side, the ranch was eternal, enveloping, life-giving, exciting, familiar, and unknown. To this day, I go there and feel renewed, exultant, alert, and complete. This, too, may be what it is like to be a mother's daughter.

In contrast, what I saw in the human mothers of children my age was not impressive. Growing up in the 1940s, I saw mothers as leading miserable, narrow lives. It seemed they were always available, living out their repetitious routines. They seemed centered on everyone but themselves, except for their special kingdoms, for which they got little respect from the world at large: clothes and makeup, house and garden, schools and community. As I saw it, they were always poking their noses into their children's business, talking with each other on the telephone, gossiping and complaining.

From my vantage point of relatively self-sufficient living in the wilds, I thought that growing up to be someone's wife and mother could only be like dying. As far as I was concerned, a house was to keep the rain off, to store food in, and to hold the treasures I collected. While I was growing up, I cleaned my room twice a year—luckily it was in a remote part of the house, and no one harassed me about it. Perhaps they did not even notice! To this day, housecleaning seems totally unnecessary to me—twice a year should be quite enough.

The Great Mother-Ranch, though, makes an excellent model for the female world, and it surprises me sometimes that I failed to transfer that experience consciously to the human level. There is, however, one realm in which I did make the transfer, though I was not conscious of it until writing this article. That realm is my psychotherapy practice. Having little or no maternal development in consciousness, I tend to be heavily over-mothering *unconsciously*.

In my early years of work, I fell into a lot of trouble regarding dependency issues in my clients. Knowing myself to be unmotherly, I could not understand why so many people became so dependent on me. Finally, via my own analysis, I began to see what was happening. For some years I had taken very little time off and was available by phone seven days a week, twenty-four hours a day. This style served to inform my patients that they needed that much availability from me, or else why would I offer it? It did at last occur to me that I needed them to need me; that is, I needed *them*. When I saw that, I already needed them less because I had a new handle on the problem. I unlisted my phone and started leaving the city for the Gold Country for three days a week where we had no phone.

One of the ways I discovered to replace this sort of negative mothering with something better was to make room in my office for people's children and animals. It took hearing one of my colleagues mention the stream of livestock, babies, and children appearing with women (and occasionally, men) in the waiting room for me to realize that there was something extra happening. As I became conscious of my purpose in nonverbally inviting pets and children, I began to do more with the opportunities.

Only once have I suggested out loud that someone bring the family pet to a psychotherapy session, and that was to a person who had already been bringing one or more of her children at regular intervals. I asked to meet the pet, a one-year-old female retriever, because this woman's panics, rages, and pain were at animal levels, and she seemed stuck in them. In she came one day with her puppy. In striking contrast to this angry, storming, despairing woman, the puppy was relaxed, friendly, and interested in her surroundings. In short, the puppy was exhibiting what was missing in her owner, and the woman was shocked and delighted to see her "alter ego" sitting there on the floor, contentedly grinning at us and thumping her tail.

A young woman in her thirties with a "good girl" adaptation of the most disturbing proportions brought in her six-year-old daughter because she could not find anyone to babysit her. This particular young mother was breaking down, or rather, her old adaptation was breaking down, and she sat there angry, weeping, talking suicide, while her daughter played in my sandtray, listening to us. Eventually I asked the woman if she wanted to lie on my couch and be wrapped up in a blanket, which she immediately did. Her daughter came to the couch, too, and crawled in beside her mother and the two of them held each other while the woman and I talked.

After they left, I looked at the sandtray. There was a tight scene of a globe-like object on a mound of sand closely surrounded by several women and animals and a mouse dressed up in a nurse's uniform, carrying a large hypodermic needle. I put these figures away and then ran my fingers through the mound of sand to see if anything was buried. Sure enough, up came a lantern and a peacock, and I felt real relief, even found myself grinning. That six-year-old daughter, with a lantern for light, was in good enough relation to the situation that I felt I could anticipate recovery for her mother, with beneficial results for the daughter.

What I am trying to say here is that the unconscious mother that I am *can* work well—in the same sense that a wilderness setting permits me the fullest experience of myself. I can provide room for the instinctual, biological aspect which for so many of us is the neglected part. And while I would not be a Jungian analyst if I were not entranced with the spiritual, fantastical, symbolic realm, the fact is that my heart and soul are in the world of the body, animal life, and the wild environment of nature.

By way of contrast to fathers' daughters, I would like to try to say something about full mothers' daughters. This is very difficult for me; as a full father's daughter, I have felt "other" and estranged from the personal Mother World. What I can try to do is to transliterate my experience of the ranch as Great Mother to what I imagine the experience of a flesh and blood powerful personal mother might be. If I remember the behavior of animal mothers, it seems quite easily described, but I am not sure it is representative. If it is, I would describe real mothering as being nurturing, both in feeding and in physical contact. It is being as accessible as possible, given the need to hunt and find shelter. It is being totally centered on the needs of the baby or babies, until some point at which they are thrown out. They are usually still pretty inept, and they go through a powerful abandonment that demands growing up fast. At the point of launching, the young animal enters the world of kill-or-be-killed, while the animal mother quits mothering until her cycle begins again.

It seems to me that our middle-class culture keeps the young under surveillance and protection too long and too tightly. By the time school starts when children are five, they can begin to look after themselves far better than we may have been led to believe. My own experience as a child was of near-total freedom from age seven on. This coincides with the study by Joseph Chilton Pearce published in *The Magical Child*, in which he suggests that it takes a child seven years "to structure a knowledge of the earth matrix and shift from mother as safe space to earth itself."

What is unknown territory for me is our civilization's way of mothering. If I extrapolate from being a *human* child in the wilderness, I would guess that the human child in a *civilized* setting experiences some of the ongoing dominance, ruthlessness, and demand to be accommodating that the Great Mother Nature imposes in the wilderness. I would guess that the human child in civilization must adhere to, accommodate to, its personal mother's culture-based projections of appearance and behavior, or else be rejected. In such ways the personal mother may become merged with the Great Mother archetype in the daughter's mind, because the Great Mother makes demands about appearance and behavior to ensure survival. It is a long haul to differentiate between the personal mother and the archetypal mother.

The Great Mother in nature never lets go; the container is permanent; there is nowhere else to go. Even the patriarchal aspects of hunting, fighting, territoriality in animal life are under the aegis of Great Mother Nature.

The difference between the animal mother and our Western human mother is in the development of consciousness, in the capacity to be objective, self-aware, to differ and decide. But insofar as we women have been defining ourselves in relation to men for the last 2,000 years, our consciousness will be oriented toward pleasing or displeasing men. Either way, we are functioning in a reactive way rather than from a base consisting both of biological energy and mental process.

The animal mother acts out of her instincts, her bodily directives. Human mothers have been reacting out of competition, ambition, envy, and pride, insofar as the Masculine principle has been present and deformed in us. Thus our daughters may be similarly deformed, though actually I think the last twenty years have eased this situation some.

I can see instinctual mothering as a good mode for a child in the first few years, without particular regard for masculine interest. But what happens next between mother and daughter? How do they re-create their relationship into an alliance and move out of the container and contained situation of animal mothering? How can they develop their human relationship and move the archetypal one into the background?

Now I would like to discuss the mother-daughter experience from the other side, from the point of view of being the mother of a daughter, rather than being the daughter of a mother. My own experience as a mother was unsatisfying, both for me and my daughters. I think I could have done a good enough job if I had only been able to make the transition from what I knew from nature to my city life, but I had no idea of that. Incredible as it seems to me now, I saw my newborn daughters as unknown phenomena. I did not realize that I knew all I needed to know. I thought I had to turn to Dr. Spock, to the pediatrician, and to the neighbor for guidance. I who had mothered so many different beasts (including a horned toad for quite a while!) turned pale and helpless when presented with a hairless, squawking human baby. Even with "natural childbirth," still quite rare in 1953 and 1955 when my babies were born, I did not quite realize they were flesh of my flesh.

Perhaps the context of the sterile hospital and uniformed personnel conveyed to me the impression that babies were to be understood only after long training. The nurses, many of whom I am sure had not yet had their own babies, dealt with me very kindly but as though I were a bit of an idiot. And because I was still very at sea in this civilized world (I was 21 and only three years off the ranch), I bowed to their clearly superior knowledge. The intricacies of feeding, diapering, sleeping, handling were—this amazes me now—*taught* to me. It never dawned on me that this was instinctual knowledge sitting within me, waiting for me to hear. And the nurses and doctors played into my rejection of instinct.

I remember being given the care of a tiny orphaned calf. It did not know how to drink from a bucket, so I put my hand into the milk, then poked my milky fingers up into the calf's mouth and lured him down into the milk. He sucked my fingers for awhile, then kept on sucking the milk after I withdrew my fingers. I was eight or nine years old at the time. No one told me to do this maneuver; I just knew.

On the other hand, I can see the old patterns still haunting us. I know a woman who has a very slim baby. The woman tends to overweight. The baby is wonderfully lively, getting on with all the new projects of development: crawling, turning over, teething, talking, and is clearly delighted with herself and her mother. But her mother is worried about her daughter's weight being less than "normal," while her height is more than "normal." The mother wonders if she has enough milk for her baby, if there may be something wrong with the baby, if the doctor disapproves of her mothering because he keeps checking her baby against his charts. It is so sad, because it is clear she has a very happy daughter and they have made a very nice fit together. No colic, little or no fussing or crying, sleeping peacefully and developing well. Yet this young woman is as haunted as I was with my two tall, thin daughters.

I remember that the pediatrician recommended that we have our daughters' hands x-rayed to determine how complete the bone development was. At a certain age—six or seven or so—it was thought to be possible to determine their ultimate height. Given that there are six-footers on all sides of the family, men and women both, there was reason to suppose that our daughters might grow "too" tall. Mercifully, the x-rays led the doctors to think they would grow to be only a little taller than average, so they let us be. Otherwise, there were tentative plans to bring the menses on early to stop growth. This appalls me now, this effort to manipulate nature. But at the time I was so divorced from my animal self that I thought it was all perfectly reasonable. After all, it was "scientific."

It was during this time that I became very attached to a woman who lived nearby. I think she was a full mother's daughter, who in turn grew up to mother as she was mothered. When I met her she had five children, plus a husband who called her "Mummy." I was awed by her spontaneous, fullhearted, all-encompassing mothering. I was in my early twenties with first one child, then two children, and this remarkable woman simply embraced all three of us. My husband was gone to the city from seven A.M. to seven P.M. every day and most Saturdays, and I was sunk in what I had been taught was motherhood. My neighbor was crucial to our getting through this time. Before she could walk steadily, our first-born crawled the long, gravelly distance to my neighbor's house if I did not take her there early enough in the day. Taking my children there was an excuse to go there myself. It was not any one thing that was so wonderful, just the whole warm, noisy place.

Several years later, the situation reversed. My neighbor's oldest child, a girl of about ten, began coming the distance to see me to complain about the way she felt supervised and dominated. A few years after that, she came to tell me about her boyfriend and ask advice for getting along with him. She could not talk with her mother because her mother became upset about sex and about how young she was, and one day, her mother read her daughter's diary for information about the relationship. Understandably, the daughter was frantic. She said, if she ever got married, she would never have children. (When she did, in fact, get married, it took her ten years to decide to have a baby.)

My neighbor came to see me, too, and turned to me for illumination on the situation. She just did not understand that things had changed, that it was no longer appropriate to be animal-mother to her daughter. I thought, at the time, that between the two of us, all our children got more or less what they needed.

It may have been the feeling of estrangement from the world of wilderness and wildlife, part of the price of being a father's daughter, that helped me begin the process of shifting my identification from the male world to the female world. This began with receiving from my mother through the mail the first draft of what was ultimately, twelve years later, to become her book *Death of a Woman*. In its original form, it was purely a mother-daughter story. The young woman who was my mother's patient was dying of cancer, and my mother was attempting to open up for her a view of the rest of her life that she was not going to have. The patient, Sally, was my age at the time, thirty-seven. In the six months they had together, the feeling relationship she had with my mother ran the whole gamut of mother-daughter feelings, from negative at the beginning, to acceptance in the middle, to love at the end. Suddenly, I felt my mother as *mother*. Until then, I had not known that she experienced feelings toward me as her daughter. But from the record she kept of her reactions to her young patient, I felt her capacity to feel motherly and concerned, even perhaps toward me. And this feeling opened up the second half of my life.

What made it possible for me to find my way into a satisfying relationship with my mother after that was finding a common ground on which we could meet as two persons. This we did on the ranch, the archetypal Mother to both of us. Thus we seem to have found an equality, a sistership—a twinship, even. (It also helps that we are the same type, according to Jung's theory: introverted sensation-thinking types.)

Even as she grew up in a literal twinship, with her brother, Clinty, so did I grow up in a figurative twinship with my cousin, Jimmy. Now my mother and I seem twins to each other, and we each again have a person who knows without effort a similar experience of life, especially as it is experienced through terrain, animals, and physical activity.

For several years, she and I had another common ground, namely horsepacking in the high Uinta Mountains of Utah. For a week each year, we rode and camped at altitudes of 9,000 to 10,000 feet with a few others, and thus re-knew our childhoods as ranch children. Though we were "cowboying" in different eras, our experiences must have been similar. We would go out with the cowboys to round up the cattle in the same canyons, ride on the same incredibly dusty roads to and from the places where we were working the cattle. The cowboys were different ones, but they were of the same "good daddy" archetype. They taught us what we needed to know to be able to help them, and we felt strong and useful as we rode out every day at dawn.

A different sort of meeting ground for us is the world of ideas. We have entered into a veritable binge of idea talk, argument, irreverence, and collusion, pooling our experiences as mothers to daughters, and daughters to mothers, and both to each other. We have had many discussions about each other's articles and talks and are writing a book together on the psychology of the wilderness.

We also have made some presentations together on the subject of the cultural shift from a "man's world" to a world which welcomes both men and women. After 35,000 or so years of psychic power being invested in matriarchy, it seems understandable that we should have had 2,000 to 3,000 years of patriarchy. Collectively, we needed a shift toward men, so as to develop in a broader way as a species. We needed some objectivity, judgmental thinking, and the organization and advance of knowledge. The eternal round of nature could have been the orientation for our species forever, but curiosity and the love of challenge and exploration, also characteristic of our species, urged us on to a more masculine effort. Seeking, conquering, inventing, all contributed to the shift of power from women to men.

That shift, however, became so exaggerated that inevitably the pendulum had to swing back. Even as I finally realized that my identification with the father world was limiting my life, so is our society coming to the same conclusion. And thank goodness, for I doubt that I would have found my way to my female center without cultural energies pressing in that direction.

7 · MOTHER OF MOTHERS: THE POWER OF THE GRANDMOTHER IN THE FEMALE PSYCHE

· · · · · · ·

Berkeley psychotherapist Naomi Ruth Lowinsky has given a name to the generations of women who carry within them the history and biology of a family: a grandmother, mother, daughter, and great-granddaughter make up a "motherline." Lowinsky has been studying adult women with adult daughters for many years, but in this paper she focuses on the grandmother as a key link in the chain.

The grandmother is not only a tie to female ancestors; she also symbolizes, for female family members, their future as women. In this timeless position, the grandmother can serve a paradoxical function: she can join a mother to a daughter by separating them, by offering them a less personalized, more objective stance than they can probably attain on their own. In this way, she serves a transcendent function to the two younger generations, creating what Marion Woodman refers to as the triple goddess: virgin, mother, crone.

On the darker side, many grandmothers are a source of the wounded Feminine in a family; they carry a history of suffering and transmit it, consciously or not, to later generations. This wound, if not transformed into a source of healing, can lead to deep patterns of devaluation and even self-destruction.

Lowinsky asks difficult questions: How do we find new forms of authentic femininity yet honor and include our biological and emotional female sources? How do we differentiate from the feminine self within our motherlines, when it is also precisely what we need for our own healing? And how do we participate in the motherline without bearing children?

Naomi Ruth Lowinsky, Ph.D., has published poetry and prose out of her experience of the Feminine since the early 1970s. She is the founder of the Psychotherapy Institute Journal, a faculty member of the Women's Therapy Center in El Cerrito, California, and maintains a psychotherapy practice in Berkeley.

Mother, who would have thought
I could grow older
than your mother?

CAROL GORDON[1]

Grandmothers loom behind parents, casting shadows, evoking the mysteries. Less familiar, less everyday than the mother, a grandmother is a woman of another time, telling stories out of long ago, when she was a child, when mommy or daddy was a child, when we of the present generation had not yet been dreamt of.

When the grandmother enters consciousness, a great archetypal pattern is evoked: the two become three, the mother-child dyad opens to include a third generation. These biological relationships are channels through which symbolic meanings flow. The personal mother is thrown into relief. She is seen as one of a long line of mothers forming a pattern that lives in the female body and is expressed in the meeting of the three: maiden, mother, and crone. The grandmother holds these three in her body and psyche, the maiden and the mother she was, the crone she has become. The wholeness of the feminine self is evoked, and the granddaughter's potential development is stirred. Someday, perhaps, she too will have a granddaughter to whom she will tell the stories of her female line. Grandmother consciousness opens a woman to images of the past, to the face of the future, and to the symbolic pattern of a woman's life.

Modern women in our culture have been in rebellion against this ancient pattern of the Feminine. In a great collective leap we distanced ourselves from the lives of our mothers and grandmothers. "Biology is not destiny" was the battle cry against the great unconscious undertow of pregnancy and nurture that keeps women in thrall to the needs of others. Speaking the language of ego, we insisted on our right to make conscious choices, whether or not to marry, to work, to have children. What we did not know, because we had moved so far from the life patterns of our mothers and grandmothers, was how those choices would play out over a lifetime. We might mourn the unborn children, the unlived relationships; we might feel ripped out of our connection to the cycles of the female body. We might find ourselves identified with patriarchal attitudes that devalue our mothers and grandmothers, that split us from our bodies and our past, leaving us wandering like motherless children in the too bright light of masculine consciousness.

How can a woman be true to her own path and yet honor the dark mysteries out of which she was born? It cannot be evolutionary to deny the ancient pattern, nor can it be evolutionary to deny one's own development. To balance these difficult opposites, a woman needs more than her mother. She is easily polarized with her mother. She needs the power of the third one, the grandmother, the one who is a generation removed and has lived the full round of a woman's life, to help her find her way. With her grandmother's guidance she can return to the land of the mothers, not as though she had never left, but with a perspective that allows her feminine self to find its roots.

GRANDER THAN A MOTHER

The psychological meaning of the grandmother is an aspect of an archetypal pattern that I call the motherline. A woman's psyche arranges itself around a core connection to female continuity and the birth-giving capacity of the Feminine. The woman who is both mother and daughter, grandmother and granddaughter, carries in her lived experience this central mystery of the Feminine. Women are the carriers of the species, the entryway to life. Even a woman who has not herself borne children is born of a woman who is both mother and daughter, is herself daughter and granddaughter, rooted in the bodies of the women who came before her. A woman's soul, her sense of the sacred, is, as Irene Claremont de Castillejo said, "imbedded in . . . her very body".[2]

Jung describes the mother-daughter bond as eliciting an experience in women of their lives being "spread over generations"[3] and thus outside the ordinary sense of time. My concept of the motherline is an elaboration of the phenomenon Jung envisioned when he wrote: "Every mother contains her daughter in herself and every daughter her mother . . . every woman extends backward into her mother and forward into her daughter." One could expand this to say that every grandmother contains her granddaughter in herself, and every granddaughter her grandmother. A grandmother locates an individual in the life stream of the generations. She is the tie to the subterranean world of the female ancestors. When three generations of women are together, a sacred trinity is evoked: the three ages of woman, the three aspects of the goddess—Maiden, Mother, Crone—which have been worshipped in many cultures since the earliest ages.[4]

My feeling for the power of the grandmother is rooted in my childhood. I remember, when my brothers and I were children, how life seemed to shift and deepen when my grandmother, my mother's mother, came to visit. It was as though another element, a third perspective, was added to the everyday struggles between parents and children. We called her Oma, the German word for grandmother. She told us stories from my mother's childhood. Her eyes were violet, looking inward, looking backward. I remember how the soft folds of skin at her throat shook when she spoke. "Once I told the children that I too had had a mother. Your aunt was about four then, your mother three. Do you know what your aunt said to me? She looked me up and down, because of course she was very little, and I was very big, and she said: 'You had a mother? She must have been a giant!!' "

We children all laughed, as we had many times, hearing this familiar tale. But looking back I see that my four-year-old aunt was onto something. Grandmothers do belong to a race of larger beings. They brought those huge creatures, our parents, into this world. The very word *grand* makes the point. A grandmother is grander than a mother, holding one in a wider circle of meanings, a larger perspective, than the tight little everyday intimacy one lives in with a mother, with its irritating ambivalence, its intensity of hope and disappointment.

This is because when a woman becomes a grandmother, an archetypal shift of the feminine self is potentiated. In the girl the entrance of grandmother consciousness shifts the two into three; the mother-daughter dyad opens up to include the perspective of a third generation. In an older woman the entrance of grandmother consciousness shifts the three into four. Because a woman is always first a daughter, she stands between her mother's generation and the generation of her children. Then, when *her* child has a child, something powerful happens in her psyche. Although her body is no longer directly involved—she is neither being born nor giving birth— her sense of self is profoundly altered. Her place in the generations has been shifted by events beyond her control. Someone else's body is bearing the children, going through the cycles. Life, she realizes, will go on without her, even as it has passed through her.

As the fourth generation emerges, as the three become four, the feminine self experiences the wholeness of continuity.[5] Integrated grandmother consciousness can hold the opposites of being involved and distant, of embodying the motherline and not embodying it. This is the larger perspective she can bring to her granddaughter: standing behind her and before her, opening doors to the deeper chambers of the Feminine, that little-known place in our culture where birth and death, body and soul, are kin, and where lives loop through time as through the figure eight of infinity, always changing, always the same.

A BRIDGE BETWEEN GENERATIONS

The concept of the motherline came to me as I was doing research on women who had raised daughters to adulthood. These women were telling their stories from the middle of their lives. They had considerable experience as both daughters and mothers. Some of them were grandmothers as well. They stood on the crossroads where the three ages of woman meet. I found, as I interviewed them about their daughters, that they would spontaneously refer to their mothers and grandmothers as part of the natural flow of their thoughts. There was an almost palpable way in which mothers and grandmothers entered the room as daughters were described.

A woman whom I'll call Carolyn described the motherline to me before I'd found a name for it. She was telling me about her feelings when her daughter Susie began menstruating.

> I can remember the date, February 14th, Valentine's Day! She came in and showed me her underpants and she said: "Have I started menstruating?" And

I said yes and I started to cry. I could just feel it was an incredible experience, that connection, that sense of being in the middle between my mother and my daughter, and that I was the bridge between generations. She said: "Oh, Mom, what are you crying for?" But I was so moved by it. It confirmed my womanhood, the woman in me. I was seeing the continuum of the women in the family, the pride of being a woman. I think I had a sense both of my mortality and my immortality.

In that moment Carolyn knew that her daughter was biologically ready to be a mother. Her place in the generations shifted as the birth-giving goddess revealed herself in a stain on her daughter's underpants. In due time she could become a grandmother, moving into that powerful relation to the feminine self when the three become four. It was a rite of passage for both mother and daughter.

In a time that devalues the biological aspects of being female, Susie was embarrassed by her mother's intensity of feeling. The sacred moment had no container. Most modern pubescent girls experience the onset of their periods as a curse, a plague, a bother. At worst their mothers feel they have to teach them about the pain and suffering of a woman's lot. At best their task is one of teaching feminine hygiene.

In native cultures it is not the personal mother who is responsible for teaching the pubescent girl about her body, for initiating her into womanhood. It is the grandmother who does this, or another older woman of the tribe. These people know what we have forgotten: that a woman's passage from maiden to woman of childbearing years is a powerful transformation, requiring the guidance of the Crone who holds the three aspects of the Goddess in her being.

We have forgotten how to honor the motherline, how to worship the power of the female procreative capacity. Our feeling for the interweaving of the generations, the integration of body and psyche, has gone underground, often lost to awareness or relegated to what we self-deprecatingly call "women's talk" or gossip.

However, as I listened to women meander in their family histories—looping backward and forward in the generations, connecting body to psyche, past to future, gossiping—I began to realize that we have not entirely lost our connection to the ancient worldview that honors the birth-giving Goddess. It made me think of the old usage of the word *gossip*, which means "god speaking through a woman" and refers to a woman who is a godparent or a member of the congregation of women at a childbirth.[6]

Telling stories from the motherline is gossiping. The women who told me their stories spoke out of an awareness that did not separate body and psyche. They spoke with awe of the birth of children and grandchildren. The physical experience of a birth was intertwined with the psychological issues between mother and child. Life was no heroic tale of mastery but was shaped by love and loss, by the twists and turns of fate. Who knows why one woman gives birth easily and another labors for days in the underworld, coming close to the dark tide of death? These women remembered their own procreative capacity as a source of meaning and danger, of joy and terrible pain, of connection and loss, of life and death. They spoke of physical and emotional pain beyond belief; they spoke of the loss of children by themselves and their mothers, and the loss of mothers and grandmothers in childbirth. A woman who had been estranged from her mother since childhood told me that their relationship began to shift when she became a mother and her mother became a grandmother. "My baby has had a baby," her mother said on the telephone, in a voice full of softness and grace.

Another woman, whose mother had died when she was ten, told me that her mother's mother also had died when her mother was a child. She spoke of her powerful yearning for her grandmother.

> As a child I longed to see my grandmother's face. I used to pester my mother about it. I just had to know how this woman looked. I said things like: "Couldn't we just go to the cemetery and dig her up?" Looking back I'm impressed that this did not disturb my mother. She seemed to understand what I was feeling.

Women long for their grandmothers because they need the viewpoint of the gossip, the woman who is not in labor, the woman who is observing the labor. The mother is always in labor, always too close, her own body and psyche involved in giving birth, in nurturing, in sorting out her daughter from herself. The grandmother has access to the objectivity of the Feminine. One generation removed from the heat and passion, she can see with the cold eye of the witch, with the irreverent eye of the gossip, with the healing vision of the wise woman. When mother and daughter fly into their polarized viewpoints, arguing on opposite sides of any subject that comes up, asserting their differences, grandmother consciousness provides the integrating third viewpoint, honoring differences, valuing both sides, seeing the struggle as part of an impersonal pattern of female development.

Often the personal grandmother is not capable of this consciousness. The woman who fills this role may be one who is not biologically related, or an older woman in one's dreams, who carries the symbolic power of the grandmother in a woman's development. A woman needs this third viewpoint, this grandmother consciousness, to initiate her fully into the motherline. She needs this as a girl, and as a woman of childbearing years, for guidance into the realm of the mysteries. She needs the grandmother as she ages, as she becomes a crone herself, to integrate this aspect of the Feminine, to become whole.

HENCHWOMEN OF THE CONVENTIONAL

Women who are out of touch with their motherlines are lost souls. They are hungry ghosts inhabiting bodies they do not own, because for them the feminine ground is a foreign place. Often they suffer because their personal mothers or grandmothers are so negative, depressed, or uninspiring that they have no access through them to the archetypal pattern of the motherline. They have been torn from their feminine selves by a patriarchal culture in which women lose their identities, lose their very names and become the possessions of men.

Paula Gunn Allen writes that among the gynocratic Pueblo Indians of New Mexico, one's mother's identity is the key to one's own identity.

> Failure to know your mother, that is, your position and its attendant traditions, history and place in the scheme of things, is failure to remember your significance, your reality, your right relationship to earth and society. It is the same as being lost—isolated, abandoned, self-estranged and alienated from your own life.[7]

In my psychotherapy practice I see many women who feel isolated, abandoned, and self-estranged. To find their way into a conscious relationship with the feminine self they need to work through their connection to their mothers, their grandmothers, their motherline. Many feel barred from access to their own true natures by a mother's punitive attitude, neglect, or abuse. Some grandmothers provide a sanctuary for their granddaughters, a haven from the mother-daughter storms. One woman, whose mother blatantly preferred her younger sister and rejected her, felt cherished and protected by her grandmother. Her grandmother's death, when she was ten, was the most painful event of her childhood. She had a recurrent dream of a white bird that she knew to be her grandmother's spirit, which came to her to protect her during difficult times. In the Cinderella story a white bird comes to sit, like a blessing from the true mother, on the tree Cinderella plants on her mother's grave. Like Cinderella, my patient must reach to the spirit of a dead woman to make a true connection to her feminine self.

However, the grandmother, dead or alive, is not always so helpful. There are negative grandmothers who bind and abuse their daughters' souls. In turn the daughters bind and abuse *their* daughters. Often I sit with a woman and experience a telescopic experience of generations of pain. I am thinking, for example, of a woman who has a tormented relationship to her body. She is constantly critical of herself for being too big, and organizes her life around running and dieting. She is actually a beautiful woman and a gifted writer, but her access to her life energy, to her body and soul, is blocked by generations of self-hating women. Her grandmother and her mother were interested in the superficial values of looks and money; life was about getting thin and marrying a rich man. The disgust they felt for their own bodies and for the instinctive Feminine continues to be suffered by their daughters.

My patient had a dream that provided a picture of this family complex. She dreamed that she had inherited her maternal grandmother's apartment.

It was clean and orderly, and she was glad to have it because now she didn't have to establish her own place. However, she discovered that whenever she came home a little old woman escaped out of the back window. The old woman had been ironing. My patient felt intruded upon. She spoke to the old woman's daughter. The daughter told her that she had no control over her mother; her mother was crazy.

In the dream it became clear that the apartment was haunted. There were great areas of unexplored sadness in the corners of the rooms. To live there the dreamer had to limit the space she occupied in order to avoid the ghosts, the crazy old woman's intrusions, and the generations of unexplored grief she was afraid to confront. She lived in the apartment as she lives in her body, by severely limiting her access to herself.

This dream provides us with descriptive imagery of a painfully common problem in the psyches of modern women. An intrusive old woman, crazy, unrelated, who breaks into one's living space to iron—this is a picture of many negative grandmothers. Her obsession is ironing clothes, smoothing out the externals of life, unrelated to the dreamer, to her feelings, to the deeper meanings of existence. She is a housewife gone mad, an old woman without any access to grandmother consciousness.

The dreamer is the inheritor of generations of unconsciousness, of maternal complexes that have never been confronted and ancient griefs that have never been mourned. Like many modern women she is the first in her motherline to begin to explore generations of pain and self-estrangement. Like many women, she cannot depend upon her inheritance to provide her with a way of living on feminine ground. Her motherline is skewed by generations of patrilineal appropriation,[8] which have taken over the power of the Feminine and separated women from their embodied source of meaning. The dreamer cannot identify with generations of despised mothers. She wants to be masculine, her body muscled and lean. But she is not a man, so she finds herself in a double bind, trying to differentiate from the feminine self that is precisely what she needs to ground her life.

In the dream of another woman the motherline is clearly symbolized. She dreamed that her grandmother, mother, and sister were engaged in a circle dance from which she was excluded. This woman had been severely abused by her mother in childhood. Her mother in turn had been severely abused by *her* mother. This woman's work in therapy has been to confront the abuse and to begin to develop an internal connection to the positive Mother archetype. Her sister has continued to deny the terrible truth about the family agony. The dreamer suffers because she feels excluded from her personal motherline. Before the dream she wanted nothing to do with her motherline. The dream helped her recognize what a terrible loss this was to her. In mourning not only for herself but for her mother and her mother's mother, she is beginning, paradoxically, to make her own connection to the motherline from which she feels so estranged.

Personal mothers and grandmothers bar a woman's access to the feminine self as long as they are perceived as larger than life. The negativity feels archetypal. Once they are brought down to size, as suffering beings themselves, the daughter can sort out her own sense of self from that of her mother and grandmother.

Every motherline is laden with sorrow and suffering, because that is a major aspect of the human condition. A distinction must be made, however, between those negative aspects that are natural to life and to the Feminine, and those imposed by a culture that has for generations devalued the Feminine. Most of our grandmothers came of age in a time that denied the Feminine, split it into angels and whores, tied women up in tight corsets that denied them contact with their bodies. Many of our grandmothers have been henchwomen of the conventional, denying their daughters' sexuality, teaching them fear of their childbearing capacity.

My own grandmother punished my mother severely for a childish game my mother played with a friend when they were eight or nine. The two friends lay one on top of the other. A baby doll came out from between the legs of one of them. They were enacting the drama of sex and birth. My grandmother found them doing this and was very upset. She talked to the other child's mother, and both children were punished. My mother's natural connection to her sexuality was deeply wounded, she tells me, by this conventional attitude of her mother's.

A GRANDMOTHER'S GRANDMOTHER

The relationship between grandmother and granddaughter is often easier, less ambivalent than that between mother and daughter. My love for my grandmother was not compromised by the difficulties my mother experienced. Sometimes, however, a daughter will be allied with her mother against a powerful negative grandmother. Such a grandmother casts her shadow over both lives. The mother never fully emerges from her status as a daughter, and her daughter is in the position of mothering her mother, protecting her mother from her grandmother, thus not being truly mothered herself.

I heard such a story recently from my mother-in-law. She is a tiny woman in her mid-eighties. A brilliant plume of white hair lights up her face and her dark eyes. I watch her with her grandchildren, with the infant great-grandson who is the first of a whole new generation, and marvel at the generations she spans. As we work together in the kitchen, she tells me stories from the motherline to which I have become attached through marriage. These days most of her stories are about her grandmothers, as though her psyche is reaching for support to the crones of her childhood. They are not happy stories.

She tells me that when she was very young her mother's mother came to live with her family. This was supposed to be a help to her mother, who was "frail." Her mother's first pregnancy had brought triplets who died at birth. "She was torn by that delivery," my mother-in-law says, shaking her head in the way women do about the terrors of childbirth, "and she never really regained her strength. After my sisters and I were born my mother had trouble keeping up with all the work. Her mother came to help, to do the cooking. But this was very hard on my mother because my grandmother took over the kitchen. My mother had three daughters, and she wanted to be the one to teach them how to cook. She felt pushed out of place by her mother, the life squeezed out of her. I remember when I was fifteen I came into the living room and my mother was lying on the couch, weeping and weeping. 'What's the matter, Mama?' I asked. 'I hate my mother!' she said. I was shocked. We never said such things in our family. That was the beginning of her nervous breakdown. She screamed and cried a lot. Finally her mother died, and then she began to have a life. But by that time I was grown up and out of the house."

My mother-in-law tells another story. Her father's mother, she tells me, bore ten children and buried six. Cholera, measles, ear infections, these things killed off the children of the poor. When her father was a boy of twelve, his mother fell into a melancholia so deep that she was institutionalized for the rest of her life. The young son had to go to work to help support the family. She remembers going to visit this grandmother at Walker's Island, a place where the insane were kept. Drained of life energy, the old woman didn't talk or eat much. But when they visited, the grandmother checked the girl's scalp and that of her sisters for some unknown disease she feared they might have. Caught in perpetual mourning for the children she had lost, she reenacted a blind ritual of protection but was lost to real human contact.

"I didn't tell my husband about this grandmother for a long time," my mother-in-law tells me. "I thought these things were inherited, and I was afraid someday I'd lose my mind too."

It's a rare motherline story that does not contain such terrible suffering. My own grandmother bore six children and buried three. Her mother died in childbirth when she was two. I have been haunted by my grandmother, the orphan, and by my grandmother's dead children all my life.

In a rare moment in the history of our species, many of my generation were born into a time, a culture, and a class in which we expected each child we bore to live a full and healthy life. We are currently shifting into a new darkness, with AIDS and babies born addicted to terrible drugs. How quickly we have lost our hold on the fantasy of controlling our fates.

My grandmother, my mother-in-law's grandmother, women transfixed in a terrible Demeter mourning, remind us that death and loss and mourning are an inescapable part of life. If you follow many a motherline back, you'll find a woman like my mother-in-law's grandmother who falls into the underworld and never finds her way back into life. This unredeemed suffering lives on in her children and her children's children like a curse from an angry fairy. The negative aspect of the Goddess is being denied, and she won't stand for it. A new consciousness requires the confrontation with the dark, a surrender to mourning and loss, a surrender of control.

ON KNOWING THE MOTHERLINE
WITHOUT BEARING CHILDREN

Everyone is a product of the motherline, but not everyone lives out the motherline biologically. Not everyone becomes a parent or a grandparent. The motherline lives also in the bodies and psyches of women who never give birth. It is an archetype that can be potentiated without the physical involvement of biology. This truth was brought home to me recently by the experience of a close friend, a woman in the middle of her life, who has never had children. She has no external connection to her birth mother, who gave her up for adoption. Her relationship to her adoptive mother was at best an ambivalent one. In therapy, through dreams, active imagination, and poetry, she has developed a strong connection to her feminine self.

A few years ago she married a man who has three grown sons. She has made strong emotional bonds to these young men, and when one of them married, she made a close, supportive, kinship connection to his wife. When this wife became pregnant, I became aware of a powerful psychological shift in my friend. It was as though she was catapulted into a new stage of life by the expectation of this grandchild. What impressed me was that while she had never borne a child, she had an instinctive and embodied connection to her daughter-in-law, knew what she felt, what she feared, what she needed. She contained and guided her through a difficult pregnancy, was at the hospital all day and all night through a difficult labor and delivery, and has been supporting the new mother on the telephone and in person as she struggles with a newborn who insists on constant attention.

I am aware of the constellation of a new archetype in my friend. There is a spaciousness about her attitude. Concerned as she is about mother and child, she sees their situation with the no-nonsense perspective of the Crone. She resonates to the pain but knows it will pass. She holds firm when the new mother gets frantic and scared. There is a steadiness about her I've not experienced before. It's as if she feels the necessity to carry the wisdom of the Feminine for a daughter-in-law who, despite living out the central mystery, is wildly out of touch with her own feminine self. This experience has grounded my friend. It's as if the symbolic Feminine has taken root in her body, and the Goddess is speaking through her.

This motherline archetype can live in women's professional lives as well. A woman who has never had children is in training with me to become a psychotherapist. In one of our consultation hours we both became aware of her tendency to pull away from her patients when they are experiencing very young and needy feelings. She thought this might have to do with her own early feelings of deprivation; she thought her own mother had not been very nurturing. As she and I talked about this, an image emerged from her motherline. When she was a baby, she told me, her mother's mother was dying of breast cancer. Her mother developed a breast infection when she was nursing. As the therapist in training sat with this image, she began to be able to identify with her mother's ambivalence about feeding her. She could feel her mother's physical pain in her own breast; she could feel the emotions evoked by the awful coincidence of a mother dying as a child is born. Knowing these things in her body helped orient her with her patients; she was more able to suffer her ambivalence about nurturing because she had become conscious of her mother's painful situation and the agony of life and death into which she was born. In my role as her supervisor, I had brought a kind of grandmother consciousness to her difficulty. Once she got beyond her polarization with her mother, she could bring a less constricted attitude to her patients.

Whether or not we bear children, or our children bear children, we carry our motherlines in our very beings. Consciousness of the Grandmother archetype guides us in our development, allowing us to unfold in harmony with our feminine selves and to experience the cyclical nature of life, not as a limitation but as a vehicle for individuation.

8 · CONSCIOUS FEMININITY: MOTHER, VIRGIN, CRONE

· · · · · · ·

MARION WOODMAN

In this eloquent and multidimensional essay, Toronto Jungian analyst Marion Wood-man portrays the triple form of the conscious or "mature" Feminine: Mother, Virgin, Crone. This trinity exists simultaneously and continuously in all conscious women, each taking center stage in awareness at different moments.

Conscious mothering, Woodman explains, can come about only through break-ing the unconscious bonds we all share with our personal and archetypal mothers. As we differentiate our own feminine natures from our mothers' legacies, both positive and negative, we can begin to re-mother ourselves in more healthy ways, as well as to mother our children more consciously.

This can be accomplished, with the help of a surrogate-mother analyst, by building a feminine ego that is strong enough to carry archetypal energy without being possessed by it. The unconscious identification with an archetype is an insidious trap, even if it's the archetype of "the good mother," because, as Woodman points out, in this state individuality is lost.

In addition, as the conscious mother awakens within us, our bodies are revi-talized. A renewed relationship with matter, the body, and the earth signifies a renewed relationship to the Feminine—an embodied spirituality. This, then, be-comes the home of the conscious virgin, the essence of feminine wholeness, containing the marriage of matter and spirit. (This archetype is beautifully portrayed as the Madonna in the next essay, by Kathleen Riordan Speeth.)

The conscious crone is the product of maturing femininity, the wise older woman (or man) who has traveled far and gained a wide perspective on life. Naomi Ruth Lowinsky describes her as holding an "objective" position; Woodman calls her "detached." She is no longer invested in the power games of society and can, therefore, be trusted to say what she sees and to love fully.

Marion Woodman is a Jungian analyst practicing in Toronto. A graduate of the C. G. Jung Institute in Zurich, she is a member of the International Association for Analytical Psychology and the Inter-Regional Society of Jungian Analysts. She has written extensively on the Feminine in her popular books The Owl Was a Baker's Daughter: Obesity, Anorexia Nervosa and the Repressed Feminine; Addiction to Perfection: The Still Unravished Bride; The Pregnant Virgin: A Process of Psychological Transformation; *and* The Ravaged Bridegroom: Masculinity in Women.

In the archetypal world, the Feminine often appears in groups of three: the three Norns, the three Graces, the three Fates. In contemporary men and women who are working on their dreams, the Conscious Feminine often appears in three distinct aspects: mother, virgin, and crone. As we separate our inner conscious mother from her unconscious shadow, we often meet a magnificent feminine figure who becomes our inner mother and guide. She helps us to recognize who we are in our Being.

With that recognition, we are gradually assimilating those parts of ourselves that we once, consciously or unconsciously, rejected. Perhaps they were not acceptable to our parents, teachers, or friends. Perhaps in our yearning to be loved, we rejected the very energies that are now most vital to our creative life. Finding those lost parts, standing to their truth, and living them in our everyday life, we bring to birth the virgin in ourselves. The virgin, as I understand her, is the mature Feminine who knows how to live her own light in her own sacred matter.

Mater is the Latin word for mother. In the process of bringing our own matter to consciousness, our body becomes the physical counterpart of our inner mother and guide. In our love for her, we honor other people's matter, and the matter who is the mother of us all, Mother Earth. Intimate and daily connection with our virgin leads us into conscious choices and painful sacrifices.

Gradually, we intuit the pattern of our personal destiny unfolding and feel ourselves paradoxically detached and totally present. In that state of mind we may one day look in the mirror and see our own crone. Her wisdom is born of conscious suffering. Mother, virgin, and crone are intimately connected at each crossroad in our lives. Bringing each to consciousness is crucial to mature femininity.

UNCONSCIOUS MOTHER

In the Greek myth of Demeter and Persephone, as long as mother and daughter are unconsciously connected, bonded in *participation mystique*, the daughter is simply Kore, the Greek word for maiden. She has no name, no identity of her own. She stays within her mother's orbit, feeling her mother's feelings, dreaming her mother's dreams. Demeter as mother and Kore as daughter make up an unconscious dyad, a symbiotic life.

An adult woman may never leave this dyad. However much she hates the way her mother treated her as a child, she finds herself repeating what her mother did and said. In her marriage she perpetuates her mother's relationship to her husband, swinging from mother who resentfully or gladly waits on "the man of the house" to little girl, Kore, who is dependent or acts dependent on her wonderful husband, who knows how to do everything.

At a deeper level, which she may not recognize, she looks to her man to give her spirit. Without a meaningful life of her own, a woman projects her own spirit onto him; life is spirited, worth living, when he is around. Men who marry women who are still locked in the mother-daughter dyad enjoy being prince with mother to serve them; they also bask in being big daddy to their little girl. The femininity of such men is equally split and equally unconscious.

The unconscious bond between mother and daughter may be uncannily strong. A mother in America, for instance, may know when her daughter in Europe goes into labor and when her baby is born. Similarly, a daughter may go into shock when her mother on another continent suffers a heart attack. Looking back over the significant turning points in her life, a woman may be surprised to find that they follow the exact pattern of her mother's life, even to the onset of a fatal illness. This unconscious bond can create an insurmountable block if the daughter feels guilty when the time comes for her to outstrip her mother, to go beyond the level of consciousness her mother achieved. A mother can feel equally guilty when her destiny takes her into a situation quite unacceptable to her daughter. Precious as their bond may be, it needs to be made conscious if either is to find her own life. A mature feminine relationship is only possible when new light is allowed to illumine the space between them.

A girl who intensely dislikes her mother may decide to be anything but what her mother is. As she becomes an adult, however, unless she becomes aware of the chains that bind her, she may appear to be everything her mother was not, but she is still a rebel adolescent, a cranky kid whose mother is the center of her existence. Sooner or later the shadow mother will throw open the back door, and the woman will have to face in herself the mother she hates. Ironically, the personal mother may then become a frightened little girl, fearful of her daughter.

Often in dreams, as in life, the mother, especially if she is a widow, becomes the daughter of her own child. Unable to care for herself properly, she looks to her daughter for mothering. No longer able to see or hear as she used to, unable to cope in a world in which her values are not honored, she becomes disoriented. She looks to her child out of eyes tremulous and perplexed. The daughter, feeling guilty because she is hostile toward her aging mother, may need to examine her own victim-tyrant complex. This old woman who once seemed omnipotent is now losing control. She is forced to surrender to Fate. Facing that in mother, daughter faces it in herself. She can become angry and act like a tyrant, or she can become conscious and break the cycle. An uneasy truce may tremble between them. Both may mellow if they surrender to what is.

As we delve deeper into unconscious mothering, we come closer to the wellspring of archetypal energy. Since we are trying to understand the unconscious dynamics that undermine our conscious intent, we need to understand what archetypes are. Here is Jung's description:

> Their origin can only be explained by assuming them to be deposits of the constantly repeated experiences of humanity. . . . The [archetypal] images contain not only all the fine and good things that humanity has ever thought and felt, but the worst infamies and devilries of which men have been capable. Owing to their specific energy—for they behave like highly charged autonomous centers of power—they exert a fascinating and possessive influence upon the conscious mind and can thus produce extensive alterations in the subject.[1]

In Jung's model of the psyche, the complexes (mother, father, savior, etc.) live in the unconscious like big onions. In attempting to become conscious we are peeling the layers of these onions. These layers have to do with our personal history, personal parents, personal associations. When we peel one layer, every other layer resonates. Gradually we realize there is something awesome at the core of the onion—something over which we have little control. And when we have thoroughly explored that, there are still all those other onions to deal with.

The energy at the center of an onion-complex is what Jung calls an archetype. We cannot see it; we can only see images of it. Like a magnet under a piece of paper, we cannot see the magnet itself, but we can see its power if we throw iron filings on the paper and watch them taking a shape determined by the magnet underneath. The images on top may change, but the archetype itself is eternal. It is also Janus-faced, with positive and negative sides. The ego is powerless if it is not strong enough to hold the tension generated by the opposites within the archetype.

When we work on dreams about our personal mother, then, we are peeling an onion whose core is the Great Mother—nourishing and containing, but also devouring and restrictive. This is why Jung said there is no such thing as an unimportant dream. Every dream, if it is meditated upon, ultimately resonates in the archetypal core. In other words, when we are dealing with our relationship to our personal mother, we are at the same time dealing with our relationship to the Great Mother. At the core is the archetype, the magnet that can, when constellated, instantly overwhelm the ego. Where the ego is frail, still locked in an infantile relationship to a parental figure and therefore unable to hold a standpoint, it becomes identified with the archetype: it unconsciously acts out what the archetypal energy dictates.

In the mother-daughter dyad, for example, individuals identified with the archetype simply swing from mother to daughter without recognizing their own feelings and thoughts. For a food addict, the archetypal energy may burst out at the smell of muffins. Driven by a force over which she has no control, the child gobbles the nourishment she craves. But Mother

Muffin is matter, not love. Satiated physically by her muffin binge but still unfed, the addict swings into ravenous mother. She may experience rage against herself and Fate. She may fall into depression caused by the futility of her actions. As she plummets deeper into the darkness, the negative mother sucks out her life energy, leaving her paralyzed. The shadow mother, the evil witch, is present in the carbohydrate stupor. Until an individual builds a container strong enough to *relate* to the archetype without *identifying with* it, the ego is the victim of archetypal power. It has not the strength to say no.

Archetypal energy is our greatest blessing or our greatest curse, depending on our ego strength. If we *identify* with the positive side of the Great Mother, we think of ourselves as Big Momma, capable of nourishing every need of everyone and everything that pleads for help. We become inflated. "My breast is full," we think. "If you don't drink, God help you," to which a conscious person would respond, "And if I do, God help me."

No one is the Great Mother, and if we act as if we are, we are unconscious, possessed by an archetype. We mistakenly identify with its power and instead of recognizing power for what it is, we call it love. Yes, we have milk, but instead of nourishing our own creativity, it drowns others. Unless the power drive is brought to consciousness and seen as destructive, mother and children come to a "woman's breasts and take [her] milk for gall."[2] The starving addict who can't stop eating goes to sleep smothered in her own huge breasts.

An unconscious mother is identified with an archetype. Its most basic drive seeks to allure the male in order to procreate the human race. Mother Media's breasts overflow with such images. And what a deluge of poisoned milk is poured out when it comes to feeding the children! Television at its worst is mothering gone wrong. There is little that is personal, little that cares about the individual. Most is for a cause—money, matter, materialism—Mother concretized, enthroned in our patriarchal living rooms.

If "mother love" (whether from mother or father) is motivated by a cause, it is tainted. If a woman's cause is her children, whose lives are to exemplify what a good mother she is, her children will be performers. In their hearts they know they are not loved for who they are, and in their despair they do their best to please. Mangled by power, they know no other reality. As they have been trained, so they train others. Masochism and sadism are two sides of this coin. The pyramid of power builds— personal, national, international, environmental.

CONSCIOUS MOTHERING

Unconscious mothering can be transformed into conscious mothering when the feminine container is strong enough to open to archetypal energy and allow the love to pour through, at the same time recognizing human limitations. A mother who genuinely loves her baby, who honors her body through which the gift was given, who celebrates her sexuality, creates a container for her child. The child learns that its own little body is its home on this earth, that it has respected boundaries, that its feelings and needs are recognized. Instead of using the child to mirror her, the conscious mother mirrors the essence of the child—its delight, its anger, its imagination, its growth. Rather than concentrating on the product she is creating, she delights in her child's process.

In most analytic processes, the analyst (male or female) begins by taking on the mother projection, and usually the need for that projection deepens until the most painful abandonment feelings are dealt with. People enter analysis because life as it is seems not worth living. They sit in their expensive designer clothes or jeans and sneakers, but their costume and makeup do not hide their deep sense of rejection. Their inner child was never mirrored. The analyst then has to watch constantly for flashes of soul that break through the facade—little asides, covert mutterings, body movements that belie the well-modulated voice. When these are mirrored back by the mother analyst, analysands may feel embarrassed, guilty, or relieved. They have been well trained to stay on the iron tracks and hide their souls—as their dreams of trains, superhighways, and steel corridors make abundantly clear.

As the superstructure that controlled their performances collapses, analysands begin to realize how weak their ego structures are. Without the critical voice that says, "You should," they lack the self-identity to make decisions and act on them. Lost little girls appear in their dreams with all the personality difficulties of a three-year-old or a twelve-year-old trying to grow up. The analyst mother mirrors the process, builds trust, receives the child, but never makes the decisions. She encourages analysands to find ego support in the real feelings manifesting in their own bodies. This process is the foundation of embodiment and gradual empowerment.

As time goes on, another little girl appears in dreams. She often emerges from the filthiest, most abandoned hole in the house, but her glowing eyes and indomitable spirit radiate light in the darkness. She is unique. She is the soul child.

The ego is a psychological structure that we build as an interface between inner and outer reality. Without a strong ego, the outer world can become a highly threatening environment. The soul, on the other hand, while it can be the prisoner of a threatening environment, has a life of its own, which, as we become more aware of it, transcends that environment to inhabit a world which we identify with those persistent values that characterize the world of culture. The ego in its fully mature form is the protector of the soul, supporting it in the actualization of its most important needs.

While both ego and soul need sensitive care, the soul's needs are very different from the ego's needs, and the despair of the abandoned soul is very different from the despair of the abandoned ego. Moreover, the resultant repercussions in life are of a totally different degree. To distinguish the difference, individuals need to check the depth of their feeling response.

"What has happened during the past few hours? Does it belong to accident or essence? Is it hurting my ego or is it a betrayal of my soul? Is this merely a passing disturbance or is soul involved?" There is a deep connection between the two little girls, but initially they need to be differentiated.

The soul child does not usually make herself known in dreams until she is sure she will be welcomed. Often she first appears as a little animal or bird, sometimes a childhood pet that has been left to starve. Sometimes she transforms into a child hiding in the attic or lost in the furnace pipes of a basement room the dreamer never knew existed. But she won't die, however cruelly she has been bludgeoned. Often she reappears in the ra-diance of a newborn girl. Whatever horrendous life stories are being told, the little soul shines out from behind the garbage and sits up in the chair and says, "I'm still alive. I want to live. Love me."

Here is where conscious mothering and virgin meet. Those men and women who were deprived or abused as children must learn to mother themselves; that is, they must accept the fact that their own mother did her best, or her worst, but she too was an unconscious victim of patriarchal power. Instead of blaming her for not giving them what she herself did not possess—a healthy model of femininity—and shirking responsibility through the victim role, they can move through the depths of their rage, forgive, and take responsibility for mothering themselves. It is an anguished process, but if they are in touch with their dreams, they will eventually contact the positive side of the Great Mother. She will teach them how to discipline their lives.

"Discipline" is a bad word for many people because they associate it with power. Nevertheless, the positive mother, like animal mothers, de-mands discipline. Destructive habits have to be broken. *Discipline* comes from the same root as *disciple*, meaning pupil. Just as we see ourselves in the pupil of another's eyes, so in being receptive to discipline we see our-selves through the eyes of another. When we are mirrored in the eyes of someone who loves us and accepts us in our essence, our soul is released.

Through the loving discipline that comes from dreams, a friend, or a therapist, we can learn to claim our own body as our own loving mother. She is our matter whose wisdom grounds us and keeps us in touch with the slow rhythms of nature. Loving her we can give up the driving will that keeps us walking a tightrope over an abyss. We can surrender to the life-force that makes us glad to be alive, glad to be a part of the soul that abides in all living things. From her the virgin is born.

THE CONSCIOUS VIRGIN

Virginity, as I understand the word, has to do with mature femininity uncontaminated by other people's projections. The virgin lives her own essence. Like the virgin forest, she contains the seeds of countless possi-bilities. She reflects the Divine Feminine that resides in and resonates through all the senses of our body so long as we live on earth. She is the maturing and mature soul child, the feminine container, strong enough and flexible enough to receive the masculine spirit. She is the consciousness that radiates through matter and lives after matter returns to dust.

The virgin in men and women in our culture is starving. While she loves homemade bread made by loving hands, her divine essence needs another kind of food. As conscious mothers it is our responsibility to give her the best possible nourishment.

We are powerless, however, to feed her as long as we allow ourselves to be imprisoned in manic activity. The predominant rhythm in our society is nothing short of insanity. Driven by ambition, competition, perfectionist ideals, or the sheer necessity of keeping a job that demands a frenetic pace, people hurtle into space. In their dreams, they leave their souls impounded with Nazi torturers and their bodies filled with vacant rooms. Because they are separated from their source, they want a "high." They want it fast and they want it concrete—drugs, gambling, shopping, drinking, eating, sex, all of which can be destructive, unconscious efforts to fulfill soul needs. Addicts want to transcend, as does the soul itself, a boring, humdrum existence. They mistake that existence for "the human condition."

But we are human beings, and transcending our humanness cannot come through a fast escape into an altered state of consciousness that cannot be integrated into daily living. Escape compounds the split between spirit and body. We may fall into a bliss state in a timeless, spaceless world—the womb of the Great Mother—or we may fly into a state of possession. But possession by stupor, ecstasy, or frenetic energy is unconsciousness. The ego is not functioning and, therefore, the treasures of the altered state are not brought into consciousness to nourish the soul. In other words, one's standpoint and attitude toward life are unchanged; trapped in the old complexes, we are impaled on our own fascist sword. Genuine transcendence involves a container strong enough and flexible enough to surrender to another reality and to bring back into life the treasures it has experienced; then "the human condition" takes on rich and textured meaning.

The treasures of the sacraments that once incorporated daily living into a divine plan brought grace to millions of believers. Now many people have no container to experience those treasures, let alone bring them back. The projection that once went onto a great and loving father-God with a flowing white beard has been withdrawn. God is dead. Many find God talk not only meaningless but offensive. What is dead is the projection. Goddess talk can become equally meaningless and sentimental if there is no inner essence that knows there is a loving presence that lives within all creation.

God and Goddess can no longer be projected. They are inner experiences through which we discover ourselves, nature, relationships, and the imperial moments that are gifts we cannot understand. Soul-making goes on in the body.

Since, to quote William Blake, the body is "a portion of Soul discern'd by the five Senses, the chief inlets of Soul in this age,"[3] we children of the patriarchy have to learn to love matter, the goddess in her mother aspect. We do not naturally surrender to the comfort of her womb. We do not hear her slow heartbeat. We take only a fleeting glance at the dying fingers of winter clutching at the triumphant buds. We rarely pause for a lungful of spring, for skin saying thank-you for sun or the taste of rain. So warped are our sensitivities that we have to *learn* to honor nature, to honor our own bodies. We have to reconnect with the primal wisdom that assures us that we are loved, that life is our birthright, that we need not prove ourselves or justify our existence. With that knowledge in our bones we can accept paradox. Life is no longer broken into right and wrong, light and dark, birth and death. Everything is part of the awesome mystery when we are conscious enough to receive the messages from our virgin soul.

Consciously relating to the Great Mother is coming back to the garden and recognizing the place for the first time, recognizing that it *is* a garden and that we have dishonored it. Consciousness takes an ego stand and refuses to identify with devouring appetites for food, drink, sexuality. It refuses to fall into compulsive behavior. By standing firm against the power principle that operates between mother and child, consciousness opens the way for love.

Now, who is the daughter? Who is the virgin who sits on her mother's lap, the virgin born of a conscious womb? Primal femininity the virgin shares with her archetypal Mother; her identity, however, is her own. That identity is *soul*. The virgin who has broken her identification with the mother, while still remaining grounded in the mother, is a transformative aspect of the Feminine. In her, matter is permeated by light. She lives at the point where matter and spirit touch and do not touch. She is the bridge between heart and head. The meeting in a dream is the image, neither completely outside in the world of the senses nor completely within the psyche. Psyche and soma meet in metaphor. Because the soul is eternal essence living in matter, the images of matter bestowed by the five senses carry within them the food of the soul.

Whatever exists in the world of the senses has a symbolic dimension that exists the moment the soul is consciously in the body. Thus, food is both physical and symbolic. Without that dimension, soul is neither present nor fed. Images are the soul's natural food. Metaphors heal because they speak to the total person through the imagination, feelings, and mind. For this reason, Jung believed that the contemplation of dream images was the pathway to wholeness.

Without the nourishment of imagery, the soul lies huddled in the gap between dark, opaque matter and disembodied spirit. If we understand how metaphor works, we can understand why visualization is so valuable in healing the sick body and crucial to feeding the creative soul. The images have both a literal meaning in the actual world and a symbolic meaning in the soul world. Both are simultaneously present. This simultaneous presence of the literal and the symbolic is metaphor. It points in both directions.

By definition, metaphor is a transformer. In Greek, it means a transporting from one place to another, a transforming of energy from one level onto another. All language is, in fact, metaphor—words standing for something. Much of our daily talk is metaphor: "She chewed me out. I can't stomach him. Let's make a clean breast of it. She's a peach, a princess, a Pollyanna. He's a prick, a prince, a paragon." Metaphor is colorful language because it carries an emotional and imaginative charge as well as a meaning.

Take, for example, the familiar lines of Macbeth when he learns that his wife, once his "dearest love," is dead:

> Tomorrow, and tomorrow, and tomorrow,
> Creeps in this petty pace from day to day
> To the last syllable of recorded time,
> And all our yesterdays have lighted fools
> The way to dusty death. Out, out, brief candle!
> Life's but a walking shadow, a poor player
> That struts and frets his hour upon the stage
> And then is heard no more.[4]

Like many students you may have wondered why Shakespeare was not smart enough to say what he meant, as you may wonder why your dreams don't say what they mean. Suppose Macbeth had said what he meant: "I'll end my empty, short life." Would those words capture the total collapse of everything a great man once was and ever hoped for? Would the imagination be fed with the image of the spark suddenly disappearing into nothingness? Would the heart resonate with the keening of Lady Macbeth sleepwalking with a candle, groping in a world in which "'Twas lighter—to be Blind"?[5] Would we see the candle of her life, like the candle of our own lives, flicker into darkness?

Without the metaphor the mind may be fed, but the imagination and heart go hungry. Without the pondering in the virgin's heart, the banquet table in dreams may be laden, but the food is not assimilated and the soul starves. There is nothing sadder in analysis than to see dreams rich with healing images, but the dreamer is unable to eat; that is, consciousness either is unable to or refuses to take the time to bite into, chew, swallow, digest, and integrate what is represented by the healing images.

So long as a dream is not brought into a conscious container, the metaphors we are dreaming are enacted in our bodies and in our relationships. If, on the other hand, we work hard on associations to the dream images and allow the feelings, imagination, and mind to move in and through and around the symbol, inevitably we are silenced by the rightness of the metaphor. There is a moment of yes! or oh, no! when the truth resonates through our whole being—sometimes a painful truth, but nevertheless a truth that leads toward freedom. The virgin has been fed.

The raw honesty of the images from the unconscious can strike us dumb with tears or laughter, often with both, because the image moves on that fine edge of the absurd between tragedy and comedy. If the ego can assimilate the point of view presented by the unconscious and see itself objectively, then it can find a new standpoint. It can observe itself suffering but at the same time experience the suffering as pangs of birth.

The ego that is relating to the virgin soul is motivated to reflect on the dream images through painting, dancing, singing, sculpting, or writing, thus allowing the healing process to transform what would otherwise be dead images into life energy. Transformation takes place through metaphor. Without metaphor, energy is locked in repetitive patterns. The unconscious Medusa witch traps energy in stone. In the creative matrix, the symbol flows between mind and matter, healing the split.

In children, the split has not yet taken place; thus for them the world is still a magical place—soul still infiltrates matter. Uncanny wisdom slips out of their mouths, but it is not conscious. In the growing-up process in our culture, rational thinking supersedes soul perception to such a degree that imagination is stifled. Without it, spontaneity and creativity petrify. Eternal essence is no longer perceived in daily living, and life becomes a repetitive treadmill. The feminine receiver is so shut down that nothing genuinely transformative registers. The contraries (spirit/matter, masculine/feminine, etc.) cease to be perceived as living paradox; without their tension, humor, wit, playfulness, the salt that gives life its savor is not there. Laughter explodes when two different realities collide, and if we are to live the divine comedy, we have to be holding the tension of the paradox between those two worlds.

If our conscious virgin is strong enough to receive, then the moment that contains finite and infinite does happen. Light in matter does open to light of spirit. Without a receiver for Mozart, his music is noise. Without a receiver for dreams, they are meaningless.

Light in matter is the light that comes to the soul through the medium of the senses. That light is different from the spiritual light that suddenly announces itself and changes the vibration of every cell in the environment. A concert pianist, for example, may have created a superbly sensitive container through technique, but if he or she also is receptive to spirit, then something transcendent may happen: suddenly musician and audience *become* music—infinite penetrates finite.

The conscious virgin sitting on the lap of the conscious mother is an image of the soul alive to its own values, needs, and possibilities, grounded in a body whose cells are attuned to every variation in the harmonics of the soul and capable of opening to more subtle variations.

The virgin is light (consciousness) in matter. She is in the continual process of becoming more light through the wisdom that is forever being revealed to her through matter and spirit. She is the personification of the redemption of matter. She becomes the ravished bride of the true bridegroom.

The Black Madonna is another aspect of the transformative Feminine, that unknown realm—part spirit, part matter—in which metaphor is born. In the dark room of the subtle body, our spiritual condition, like negatives put into a developing bath, is gradually transformed into pictures we can see either as dreams or physical symptoms. This process happens in the womb of the Black Madonna. She is related to Sophia, the Greek word for wisdom. When the church fathers were translating the Old Testament, they chose to use the abstract word *wisdom* rather than the personified image *Sophia* for the feminine side of God.[6] The Old Testament has a different resonance when Sophia, rather than Wisdom, plays around His throne. The body/soul responds to Sophia; the mind responds to Wisdom.

The split that has taken place between body/soul and mind can be healed through images, but few people have experienced that healing. The wisdom of the soul is just beginning to enter consciousness. That is partly why it appears as the Black Madonna. Partly, too, this figure is black because we know so little about the mystery of the subtle body, that still point where matter and psyche meet. Moreover, the redemption of matter, the sacredness of our own bodies and that of the planet are still far from our consciousness.

At this point we can only vaguely guess at what the sacredness of matter means, but the images that appear in dreams—like the long-distance telephone calls from "Mother"—suggest possibilities beyond our comprehension. Imagine a world in which communication is possible without the encumbrance of wires and telephones. Imagine a world where human beings would listen to the wisdom of the deep through dolphins who know the secrets of Grandmother Ocean. Some vast unknown lies ahead.

THE CONSCIOUS CRONE

Feminine growth is cyclic, not linear. As mother and virgin mature together, the crone is implicit in their maturing. As the virgin surrenders to her destiny, she goes through crossroad after crossroad. Hecate, goddess of the crossroads, is the crone.

In Europe today, there are still cairns at crossroads where people were faced with going down an unfamiliar path into the unknown; in their fear, they offered a stone to Hecate to give them heart. Symbolically, crossroads represent moments in our lives where the unconscious crosses consciousness, where the eternal crosses the transitory; in other words, times and places where a higher Will demands the surrender of our ego. The crone has gone through her many crossroads; she has reached a place of conscious surrender where her ego demands are no longer relevant. She is a surrendered instrument and therefore detached.

Detachment does not mean indifference. It means she has been there. She has suffered, but she can draw back from the suffering. She suffers more pain in the presence of an unconscious person than that person can be aware of, but she can hold the pain and look at it at the same time. She is not indifferent or withdrawn. She is there, totally present. She can be who she is and live her naked truth. Therefore she is like a tuning fork in her environment; being so real herself, she rings a true tone. Others are brought into harmony with that tuning and respond with what is true in themselves. Or flee.

The crone can afford to be honest. She is not interested in playing outworn games. Near her, others can experience their own essence. Her flat-out truth sometimes makes her hard to take. But her truth is the measure of her love. She has nothing to lose because who she is cannot be taken from her. She has no investment in ego and so she can love with no desire to control. She has no reason to persuade. In her eyes you can see your true self. She is the perfect mirror. You can trust her discipline.

In the Middle Ages crones, both men and women, were often mistaken for witches. They lived outside the collective—as many do today—and were lucky if they escaped being burned at the stake.

Conscious crones are magnificent creatures. I have been fortunate enough to know a few. One was a man, Dr. E. A. Bennet, my analyst in London, in his eighties when I knew him. I had been in analysis about six months and was still trying to be a good girl. On Christmas Eve I received word from Canada that my little dog, Duff, had been killed. I was stunned, but my session was at six o'clock and I decided not to waste the time talking about my dog. I went to the office and talked about my dreams. At the end of the hour, Dr. Bennet was very pensive. "What is wrong?" he asked.

"Nothing," I said, putting on my coat as quickly as possible.

"Well, you haven't been here," he said.

"My dog was killed," I said. To my astonishment, Dr. Bennet began to weep. Dr. Bennet crying over my dog! I thought.

"How could you waste Christmas Eve chattering when your soul animal has died?" he asked. His tears broke the dam in my heart, and I cried. His feeling made me feel what I was doing to my feminine soul. Then my analysis truly began. No longer a fascinating intellectual study, it became a soul journey.

Another crone I loved was Barbarah Hannah, one of my Zurich analysts. She was also in her eighties when I knew her. She told the truth and she told it straight. During my analysis, I came to one of those crossroads where my ego desires were completely scuttled by what I call God. I arrived in her presence a burnt-out shell. She looked at me. She said nothing, but her love was palpable.

I sat beside her in silence. It was like being in a womb, enfolded in the love quietly beating in her heart. She didn't tell me what I should do. Neither of us had any idea what to do. She held me in her love until my soul was once again embodied and I was present and strong enough to walk into the unknown.

Mother, virgin, crone—all three mature together into conscious femininity. For centuries the redemption of matter has been discussed as a theological concept. Now our bodies and our planet are confronting us with decisions that make Conscious Femininity imperative and the redemption of matter crucial to our survival. Each of us needs to look into our heart and ask the questions "Do I love my femininity enough to honor her with time and energy? Do I believe that she can be released from the prison of power into her radiant empowerment?"

9 · THE MADONNA

· · · · · · ·

KATHLEEN RIORDAN SPEETH

In this beautiful work of active imagination, author Kathleen Riordan Speeth draws a timeless portrait of the Madonna, the woman in whom the personal mother meets the divine mother, the individual meets the archetype. She evokes the mystery and magic of a virgin birth in which a woman who is whole unto herself contains and brings forth a child who is whole, who is in her and yet not of her, who has his own destiny. The virgin/goddess gives birth to the son/god; spirit gives birth to matter, which gives birth to spirit.

At the same time, Speeth portrays the elements of every childbirth: the fatefulness of conception, the fullness of gestation, the painful intensity of labor, the ultimate self-sacrifice. Every mother, as the source of life, becomes as well the source of death. At every birth (and at every death), Life appears and disappears in a single numinous moment, while life drones on.

Speeth's portrait in words brings an encounter with the Face behind the face of every woman: mother as creator, woman as divine source of life.

Kathleen Riordan Speeth is a psychologist in private practice in New York and California. Her interests include the psychodynamics of creativity and transcendence and the conduct of life as a work of art. She is the author of The Gurdjieff Work *and* Generativity *(forthcoming).*

This portrait arose from my experience as a mother, my studies of motherhood in art, literature, and ego psychology, and also from the influence of David Rosenmann-Taub, to whom I would like to acknowledge my gratitude, in particular for his unpublished reflection "Maternidad" and in general for his profound understanding of human nature and evolution, upon which my own perspective depends.

Amid the nodding roses sits a slender girl in blue, the book of Isaiah on her knee. Under her foot, the serpent's head is bruised. The moon beneath her reflects the light above. Dawn entwines her hair. In the stillness, aromatic with cedar, a dove coos. Then, in the breeze of morning, in a flutter, Mary is not alone. She looks up, astonished. The seal falls away from the book. She understands.

Mary is the chosen one. She has learned the news. In a moment's hesitation, a line appears between her brows, for the end is nailed upon the beginning. Choice. She sees it plain. Must it be? Time stands still. The dove is silent. Heaven and earth await her . . .

Yes!

Accepting her lot, she is transfigured. Gladly will she mother a baby. Her heart is full. With happiness she says yes to the white-lilied, winged messenger who interrupted her reading. Yes, I will. There is no withholding: her simple heart sings one note. She agrees. Blooming with yes, she is fragrant with grace. I accept. Thy will be done.

Nothing will stop Mary now, or deflect her from her purpose. She never changes. The cosmic egg is penetrated only once. Nevermore will it receive the visitor. Now the blessed zygote secretly makes miracles of loaves and fishes within her. One becomes two, becomes four, ever sculpting, never resting. Curtained with flesh, hidden in cascades of blue tunic, the pattern forms itself in the busy sphere within, cradled by her whitened human bones.

Mary is a maiden, warm and clean, kind mannered. Amiable and mild, respectful of her family and her world, she must now soar beyond convention. The birth will forfeit social honor. Who is the father? Eyebrows are raised. People smirk at the answer, sneer at the mother, and drive her out. Where are her friends? One kinswoman stands beside her, though her neighbors are of two minds. Many shun her. Others aid her but in secret. Sensing that light must cast its shadow, she has the strength to bear surprises, insults, and humiliations, for her child's sake.

Nausea. The fruit of this earth is speckled with corruption, the flesh of animals is putrid. Distaste fills her mouth. Intolerant of dirt, she swallows no impurity, but happily the second apple is unblemished. It is tartly sweet. She adds to it her bread and wine, forming the body and blood of the growing child.

Slenderness renounced, she assumes a global form, glad of how the roundness shapes her. She wears her apron high. Upon it tremble breasts filling with anticipation. Beneath it a new life bakes. She contains her joy, sitting on the bench under the cedars in the rose garden, knitting little things or reading.

Walking among the flowers her step grows deliberate. What is this? She stands still. The thorns come into focus, under the petals. Why this whisper? It is a warning. Someone has talked. A rumor was told the power holders. The life within her is threatened. Slander and gossip infest this place. She senses the menace, listens and escapes, accompanied in her night flight by a man who trusts her but is not the father of her child. He will protect what is not his seed. In his devotion for the unwed mother, he takes her unto himself and into his protection.

Her calm is changeless. Safe again, she waits. Yes envelops her. In pregnancy she knows herself as the divine surround, the matrix of the world. Under her heart stirs the hope of generations. She is truly Mary, being what Mary is. She knows herself and is thus sinless, without beliefs, with certainties.

The sun comes and goes, comes and goes. She moves and rests with the rhythm of days and nights, her hope inward, brooding. She is the holy envelope in which all evolution retells its tale. The long journey from gills to lungs takes place in her inner ocean, nourished by the manna of her pulsing cord. She is the eternal stasis in which time swims upstream.

For the tenth round the moon circles her body. At one moment she gazes faraway or inward. She leans heavily on the proffered arm. Her hour has come. The man finds her shelter. In her lying-in she needs a haven—anywhere will do. Couched in a fragrance of hay, encircled by soft-eyed oxen, all her attention is given to birthing. Breathlessly laboring, she must be cared for herself. The man kneels nearby. Thunderous convulsions storm her body. Colossal forces can maul her or let her live. Mary forgets her name. She is gripped and released, lifted up and smashed down. In the face of heaving nature, what can the man do? He is only a bystander. His eyes are tense. She wrings his hand. He dries her forehead. The gentle bovine munching in the stable drones on irrelevantly.

Mary is approaching motherhood. She strains forever and ever, making the gate. Her belly rises like a mountain: a rock must be rolled away from the entrance to the cave. It moves and hesitates, it rolls and stops. Push and pause, and again bear down. Such effort! What weight!

Her abdomen clenches—a furious fist, held up against the tyranny of this impermanent world. The fist gestures and shakes, signaling rebellion, heralding creation. Then little by little the palm unfurls and opens. At one moment all is quiet.

Now!

Her eyes widen in amazement. She lets go the ripened child. She becomes the corridor of life, bridge to the ten thousand things. She yields up her treasure, giving light to her little one, the one who must die. She can shield him no more. The crown appears, then the little king glides into the world of forms. His voice is a baby's cry in the darkness.

Gladness. Untethered, he is himself now. They are two now. She holds him close, warms him, cleans him while the man who loves her attends them. He recognizes the child. The holy family.

The Madonna has at last given birth. Something that was inside is outside. Part of herself. A human being. Her own son—yet not her son at all. He is no one else's on earth—and everyone's. The newborn is her center.

The innocence she has cushioned with her own red human blood has pushed forth and now, pale and closing, she must offer the white blood of her breasts, and she does so spontaneously, gladly. It is her pleasure. This first suckling is momentous for the woman, stretched and bleeding, who will henceforth be called not by her given name but by the universal, mantric name, Mama. She is Mary, *mère, mer, mare*: the sea, mother of pearl, fulfilling herself in being background for another.

She receives the gifts of those awaiting him. The babe is welcomed. She shows him to animals and men and women, held in her arms, swaddled with white. These few adore him. Earth and heavens shiver with the change.

A single light dazzles the night sky, punctuating darkness with an excla-
mation: welcome!

Gracefully do the mother and child give attention and gratefully receive
it, as with one mind. In the beginning baby and mother are one, and that
one is baby. Thus the divinity the mother sees in her newborn is also hers,
and she proves it with the impossible, the saint's maneuver: she puts another
before herself.

She keeps her babe in comfort, her blue-white milk is honeyed. Smiling, she holds him close. The baby rests, secure in a heaven of her making.
The familiar drumming of her heart—da rump, da rump, da rump—is as
calming as the tides of her breath. The melody of her voice, familiar from
the womb, lulls him. Well held, the baby relaxes. Carried with care, he
enjoys moving securely. Well fed, he blossoms and chortles. Steadily nurtured, he asserts dominion over this world as his mother adapts, adapts,
adapts to his needs.

The thriving infant feels at one with all. He knows no limitation. He
is everything, master of all. His mother is the source of comfort, without
thought of herself. To her the child is central, she is peripheral. To her
child it is the same: he is the axis and she the surround. She forgets herself.
To love is to study the other. The baby is her natural subject to understand.
She finds just the right ways to hold him, to snuggle him, to jiggle him,
and she learns lullabies to help him overcome his agitation. With her feminine self-sacrifice, she is indeed a goddess, the embodiment of givingness
without bounds.

As the child begins to emerge from this blissful union, he realizes his
mother appears and disappears. While she is out of sight he forms her image.
When she returns he corrects, makes more vivid, perfects an internal icon
of the holy mother.

The baby creeps away, always looking back to his mother for refuge.
Mother was a breast. Now she is a breast and a lap. She is the snug nest
to which he can always return. One day he wanders out of her sight,
absorbed with the things of this world. Then he races back to pull himself
up on her skirts, to find her arms. She welcomes him, embraces him, calms
his fears, consoles him. Knowing she is there, he can go bravely abroad.
She is his home, his lady luck, the shrine of goodness.

Mary lets him go. She is not a sea that drowns or smothers, but
supports. Involved in his own love affair with the world, he does his own
things. When his adventures bring him home in tears he finds her there,
ready to console him. Whether he is hurt or joyous, she is tender. In the
amplitude of her concern, she intercedes for him.

Madonna. My lady. She is a gentle woman, capable of restraint. She
who said yes can also forbid. She civilizes. When she says no it is for the
child's sake, not her own convenience. Once she refuses to open the door
to strangers, and her command of silence is strong. The little one secreted
under her blue mantle holds his breath. The soldiers pass them by. Very
near, then farther and farther, women scream and keen as their nurslings'

necks are twisted. The child obeyed his mother; thus he lives. She is worshipped as divine protectress.

The child has faith in her and in himself. He plays with pomegranates on her lap. He examines the dazzling globe in his hands. He dawdles under the victorious palms, near the well, in the enclosed garden, or races through the lilies and the roses. His mother watches, to attend him now, because she cannot deflect his inexorable destiny. Vital and sweetly intelligent, he flourishes.

As he grows he gains skill and knowledge. He learns the scriptures. The rabbis are amazed, the mother is proud. But she never changes. Whatever he will be, he will be. He is a youth, a worker, a dreamer. One day he goes off, she knows not where, but she stays serene, peaceful in her garden, trusting that he will come back eventually. She is happy with his goings and glad with his returnings.

The son's days and nights are his affair, not hers. In freedom he lives as he must. He goes his own way, following his own light. Taller than his mother, he reveres her, and what little she asks he provides. Standing on a hill, he speaks his mind. People gather. A few are convinced but others disagree. Some are soothed, inspired, or healed. Some wake up from deathly slumbers. Standing apart, the mother knows him: mild with the meek, he is resolute against worldly power. He takes chances. She is behind him.

His time has come. It must be. She is helpless to prevent the happening. Though her sighs wrack heaven and earth, in her grief she never changes. He breathes no more. What has been offered through her to the world has just as mysteriously been taken away.

She holds her dead son in her arms. As always, she bears his weight. She is still the lap, still the surround. She accepts her son, his corpse she washes like an infant, and his grave clothes are swaddling shrouds. The rock is heaved from the cave, now and always.

Mary is alone in her unfathomable destiny.

Mary sits in the rose garden, draped in blue. Under her foot the serpent sucks its tail. The moon beneath her reflects the light above. Night entwines her hair. In the breeze, aromatic with cedar, a dove coos. Though the lilies nod, she never changes. A pregnant star amid eternal darkness, she enfolds the inner Man in her vast, virgin womb. He is forever safe under her rocking heart. Her time will never come; her hope will never end. Though the book on her knee lies open still, she cannot understand. She is the chosen one: *Maria*, the pregnant madonna, the Madonna.

· · · · · · ·

PART 3

RE-FATHERING
OURSELVES:
HEALING OUR
RELATIONSHIPS
WITH MEN
AND THE
MASCULINE

The girl and the woman, in their new, their own unfolding, will but in passing be imitators of masculine ways, good and bad, and repeaters of masculine professions. After the uncertainty of such transitions it will become apparent that women were only going through the profusion and the vicissitude of those (often ridiculous) disguises in order to cleanse their most characteristic nature of the distorting influences of the other sex.

RAINER MARIA RILKE

Opening to the Conscious Feminine also requires a new relation to the Father World, the realm of life that contains men and the Masculine. For women, this includes our personal fathers, husbands or lovers, sons, and brothers. It also encompasses our animus, the unconscious masculine element in our psyches, which can become a key to spiritual growth when it holds its proper place in relation to our feminine egos.

At another level, this realm contains the Father archetype, the transcendent image that exists within and beyond the personal world of men. This includes both the patriarchal (male-dominant) institutions of our society and their ruling patriarch, the Divine Masculine image we have been taught to think of as God.

(In contrast to women, for men the Father World is the birthplace of ego identity. For them, it also would include the sphere of the newly emerging men's movement, which is giving rise to a sense of brotherhood and community for men.)

The Father World (also commonly known as "the real world") is for women the world of the Other. From the beginning, our love affairs with our fathers are typically complex and convoluted, whatever their style.

When we start to clarify and make conscious their hidden dynamics, we take a major step toward clarifying our relationships with all men, as well as with the Masculine principle. This is the beginning of *re-fathering* ourselves.

Like our mothers, our fathers could not meet the more-than-human needs we projected onto them as children. Sometimes, sadly, they could not even meet the all-too-human needs as well, perhaps because of their own insufficient parenting. So most of us have greatly wounded feelings in relation to our fathers, ranging from intense hatred to idealized adoration, and everything in between.

To develop psychologically, we need to carefully examine these feelings and their ripple effects on our lives. We need to look closely at how we have owned and disowned our fathers' qualities, how we have identified with our fathers and become like them, how we have feared them, and how we have rebelled.

For example, in one kind of relationship with a father, a loving daughter may have knowingly adopted some of his traits or even tried to fulfill a career wish that belonged to him. With a different dynamic, another daughter may have veered off in the opposite direction simply to thwart her father's will. In the one case, she tries to live his unlived life; in the other, she tries to escape his influence. In both, she is trapped in a dynamic that is determined by her (probably unconscious) intense feelings about him, not by her own adult choices.

Our fathers also have great impact on how we experience our feelings of power and attractiveness as women. A father's anima (internal feminine image) can be carried unknowingly by a daughter, giving her a sense of sway over him yet trapping her in his personal pictures of beauty and femininity. Alternatively, a father may devalue a daughter's style of femininity, criticizing her growing shapeliness or her tomboyish ways and destroying her budding feelings of self-confidence at a young age. She begins to yearn to be a woman other than the one she is.

Later in life, as we are attracted to lovers and mates, our fathers (now fully internalized within us) continue to affect our choices and behaviors. Some women seek their fathers in other men, forever searching for the "one that got away." Others seek their fathers' opposites, their shadow qualities, for these women are determined (even unknowingly) not to re-create the father-daughter relationship.

For instance, I know one woman whose father remains a very loving and involved presence in her life. He is a great conversationalist who spent his life creating success in business and who highly values a knowledge of politics and history. For years, this woman has become involved with men who, unlike her father, remained unworldly and unaccomplished financially, and whose priority has been to develop their emotional and psychic abilities. In effect, she has sought out her father's opposite, almost as if one man of his kind is enough in her life.

For all these reasons and more, it's essential to begin to sort out the complexities of this primary relationship. Whether we are overly identified with our fathers or overly rejecting, we are not free to create a femininity of our own until we detect his invisible hand on our destiny.

Her father and other father figures in a woman's life are also the source of her animus—the masculine element within. So re-fathering involves awakening and separating out this element in the unconscious. Jungian analyst Andrew Samuels calls the animus the "inner figure of man at work in a woman's psyche."

These two archetypes, or underlying universal psychological patterns, were uncovered by Carl Jung in his clients' dreams and behaviors and corroborated in fairy tales and myths. He came to view them as basic building blocks in the human psyche. Jung used the terms *animus* and *anima* as they derive from the Latin *animare*, which means to enliven, because he believed they act like enlivening souls or spirits to men and women.

Jungian analyst John Sanford, in his book *The Invisible Partners*, explains that our animus is usually difficult to detect. Like men who, identified primarily with the Masculine, project their femininity onto women, so women, consciously identified with the Feminine, project our unconscious masculine side onto men. For this reason our animus appears to belong to someone else, such as a lover who appears to be the living image of "the perfect mate." Sanford calls these projected unconscious elements "the invisible partners" in our male-female relationships.

Sanford adds that if a woman projects onto a man her positive animus image—the savior, hero, and spiritual guide—she overvalues him. If he does the same and sees her as his ideal woman, their projections will match, and they will declare that they are "in love." In their fascination and attraction, they may come to feel completed only through each other, remaining blind to the mechanism of projection that creates their reality. If, on the other hand, she projects her negative animus image, he becomes a source of disappointment, even betrayal; if he does the same, she becomes a "witch." This shift often follows the initial phase of a love affair, when the projections begin to burst.

To begin to understand the role of animus-projection in our relationships with men is to begin to discriminate between what is "in here" and what is "out there." When we learn to own the masculine side of ourselves, developing our own source of autonomy and spirituality, we can begin to be free of emotional dependency on men.

There is a flip side to projection of the Masculine onto men: a woman's overidentification with the animus within. This necessary psychological stage is widespread among women today. In our efforts to be free of stereotyped patterns of femininity, which stem from projecting all masculinity onto men and receiving their feminine projections, we have adopted instead a "masculinized" way of coping, becoming "daughters of the patriarchy."

The language to describe this phenomenon is unfortunately simplistic, I believe, and lacks the depth we need to accurately reflect the complexity of what is taking place. It is said that a woman with a highly developed animus becomes overly aggressive, intellectual, and power-hungry in an effort to end patterns of passivity, dependency, and moodiness. In the 1960s, for instance, many feminists wished to dispel the myth of biology as destiny and to prove women's capacities to think clearly, handle authority, and achieve what some men can achieve.

As a result, some women grew addicted to the heady rush of productivity, becoming workaholics and taking it upon themselves to be "superwomen." They may sacrifice loving relationships during this time in order to develop their personal power. Others find that their relationships with men suffer from a loss of clear gender boundaries. Some observers have remarked that during the heyday of feminism, many men became more "receptive," "nurturing," and "sensitive" in response to women developing what men perceived as "masculine" traits.

The light side of this, of course, is that, for the first time in history, large numbers of women have had and will continue to have a tremendous impact on a patriarchal culture. Through a greater use of our wide-ranging capacities, we have begun to leave our mark on every field of endeavor.

In addition, again for the first time, male-female relationships can become a vehicle for the growth of consciousness through an increasing understanding of projection and the withdrawal of those projections from our loved ones. The suffering that results from unclear gender boundaries brings with it the exploration of deeper forms of love, and more meaningful connections that can emerge only after the anima- and animus-projections have died.

When women no longer place the Masculine outside of ourselves (on a man or on society), the animus is no longer unconscious and we can no longer be called animus-possessed. Conversely, when men no longer place the Feminine outside of themselves onto women, they are no longer in the clutches of an unconscious anima. This, then, portends a huge shift in our intimate relationships, as well as in our creative lives. And it calls upon us to develop a new language that goes beyond Jung's classification, which was more appropriate for his time.

We are in the midst of these psychological transitions today. Many women have emerged out of the unconscious Feminine into a more focused, active masculine style. However, the next step also has begun: women have begun to report feeling dissatisfied with the limits of these newfound ways, mourning our lost femininity.

Jungian analyst June Singer calls this syndrome "the sadness of the successful woman." It stems, she says, from losing touch with our femininity by giving priority to developing individual identity at the cost of relationship values. Singer is not proposing that women undergo a regressive return to being full-time caretakers; rather, she is suggesting that deep feelings of conflict will erupt when life is one-sided, such as when the goals of career do not validate the feminine self.

This trend signifies a new stage in women's development. We can predict the beginning of the breakdown of animus-identification, and with it the beginning of emergence out of the Father World and into Conscious Femininity.

I do not believe this developmental step in individuals is age related, like the onset of puberty; however, I think it frequently coincides with midlife or a few years later, because it demands a certain kind of psychological maturity and a certain degree of worldly success that takes time to achieve.

In this section you will find four poignant essays about women in the Father World.

Linda Schierse Leonard's piece on redeeming the father explores her own personal work in this area, her efforts to recognize her entanglement in her father's shadow qualities and to free herself for a more conscious relationship to the Father World. The result, unforeseen to her initially, is her discovery of a new feminine spirit, an internally derived source of authority.

Manisha Roy describes the need for women to live out the animus stage, as well as the dangers of becoming stuck in it. She points out that this explains the inner dynamics of certain social trends, such as role confusion in relationships, female-initiated divorce, feminism, and the baby boom among baby boomers. And she suggests that the spiritual function of the animus, to guide the ego to reconnect with the Self, can be fulfilled by women today.

Jane Wheelwright sees the breakdown of animus identification as a key gateway to developing conscious femininity. She notes that it often takes some kind of trauma to wake up a woman from the status quo: a bodily crisis such as illness or post-partum depression, or a relationship crisis. Like Manisha Roy, she prescribes psychological work with a woman who can model and evoke new feminine patterns.

Polly Young-Eisendrath tells how feminism awakened her to the nature of reality-making in a patriarchal culture. Because our male-dominant institutions and language define women as lacking in relation to men, we inherited a collective identity crisis. This cannot be healed, Young-Eisendrath believes, by a psychology that maintains a gender bias. Therefore, she rejects the classic interpretations of Feminine and Masculine and seeks to redefine the animus and its development in women in a way that includes feminist insights.

Entry into the Father World, then, is an inevitable and needed step in women's development. And so is emergence out of the Father World. It will mean a new way of life at every level—personal, interpersonal, and cultural.

10 · REDEEMING THE FATHER AND FINDING FEMININE SPIRIT

· · · · · · ·

LINDA SCHIERSE LEONARD

San Francisco Jungian analyst Linda Schierse Leonard, in her best-seller The Wounded Woman, *struck a chord in the hearts of hundreds of thousands of women when she urged us to uncover the hidden and sometimes messy wounds within our fathers, and to trace their legacies within us.*

In the book, Leonard describes two underlying patterns that develop in women as a result of deficient fathering: the puella, or eternal girl, who adapts to become pleasing and attractive to the male world; and the armored Amazon, who adopts masculine ways to succeed in a man's world. Both archetypes are shaped by the demands, explicit or implicit, of the personal father and the cultural fathers. They are not of our own making.

In the selection I have chosen from this book, Leonard ties her theme of cleansing and renewing the relationship to the personal father to rediscovering our own feminine nature. The fairy tale that follows, along with Leonard's insightful commentary and personal revelations, reveals the father's lack of wholeness through his deval-uation of the Feminine; ironically, only the Feminine can heal him. The daughter's quest, in the name of her father, becomes her own quest of self-discovery.

To redeem her father, then, a woman must come to see both his dark and light sides—his anger, lack of control, and incompleteness; his power, creativity, and generosity of spirit. Recognizing these multiple realities in him permits us to see them in ourselves, to have a more direct relation with our own darkness and light. We can then re-father ourselves and awaken the Masculine principle within us, which leads to a healthier, richer balance with the feminine self.

This piece is reprinted from The Wounded Woman *with permission of the original publisher, Ohio University Press.*

Linda Schierse Leonard, Ph.D., is a Jungian analyst and existential philos-opher with a private practice in San Francisco. She gives workshops and consultations across the United States. She is the author of The Wounded Woman: Healing the Father/Daughter Relationship; On the Way to the Wedding: Trans-

forming the Love Relationship; *and* Witness to the Fire: Creativity and the
Veil of Addiction.

"Where are the myths and stories of feminine quests and courage?" is a
question I frequently hear women ask. Where are some models for feminine
development? One story that helped me in my own quest is a fairy tale
from the land of Tadzhikistan, which borders on Afghanistan in the south
and on China in the east, a land whose culture and language are akin to
Persia. [It] is entitled "The Courageous Girl."

An old man who longs for a son but instead has three daughters falls
ill and becomes blind. In a faraway land there is a surgeon who has medicine
that can heal blindness, and the father laments that he has no sons to get
the healing medicine, believing this task to be impossible for the daughters.
But after the eldest daughter entreats him to let her try, he agrees.

Dressed in men's clothing for the journey, she sets off and encounters
a sick old woman and gives her some food. The old woman says it is
impossible to get the medicine, for all brave lads who have tried have
perished. Upon hearing this, the eldest daughter loses all hope and goes
back home. Then the second daughter wants to try, and although the father
discourages her, she sets out on the journey, also dressed in men's clothing.
She too encounters the sick old woman, giving her something to eat, and
the old woman tells her it is very difficult to reach this goal and that she
will perish in vain. So the second daughter loses courage and goes back
home. Whereupon the father sighs heavily, "Ah, how pitiful is a man who
has no sons!"

The youngest daughter's heart is struck by these words and she im-
plores her father to let her go. At first the father tells her it is better to stay
at home than venture forth in vain, but finally he accedes once more. So
the youngest daughter puts on men's clothing and sets off on the journey
to get the healing medicine. When she encounters the old woman, she greets
her politely, helps her wash, and gladly feeds her. The old woman is impressed with the tender and pleasant way of this youth but says that it is
better to stay with her or return home, since such a tender lad will not
succeed when so many tall, strong men already have failed. But the girl
refuses to turn back. And because of the kindness and courage of this youth,
the old woman reveals how to get the medicine.

The surgeon who has the medicine requires the seeds of a tree whose
fruit has great healing power. But this tree is in the possession of the Dev,
a three-headed evil monster. To reach the tree, the girl must perform some
kind acts toward his animals and servants and then take a fruit while the
Dev is asleep. And for protection against the Dev, in case he should come
after her, the old woman gives her a mirror, a comb, and a whetstone to
throw backwards over her shoulder to stop the Dev from following her.

When the youngest daughter reaches the Dev's dwelling, she sees that
the gate is dirty and warped, and so she quickly cleans it and hangs it
straight. Inside she sees some huge dogs and horses chained against different

walls, but the hay is in front of the dogs and the bones in front of the horses. She puts the hay by the horses and the bones by the dogs and goes on. Then she meets some servant girls whose bare arms are burnt because they have to reach inside a red-hot oven to bake food for the Dev. She befriends the servant girls and sews a protective sleeve for each one. Grateful, they tell her that the tree has no fruit, but that a sack of seeds from the tree is under the Dev's pillow. If all his eyes are open, it means he is asleep and she can take the seeds.

The girl finds the Dev asleep and takes the seeds, but the Dev awakens and shouts to the servant girls and the dogs and horses to catch the thief and tells the gate to shut. Because the girl has helped them, they all refuse to obey, and so the Dev sets out himself to pursue the girl. She throws over her shoulder the mirror, which turns into a swift river, and this stops the Dev for a while. But soon he catches up with her, so she flings back the whetstone, which turns into a mountain, barring the Dev's path. When once again he catches up, she throws the comb back over her shoulder and that turns into a gigantic dense forest, too great for the Dev to penetrate, so he gives up the chase and returns home.

Finally the girl reaches the surgeon's house. Since she has the seeds and since she has been "a daring and courageous young man," he gives her the medicine to heal her father's eyes and half of the healing seeds as well. The girl thanks him from the bottom of her heart, and the surgeon invites her to remain a few days as his guest.

However, one of the surgeon's friends suspects her true identity, that she is a girl in disguise. The surgeon can't believe that such a daring, courageous hero who has done this most precious deed could be a girl, so the friend suggests the following test: to put white chrysanthemums under the pillows of both the surgeon's son and the girl, who are staying in the same room. If the daring hero is a girl, the flowers will wither, says the friend; but if the hero is a young man, the flowers will stay fresh. The girl, guessing this scheme, stays awake all night and just before dawn finds the withered flowers under her pillow and replaces them with fresh ones from the garden. So when the surgeon finds the flowers in the morning, both bundles are fresh. But the surgeon's son has been awake during the night and has seen everything the visitor has done and, full of curiosity, decides to escort this visitor home.

By the time the girl gets home, her father has become totally bedridden in his grief and rues the day he let his daughter try to get the medicine for him. But when the youngest daughter brings the medicine to her father, he soon is cured of his blindness and all his other ills. After she tells about all the adventures she has gone through to procure the healing medicine, her father weeps in joy, saying he will never again regret not having a son, for his daughter has shown the devotion of ten sons and has healed him. The surgeon's son, seeing that his companion is a girl and not a boy, declares his love for her and asks for her hand in marriage. And when the daughter says there is a deep bond of friendship between them, her father is full of joy. Thus, the fearless and clever maiden and the son of the learned surgeon marry and live happily ever after.

This fairy tale describes a father who is sick and blind, who cannot see the total value of the Feminine. Although he loves his daughters dearly, he does not believe they are able to go out in the world and get the medicine to heal him. The only representative of the feminine spirit is a sick old woman who knows how to get the medicine but who believes the task is impossible, even for men. The three daughters want to try. Here is an image of a wounded father, injured in his relation to the Feminine, yet only the Feminine can save him—the old woman has the knowledge and the daughters have the spunk and motivation.

The daughters have to dress in men's clothing to set out on the journey, and this shows the low estimation and mistrust of the Feminine. To show themselves as women would most likely result in immediate defeat. The first phase of feminine liberation in our culture also required that women act like men to succeed in the world. Women were not accepted by either men or women in terms of their own feminine contributions in most professions. Although the first two daughters give up and return home, nevertheless there is some progress made. They all are ready to go out in the world and try. And although the old woman tells the first daughter the task is "impossible," after that encounter, she changes and tells the second daughter the task is very "difficult."

And by the time the third daughter comes, although the old woman at first tries to dissuade her, she finally does share the knowledge needed to complete the task. As the daughters keep on trying, the older woman becomes more optimistic and finally communicates her knowledge and wisdom. This corresponds symbolically to the gradual progress made by women in their united efforts to be recognized and gain their rights. Although the youngest daughter is still disguised as a man when the old woman tells her how to get the healing medicine, she has impressed the woman through the combination of her tender kindness and plucky courage—two qualities often thought of as opposing, the former ascribed by culture to women and the latter to men. In combining them, the youngest daughter shows the possibility to integrate them. And it is via this integration that she learns how to gain access to the healing power.

The tree with the fruit that heals is in the possession of the Dev, a raging monster. The youngest daughter has to face the rage and the power of this destructive masculine figure in order to gain access to the healing power. Redemption of the father invariably seems to require facing monstrous rage and aggression, both one's own and that which the father himself was unable to integrate. On the cultural level, confronting rage vis-à-vis the patriarchal fathers has been necessary to make feminine needs and value known. The way the daughter wrests the healing seeds from the angry monster, however, is not through a head-on attack. She is considerate, kind, and helpful; she oils the gate (the entryway), feeds the animals (instincts), and protects the burned arms of the servant girls (the Feminine)—

all aspects the monster has neglected. And because she has helped them, they come to the aid of the girl rather than the monster.

These are also all aspects of the father-daughter relationship that need to be healed. The entryway between the daughter and the world has not been cared for; the feminine instincts are chained and not given the right food; and the feminine ability to handle the world (the arms) has been burned by reducing women to the status of servants. In caring for these, the kind and courageous girl is able to get the healing seeds from the monster.

But she still has to stop him in his attempt to get them back, as many women who have initially made important steps in their self-healing and growth may be attacked again by the old monstrous forces. That means they must continue to make the effort to keep their gained development and not fall back into old passive ways. To use against the monster's pursuit, the girl has the old woman's gifts—the mirror, whetstone, and comb. The mirror enables one to see oneself clearly in reflection; the whetstone is used for sharpening tools; and the comb to untangle and shape the hair, which provides a frame to one's face and identity. When the Feminine is so formed, these objects turn into natural forces which stop the attack of the monster.

Although the courageous girl retrieves the healing seeds from the monster and gives them to the surgeon, who in turn gives her the medicine to heal her father's eyes, she has one test left before she can redeem the father. She now has a relation to the physician who heals, but she cannot yet reveal she is a girl. At a certain point in a woman's development and to achieve certain tasks, it is necessary to use her masculine side. Given the social conditions, the courageous girl had to keep her disguise as a boy to fool them so that ultimately the worth of her feminine being could be valued. If at this point the girl were to reveal she was not a man, it might interfere with the completion of the task—to heal the father. For it is precisely feminine courage and ability that the father and the culture have been unable to see. This is echoed in the doctor's disbelief that such a heroic act could have been performed by a girl.

Often women who are trying to gain access to their own strength and ability give up before they have gone all the way, sometimes by getting into a love relationship and projecting their newly gained strength and power back on the partner, thus losing it for themselves. This possibility is present for the courageous girl since the doctor's son is a potential partner. But she is alert to this danger. The fragility and transitoriness of the feminine strength is symbolized by the wilting flower, and the girl stays awake all night and provides a fresh flower, which is analogous to the consciousness and action required by women to show that their feminine strength and courage are not a transitory or passing event but something permanent. And the uniqueness of this action is observed by the doctor's son so that he is interested in getting to know this person better and decides to accompany her home.

When the girl returns home with the medicine and her father is able to see again, he realizes he has devalued the power of his daughters and, weeping with joy, he is now able to see the value of the Feminine, saying he will never again regret not having a son. The doctor's son, who had cherished a deep love for his new friend, after discovering she is a girl, asks to marry her. And when the girl tells of the deep bond of friendship between them, the father joyfully consents to the marriage. So after the girl redeems the father, who then sees the value of the Feminine, the girl is free to marry—a marriage based not on cultural projections about the Feminine but on a deep and mutual bond of friendship and on the man's love and admiration for the woman's courage and knowledge. The redemption of the father, both on the personal and cultural levels, can lead to this potential—the mature union of Masculine and Feminine. And the girl, with this union, can act in her original feminine form showing all its strength and spirit.

Here is a fairy tale that provides an image of the way a daughter can heal the father's wound. And in the process the daughter gains a deep connection to her own strength and courage, to the power of her own feminine spirit, and to a loving relationship with the Masculine. How might this process of redeeming the father be manifested on the personal and cultural levels?

On the personal level, the redemption may be possible only inwardly, for the actual father may be dead or not open to a new relationship. But that doesn't diminish the importance of this task. As the protagonist of the play *I Never Sang for My Father* says: "Death ends a life, but it doesn't end a relationship." The relation to the inner father still needs to be transformed. Otherwise the old destructive patterns coming from the impaired relationship will continue. One part of this transformation process entails seeing the destructive patterns and how they have affected one's life.

Another aspect entails seeing the value of the father, for if one doesn't relate to the positive side of the father, that aspect of the psyche remains cut off, unintegrated, and potentially destructive to one's life. On the cultural level, redemption of the father also requires seeing both the positive and negative aspects of the father. And it requires changing the cultural ruling principles so that both the Feminine and Masculine are uniquely valued and equally influential.

Redeeming the father has been for me the central issue of my personal and spiritual development. For the wounded relation to my father disturbed so many important areas in my life—my femininity, my relation to men, play, sexuality, creativity, and a confident way of being in the world. As a therapist, I have seen that finding a new relation to the father is an important issue for any woman with an impaired relation to the father. And culturally, I believe it is an issue for every woman, since the relation to the cultural ruling fathers needs to be transformed.

In my own life, redeeming the father has been a long process. It started when I went into Jungian analysis. With the help of a kind and supportive woman analyst who provided a warm, protective container for the emerging energies, I entered a new realm—the symbolic world of dreams. There I encountered sides of myself I never knew existed. I also discovered my father there—the father I had long ago rejected. There was in myself, I discovered, not only the personal father I remembered. There were a variety of paternal figures, images of an archetypal Father. This father had more faces than I had ever imagined, and that realization was awesome. It terrified me and it also gave me hope. My ego-identity, my notions about who I was, crumbled. There was in me a power stronger than my consciously acknowledged self. This power rolled over my attempts to control my life and events around me, as an avalanche changes the face of a mountain. From then on, my life required that I learn to relate to this greater power.

In rejecting my father, I had been refusing my power, for the rejection of my father entailed refusing all of his positive qualities as well as the negative ones. So, along with the irresponsibility and irrational dimension that I had denied, I lost access to my creativity, spontaneity, and feminine feeling. My dreams kept pointing this out. One dream said that my father was very rich and owned a great palatial Tibetan temple. Another said he was a Spanish king. This contradicted the poor, degraded man I knew as "father."

As far as my own powers went, my dreams showed that I was refusing them too. In one dream a magic dog gave me the power to make magic opals. I made the opals and had them in my hand, but then I gave them away and didn't keep any for myself. In another dream, a meditation teacher said, "You are beautiful but you don't recognize it." And a voice said to me in another dream, "You have the key to medial knowledge and you must take it." But I woke up screaming in terror that I didn't want the responsibility. The irony was that although I criticized and hated my father for being so irresponsible and letting his potentialities go down the drain, I was doing the very same thing. I wasn't really valuing myself and what I had to offer. Instead I alternated between the unconfident, fragile, pleasing puella [eternal girl] and the dutiful, achieving, armored Amazon.

Because of my rejection of my father, my life was split into a number of unintegrated and conflicting figures, each trying to keep control. Ultimately this leads to an explosive situation. For a long time I was unable to accept the death of these individual identities for the greater unknown unity that could ground my magic—the mysterious ground of my being, which I later found to be the source of healing. So I experienced this powerful ground of my being in the form of anxiety attacks. Because I would not let go willingly and open up to the greater powers, they overwhelmed me and showed me their threatening face. They struck me suddenly and repeatedly in the core of my being, shocking me out of my controlling patterns like lightning jolts open a closed and clutching hand. Then I knew how little help my defenses really were. Suddenly I was face-to-face with the void.

I wondered if this was what my father had experienced, too, and whether his drinking was an attempt to ward this off. Perhaps "the spirits" of alcohol that ruled his being were a substitute for the greater spirits, and perhaps even a defense against them because they were so close. Since I had denied any value to my father after he "drowned" in the irrational Dionysian realm, I needed to learn to value that rejected area by letting go of the need to control. But this required experiencing the negative side, being plunged into the uncontrollable chaos of feelings and impulses, into the dark depths where the unknown treasure was hidden. Ultimately, to redeem the father required that I enter the underworld, that I value that rejected area in myself. And that led to honoring the spirits. Jungian analysis led me to this and writing has furthered this process.

Writing has been a way to redeem my father. As a child, I had always wanted to be a writer. Finally taking the risk to put my insights on paper required a lot of assertion and courage. The strength of a written word requires the writer to stand behind it. Writing required me to focus on and commit myself to the relationship with my father. I had to really look at him to try to understand his side of the story, his aspirations and despair. No longer could I dismiss him from my life as though I could totally escape the past and his influence. Nor could I simply blame him as the cause of all my troubles. Now, through my writing, we were suddenly face-to-face. Like Orual in *Til We Have Faces*, when I looked in the mirror I saw my father's face. This was incredibly painful because my father had carried the shadow side of my existence, all that was dark, terrifying, and bad. But strangely enough it was a source of light and hope as well, because in all that darkness shone the creative light of the underworld's imaginative powers. And I felt the force of its masculine energy as well. About a year after I started writing and really facing my father, I had the following dream.

I saw some beautiful poppies, flowing with red, orange, and yellow colors, and I wished my mother-analyst were there with me to see them. I went through the field of poppies and crossed a stream. Suddenly I was in the underworld at a banquet table with many men. Red wine was flowing and I decided to take another glass. As I did, the men raised their wine glasses in salute to my health, and I felt warm and glowing with their affectionate tribute.

The dream marked my initiation into the underworld. I had passed from the bright world of the mother into the realm of the dark father-lover. But there I was saluted as well. This was of course an incestuous situation and yet a necessary one for me. Part of the father's role, according to Heinz Kohut and self-psychology, is to let himself be idealized by the daughter and then gradually allow her to detect his realistic limitations without withdrawing from her. And of course with the ideal projection goes deep love. In my own development the love turned to hate, so that the previous ideals associated with my father were rejected. I had to learn to love my father again so I could reconnect with his positive side. I had to learn to value my father's playful, spontaneous, magic side, but also to see its limits, as well as how the positive aspects could be actualized in my life. Loving the Father-ideal allowed me to love my own ideal and to realize that ideal in myself. This entailed first seeing my father's value and then realizing that that belonged to me. This broke the unconscious incestuous bond and freed me for my own relation to the transcendent powers in my Self.

For wounded daughters who are in poor relation to other sides of the father, the details of the redemption may be different, but the central issue will be the same. To redeem the father requires seeing the hidden value the father has to offer. For example, those daughters who have reacted against the too authoritarian father are likely to have problems accepting their own authority. Such women tend to adapt or react rebelliously. They need to see the value in their own responsibility, in accepting their own power and strength. They need to value limit, go up to it and see the edges, but know when too much is too much. They need to know when to say no and when to say yes. This means having realistic ideals and knowing their own limits and the limits of the situation.

To put it in Freudian terms, they need to get a positive relation to the "super-ego," the inner voice of valuation and responsible judgment and decision-making. This voice, when it is constructive, is neither too critical and severe nor too indulgent, so that they can see and hear objectively what is there. One woman expressed it this way: "I need to hear the voice of the father inside tell me in a kind way when I'm doing a good job, but also when I'm off the mark." Redemption of this aspect of the father means the transformation of the critical judge, who proclaims one constantly "guilty," and the defense lawyer, who responds with self-justification. Instead will be found a kindly, objective arbiter. It means having one's own inner sense of valuation, rather than looking outside for approval. Instead of falling prey to the cultural collective projections that don't fit, it means knowing who one is and actualizing genuine possibilities. On the cultural level, it means valuing the Feminine enough to stand up for it against the collective view of what the Feminine is "supposed" to be.

Daughters who have had "too positive" a relation to their fathers have still another aspect of the father to redeem. These daughters are likely to be bound to the father by over-idealizing him and by allowing their own inner father strength to remain projected outward on the father. Quite often their relationships to men are constricted because no man can match the father. In this case they are bound to the father in a similar way to women who are bound to an imaginary "ghostly lover." (Often an idealized relation to the father is built up unconsciously when the father is missing.) The too positive relationship to the father can cut them off from a real relationship to men and quite often from their own professional potentialities. Because the outer father is seen so idealistically, they can't see the value of their own contribution to the world. To redeem the father in themselves, they need to acknowledge his negative side. They need to experience their fathers as human and not as idealized figures in order to internalize the father principle in themselves.

Ultimately, redeeming the father entails reshaping the Masculine within, fathering that side of oneself. Instead of the "perverted old man" and the "angry, rebellious boy," women need to find "the man with heart," the inner man with a good relation to the Feminine.

Redeeming the father also requires redeeming the feminine in oneself

—really valuing that mode. Part of the wounded father's problem is that he himself is out of relation to the feminine. Either he is cut off and devalues it by going the route of the rigid patriarch, or he may be too much under its power as in the case of the eternal boy who loses his own ability to act and becomes passive. The first ignores the power of the feminine, and the other gives it too much power by putting it on a pedestal and so, paradoxically, devalues its real value too.

If a woman really values herself and acts out of the unique realm of her needs, feelings, and intuitions, creates in a way that is hers, and experiences her own authority, she is then able really to dialogue with the Masculine. Neither is she subservient to the Masculine, nor does she imitate it. Valuing what is really one's own in the feminine realm is really hard because it means facing the collective as who one is. The puella tends to buy a collective view of the Feminine by accepting the projections, being what the other wants. But the armored Amazon, in imitating the Masculine, devalues the Feminine by implicitly accepting the Masculine as superior.

And what is the Feminine? In my experience, this is a question that women are now asking. They are searching, talking with each other, trying to articulate their experiences. Many women feel and experience the Feminine but don't have the words to express it since our language and concepts have been based on masculine models. So redeeming the Feminine is a challenging quest now.

While writing "Redeeming the Father," I had two dreams. The first occurred a day or two before I started that chapter. It was a horrible dream and I woke up crying for hours.

My first female analyst, the woman I loved most and who had been a mother and model to me, had died. She had sent a female messenger from Europe to give me three gifts. The major gift was a huge, hand-carved, golden toilet bowl that actually looked more like a chalice. This exquisite gift was to be in my living room. She also gave me several different pictures of myself taken at the time I first went into analysis. The third gift was some newspaper clippings. I sobbed and kept saying it couldn't be true. My analyst couldn't be dead. I wanted to call Switzerland to find out. But the dream kept repeating itself.

After the initial shock of this dream, I realized its inner symbolic meaning. The death of this woman analyst who had been a mother and feminine model for me left me on my own. But I had her gifts to take with me. The photographs were the reminder of what I looked like when I started the process of analysis. The news clippings were the reports of what had happened. The beautiful toilet bowl was the greatest gift she could give me, symbolizing the union of "highest and lowest." My analyst, through her acceptance and example, had given me the possibility for bringing out, valuing, and containing the previously rejected parts of myself—my rage and my tears—as well as my repressed longing for the positive spiritual side of my father. The dream showed clearly the importance of this gift for my life; it was to be placed in the central part of my home, the living room, and not to be relegated to a rejected corner of the house. For me, the dream provided an image for forming and containing my feminine spirit.

The second dream occurred on my birthday, a few days after I had completed writing "Redeeming the Father." In that dream, I had asked another woman analyst, with whom I was currently in analysis, to trim and shape my hair and give it a permanent for more body and fullness. For me this meant the shaping of my feminine identity and giving it more permanence and substance.

Redeeming the father was not the last step in my process of trying to heal the wound. My dreams were telling me the final secret lay not in the Masculine—but in the Feminine. The paradox of redeeming the father was that ultimately I had to give up projecting spirit onto the father and find it within the Feminine. To redeem the father meant finding the feminine spirit in myself.

I was struck in the fairy tale of "The Courageous Girl" at how necessary it was to wear men's clothing in order to get the medicine to heal her father's blindness. Other women heroines, such as Joan of Arc, also have felt it necessary to wear men's clothing to achieve their goals. Taking on "men's clothing" consciously is different from an Amazon armor. For if the disguise is consciously chosen, it can be taken off consciously as well. Sometimes it is necessary to adopt men's clothing to save oneself if one wants to go out into the world and affirm women's values. I think of Rosalind, the heroine of Shakespeare's *As You Like It*. She had to disguise herself to save her life from the evil designs of the duke who had expelled her father. And she chose to stay in that disguise to see how true was the love of Orlando, rather than trying to seduce him through accepting his feminine projections. If a woman is disguised as a man, she can see how her potential lover behaves toward her as a friend. She also can see how her work is regarded by the culture when there are no collective projections applied to it.

While I see this as a necessary step in the liberation of women, I feel now the time has come for women to wear their own clothing and to speak out of their feminine wisdom and strength. The Feminine—what is it? I don't think we can define it. But we can experience it and out of that experience try to express it via symbols and images, art forms through which we can be in the mystery of that experience and yet somehow articulate it too. Recently one woman told me she had, for the first time in her life, experienced what the Feminine is. But she couldn't articulate the experience. No words and images had come to her yet. Still that didn't negate the value, intensity, and awareness of that experience. One of the challenges women have today is not only to be open to the experience of the Feminine but also to try to express it in their own way.

I asked one of my classes to describe their images and experience of feminine spirit. This same class had described their fantasy of the good father earlier. That was not difficult for them to do and their descriptions of the good father were amazingly similar. But when it came to describing feminine spirit, they were at first stymied. The descriptions were quite different. The one common experience was that none of these women felt they could use their mother as a model. They had to turn to themselves and try to bring out their own experience.

Women are beginning to realize that men have been defining femininity—through their conscious expectations of what women can and cannot do and through their unconscious projections on women. This has resulted in a distorted view not only of women but of the man's inner feminine side as well. Women first need to become conscious of these definitions and projections and say which describe them and which do not. Men can help in this process too. For if they are sensitive to the Feminine, receptive and listening, they can add their own experience of femininity to our understanding of it. But ultimately women have to tell their own stories out of their own personal experience and feeling, but with an eye to the universal as well. When women begin to feel confident and to express the values of their own way of being, then they will enable the healing of the Masculine.

11 · DEVELOPING THE ANIMUS AS A STEP TOWARD THE NEW FEMININE CONSCIOUSNESS

· · · · · · ·

Boston Jungian analyst Manisha Roy opens yet another doorway to the Conscious Feminine. Her thesis is that a woman's animus, the unconscious masculine side of her personality, needs to be in a healthy relationship to her female ego in order for her to fully mature as a woman.

The source of a woman's developing animus is her father and father figures, while the source of a woman's ego is her mother. The animus sets two traps that can arrest our development: It can remain unconscious, becoming projected onto men (this can be seen in traditional marriages with stereotyped sex roles) or onto society (this can be seen in radical feminists who "fight men with men's weapons"). Or a woman can become internally identified with her animus, causing her to become rigid and overly intellectual, ultimately losing touch with her feminine instincts.

Roy believes that we have fallen into these traps in epidemic proportions, and that this can explain several pressing social trends: women rejecting the submissive lifestyles of their mothers and seeking satisfaction primarily from careers in order to live out their own animus development; women, in midlife or later life, initiating divorce in large numbers in order to reintegrate the archetype that was projected onto their husbands; and men feeling inadequate and confused in the face of women's increasing power and decreasing interest in nurturing. In some cases, men have responded by developing their own feminine qualities (the anima), which has led to the widespread breakdown of gender stereotypes.

Roy does not bemoan these psychological and social events, because she sees them as part of the picture of developing consciousness. She suggests that for a woman the animus can become the inner guide that links her ego to deeper sources of creativity. If it fulfills this spiritual purpose, the animus guides her to reconnect with the lost feminine Self.

Manisha Roy, Ph.D., is a Jungian analyst in private practice in New England. Born in India, she has lived and worked for many years in America and Europe and has taught anthropology in several universities. She has been trained as a cultural and psychological anthropologist and as a Jungian analyst at the C. G. Jung Institute in Zurich. She has published extensively, including the book Bengali Women. *Jeremy P. Tarcher, Inc., will publish her book on the topic of this article in the near future.*

Martha, age sixty-eight, filed for divorce from her husband of forty years. A mother whose children had left home years ago, she had gone through the so-called empty-nest syndrome and had taken up painting, in which she was trained as a young woman. She had no other skills, yet the idea of leaving the financial security of marriage did not seem to matter. "I must do this," she said. "I don't know exactly why. Something inside me keeps pushing me to get out of this comfortable, secure place. It's crazy. But I seem to have no choice.

"There were other times in my marriage when I should have left. I was angry when my husband had his first affair, but couldn't leave him. I did love him, and the children were young. Time healed that wound and many others. In a long marriage, I suppose, this is expected." She paused before adding, "It's strange that now after all these years I have this urge to get out, to do something on my own, for myself." Although she was in tears as she spoke to me, she looked determined.

Martha left the economic security of her marriage and the comfortable home she had created and loved for so many years. After the divorce she went back to school and worked evenings in a library to support herself. She needed to be out in the world of ideas, money, and productivity. She began to look more alive and to feel ten years younger.

Mary, fifty-nine, a nurse by training, was widowed ten years before we met. She had been doing volunteer work in the same hospital where she had been employed for many years. Her husband left her enough money for a comfortable life. Although quite popular among her friends and co-workers, lately she had begun to be bored. She came to therapy at this point. Her opening lines were, "I reached a blind alley. I'm bored with everything. I feel restless, as if I need to do something else, something different."

Mary also began to show symptoms of insomnia for the first time in her life. A few months later she reported a crisis. To her great shame and surprise, she confessed to falling in love with the young priest in her church. She admitted having powerful sexual fantasies that were driving her nearly insane. She was totally at a loss and in great difficulty. "I'm so ashamed," she said between sobs.

Women such as Martha and Mary, who are hit by what may be called the midlife crisis, may act in a way they themselves cannot explain. Another woman client, fifty-one, tried relentlessly to organize a basketball team with her women neighbors and became obsessed with the game. Intrigued in the beginning, her husband became embarrassed and ended up ignoring her.

LIVING THE ANIMUS

I believe these women needed to live what may be called the experience of the animus in its various aspects. The animus, or the contrasexual archetype, a concept first introduced by Swiss psychologist C. G. Jung thirty years ago, refers to the unconscious masculine aspects that have been excluded and repressed from a woman's conscious life. These masculine aspects are defined by the culture and society of a particular time. The animus is an archetype that is rooted in the collective unconscious and acts as a link between the personal and the transpersonal realms. As an archetype, its dimensions are manifested through cultural symbols. And it can act as a spiritual guide to a woman, especially in her later years.

Every woman's personality must develop by gradually coming to terms with her unconscious elements throughout her lifetime. Her female identity needs to be grounded in gender, culture, and archetypes, all of which must be in proportion and combine for her to function as a balanced biological, social, and spiritual human being. A woman's conscious personality, ideally speaking, is rooted in her body and in the archetype of the Feminine within the context of cultural history. And she also learns to be a woman by the current definition of feminine sex roles prescribed by her society and cultural norm.

However, internally, a woman's psychological maturity depends on how well her ego is aware of the unconscious both in the Feminine and contrasexual archetypes, and how well it incorporates these unlived parts into the conscious Self. In order to do that she must know how the animus manifests itself in her life so that she can differentiate between the personal, the collective, and the transpersonal aspects of the animus. This is necessary before she can integrate her unlived parts—her unconscious potentials. This conscious process of integration is vital for maintaining a healthy psychology. Otherwise the animus, a potentially healthy and creative part of her inner life, becomes a complex expressed in negative and destructive ways. An unlived animus can lead to neurosis, including severe psychosomatic symptoms.

The development of a woman's personal aspect of the animus depends on many factors: her father and father figures, her cultural images of masculinity (which may change over time), and her psychological constitution. Her ego has to relate to the animus consciously for it to have any value to her. On the other hand, her female ego depends on her early relationship with her mother and her connection to the Mother archetype, along with other factors.

Typically, a young woman experiences different aspects of her animus through projections on men and on objects and ideas that represent masculinity in her culture. Unknown male figures in dreams are often person-ifications of the animus on both personal and transpersonal levels. These figures may appear as negative judges and critics devaluing the dreamer, because, when unconscious, the animus may become quite negative and even diabolic.

She either projects the primitive masculinity onto outer men and mas-culine symbols, disowning this part of herself, or she internally identifies with the complex in a way that overpowers her feminine identity. She then becomes an Amazon, or armored woman, with competence and masculine skills but a lost feminine soul. To a lesser degree, she may copy an unde-veloped masculinity in her opinionated notions and ideas.

In everyday life a woman may be able to detect her unconscious animus by its disturbing interference in her conscious life in many forms. She may be driven to a biting comment or an insulting action despite herself. Such behavior may cost her emotionally. Soon afterward she may tell herself, "I don't know what came over me." At other times the unconscious, undif-ferentiated animus may manifest itself in the form of a collective norm and an ethical injunction such as "I should not do this." A drive toward per-fection at the cost of personal feelings and instinct is typical of animus behavior in its negative aspect.

In both psychotherapy and everyday life, one encounters women who are highly intelligent, successful professionals but are depressed and un-happy. They often engage in some sort of compulsive activity or addiction to food, alcohol, drugs, money, or love. They complain about losing control over their lives. They have a hard time forming relationships and great difficulty in expressing emotions, especially negative ones, except perhaps occasional outbursts of hysterical impulses.

Despite outward success, such women suffer from a very low self-image because of their loss of feminine self somewhere along the line. They have sold their souls to the animus, who helps them to be successful "men" but not self-sufficient women. In conversation they are intelligent and log-ical even when talking about love and relationships, and they rarely betray feelings as women who need or cherish such experiences. One gets the impression of a superficial existence without depth, camouflaged by a well-cultivated persona.

Why is it so hard for a modern woman to be herself, to be fully feminine and fully productive? The answer to this question, I believe, lies in the lack of relationship between her ego and her archetypes—both Feminine and Masculine, i.e., the animus. A look at recent cultural history may enlighten us to this psychological development.

TECHNOLOGY VERSUS FEMININE VALUES

The discovery of oral contraceptives and the rapid progress in domestic technology since World War II both had a momentous impact on the life of women in this country. During the next two decades the freedom to choose pregnancy and to cut down the time and energy spent in housework brought women out into the world of men in many ways. Some spent time learning professional skills valued in the job market, while others, lured by seductive advertisements, became major consumers. This newfound freedom from destined motherhood and strenuous housekeeping, however, came with a price.

Between the 1950s and 1970s, the challenge of building a home and family no longer rested on a woman's ability to organize and create. Housekeeping demanded mechanical skill and efficient organization of time rather than creative imagination. Women gradually began to devalue domesticity and motherhood, despite their instinctive needs and despite messages from the older generation, who still stressed marriage and motherhood as the ideal goals of a woman's life.

Meanwhile, the culture went ahead developing and using its technology to achieve the highest standard of living in the world. Education for both sexes became training for skills based on scientific and rational aptitudes toward attaining these goals. Little room was allowed for feminine qualities. Intuition, feeling, subjectivity, relatedness, emotional reactions, endurance, and many more traits we associate with the feminine style of being were repressed and devalued by both sexes.

Women grew eager to eat the fruit of masculine consciousness based on materialistic rationalism. A skeptical attitude began to permeate human experience, including the most mysterious realms—love and religion. Women began to be proud of their objectivity and their ability to question and analyze logically.

SEPARATION FROM THE MOTHER

By the end of the 1950s, the role model of the accommodating, gentle, and submissive wife/mother had already become obsolete. Women who became adults by the late '60s and early '70s hoped to attain the self-worth and independence that their mothers and grandmothers had been deprived of. Nancy Friday's best-seller *My Mother Myself* (1977) clearly voiced the need of American women to separate from their mothers and their mothers' myths if they hoped to be self-fulfilling individuals.

This separation from the mother also meant a rejection of the traditional marriage and dependency on men for economic and social security. Women began to be trained for every kind of profession and by 1980 formed more than half of the national work force, including many top positions. Women between the ages of thirty and fifty, during the last two decades, hoped to gain their self-respect from professional success, as men do.

This conscious separation from the mother's model of life and marriage also separated them from the Feminine archetype, the emotional and instinctive parts of themselves. Motherhood, the most instinctive of all feminine needs, and also other emotional needs such as dependence and vulnerability, were controlled by reason and skepticism. It seems likely that the uncontrollable addictions and destructive compulsions that emerged among many women in the next decade followed as a reaction and psychological compensation.

These women had identified with the animus in its rational and professional aspects totally. They had no understanding that they were donning the animus as a persona for the sake of social approval. They convinced themselves that they were as capable and worthy as men in the eyes of society and, therefore, in their own eyes. However, they soon began to realize that the skills needed for success at work did not help in their intimate relationships. Some tried "honest communication" or "open marriage," only to be surprised that these well-meaning intentions were often subverted by uncontrollable primitive emotions such as jealousy, mistrust, anger, and revenge.

Elizabeth, an attractive woman of thirty-two with a Ph.D., held a high position in a university research lab. Her father was a respected professor in the same field. She married one of her father's students, an equally bright and promising scientist. Within five years, her husband started an affair with a less attractive and far less-educated woman. Elizabeth was more surprised by her own jealousy and emotional outburst than by her husband's sexual betrayal.

It took her several years of painful psychoanalysis to realize that it was not her husband but she who had been betraying her emotional self. Her relationship to her husband was civilized and decent but not emotionally grounded or fulfilling. What an ordinary woman promised him, she could not. Her education had offered her intellectual skills but no wisdom and insight into herself or her man. Her ego could not benefit from the well-educated animus because it was not connected to her emotional nature, which had erupted through the marital crisis.

Why do women like Elizabeth need to identify with the rational and professional animus even at the cost of losing their feminine roots? I believe this was a necessary defense against the wounded and shameful feminine image they inherited from their mothers and grandmothers. They did not want to repeat and continue the pretentious and devalued self-image of the previous generation. In this conscious decision, women of Elizabeth's generation took a heroic stand. As in other areas, they followed men into open battle with their mothers, from whom they needed to separate to become themselves. But they fell into another kind of false identity, which was only to become apparent in the next decade.

Let us pause here to look more deeply at the wounded and shameful feminine image. It is important to understand this historical situation psychologically before we can analyze the current animus problem.

THE SOLUTION OF MARRIAGE

For the women of the 1940s and 1950s, marriage and motherhood were the most popular choice of lifestyle. In a traditional marriage the symbiotic interdependence between the partners was possible by relying on a division of labor by sex roles. Much, if not total, psychological unconsciousness was necessary for the partners to project their contrasexual archetypes onto each other. A woman projected nearly all aspects of her animus onto her husband and sons. In return, she carried the projection of her husband's (and sons') anima in its positive and sometimes negative aspects.

Such a marriage could easily create a ground for the gradual sacrifice of a woman's natural femininity in the archetypal sense. Her total unconsciousness about her inner self made it necessary for the animus to be projected out. Compared to women of her daughters' and granddaughters' generations, she was more rooted in her feminine self but less aware of her inner masculinity. And she lacked the help from her animus necessary to develop her full human potential in all aspects, including the spiritual.

Many women of that generation remained steeped in the material life in which joint bank accounts, houses, and cars—even the family itself—became possessions that were synonymous with their identities. Their economic security and their husbands' and children's achievements became essential to their psychological survival.

The implication of such dependence on men and the men's world is very serious indeed. Because of centuries of repression, the negative aspect of the animus became quite tyrannical. The power of the patriarchy that women fight against today could only endure partly because of such negative projections. Moreover, the kind of femininity these women represented is often quite primitive and conservative. This is the Feminine archetype in its most archaic form, where instinct resists spiritual transformation at any cost.

A woman needs the cooperation of her animus in its various aspects to help her transform her instinctive femininity into its more creative and spiritual goals. In this process, the animus develops itself and *serves* the ego rather than *controls* it.

Psychologically speaking, a symbiotic marriage can last only up to a point. When the children grow up and leave and both partners reach midlife, the neat structure of anima/animus-projections can no longer work. At this stage of life, the function of the contrasexual archetype is to guide the ego to reconnect with the Self. The animus wants to be internalized rather than projected out. So when a woman is released from her maternal duties, she has the opportunity to become conscious of herself in a deeper spiritual sense. However, many women in the past failed to take this challenge and did everything in their power to remain unconscious.

Helen, forty-six, was married to a successful lawyer and spent more than twenty years bringing up three children and being an efficient and supportive wife. She had everything a woman could ask for—a successful husband, healthy and accomplished children, a beautiful home, and the satisfaction of "owning" it all. She thought she was a lucky woman until five years ago, when she discovered that her husband was having an affair. She decided not to rock the boat, but she punished him by moving into a separate bedroom. A few months later her husband asked for a legal separation. She was shocked to find that he was not at all appreciative of her tolerance of his betrayal! As revenge, she flatly refused his request. Her husband went ahead with divorce proceedings. Helen had no choice but to contest. She hired the best divorce lawyer in the state and fought ferociously. She managed to win most of their property and a sizable alimony, which she sacrificed a year later to marry her lawyer, whose income was substantially higher than that of her first husband.

Within a year of her second marriage her new husband was looking for a therapist. He encouraged her to "go out and get a job or something," but Helen was not interested. She was content with her life and failed to see why he was so unhappy. Within a few months her second husband moved out. A few years later she developed chronic emphysema, although she had never smoked.

Because of her ego's total denial, Helen's animus was not available to bring her any awareness. The animus became a serious negative complex that found expression in her psychosomatic illness. Her refusal to gain consciousness turned into a chronic respiratory disease. It is quite possible that this unconscious animus-complex colluded with her equally primitive femininity to create such destruction in her relationships and with her mental and physical health.

Helen's case is an extreme example of a false identity created by total unconsciousness on the ego's part. It also shows how vital the ego's role is in developing one's animus potentials. If a woman refuses to react to life's challenges, her opportunity to become conscious is lost. It then becomes easier to understand why the daughters and granddaughters of women like Helen rejected their role models. The act of rejection in itself demonstrates a higher consciousness.

Although Helen's two husbands showed some awareness, in general during the last fifty years women's awareness has far exceeded men's, simply because men enjoyed a more privileged social position and so tended to be complacent. Life for men had been less problematic until the last decade or two, when male stereotypes began to crack.

THE EFFECT ON MEN

Traditionally, men in America have been brought up by the model of a "tough, aggressive guy" who brings home the bacon and provides economic and social security for the family. This masculine ideal reflects the image of a modern knight or an adventurous cowboy who is ready to shoot the enemy to save the damsel in distress.

An American man's other ideal is to be the romantic lover, another trait inherited from the medieval knights. Hollywood idols such as Clark Gable, Humphrey Bogart, and Gary Cooper were aggressive men who courted beautiful, love-sick, and dependent (albeit intelligent) women. This masculine ideal—aggressive, adventurous, and physically strong yet a romantic lover and a provider father-husband—has been widespread until the current generation.

By the late 1960s men brought up by this role model began to find themselves in marriages and love relationships with women who did not seem to need this machismo in their men anymore. Women's awareness of their own masculinity began to depotentiate men. In men's eyes, modern women had not only become less feminine but also more competitive in work and business. In other words, men continued to project the unconscious, dependent anima onto their wives. So the sexually and intellectually exciting anima could only be carried by a mistress or an unavailable woman.

This problem of passing one another in psychological development is one of the major reasons for the increasingly high divorce rate in this country. Women of the 1970s and '80s already have begun to withdraw the projection of the provider/professional animus from their husbands, leaving traditional husbands confused. A small fraction of these husbands may even seek homosexual alliances in which they can still carry the powerful male projection from their partners, who in turn need to live out the anima, an identification that has its roots in personal and family psychology.

Women who withdrew their animus projections from their husbands and lovers began to identify with the active and independent animus. This identification makes the relationship with outer men almost unnecessary, unless men are willing to play the roles of "wives" in the traditional sense. In this setup, some professional women today are comfortably married to house-husbands who, in turn, seem to need to live out part of their own anima.

THE EPIDEMIC OF DIVORCE

Divorce seems inevitable if the above-mentioned role reversal does not take place. Divorce initiated by women of the last generation indicates the withdrawal of the animus-projection from their husbands. These women, therefore, benefited considerably by discovering their own animus and hopefully integrated some aspects of it. Martha, my client described early in this chapter, was such a woman. Even at her advanced age, it was imperative for her to separate from her husband to reclaim her animus-projections. She listened to her instincts and made a conscious decision to sacrifice her economic and social security. She felt a strong need to develop her animus toward its ultimate spiritual goal—to guide her ego to the Self, the Feminine archetype on its transpersonal level.

However, unless a woman is aware of her psychological situation, no amount of independent activities can solve the problem of the integration of her projected animus qualities. She has to be aware of why she needed to leave her secure personal life to enter the wide world of adventure and danger. For a woman like Martha, this first step implies that deep down she was connected to her Self, which guided her to take the external risk for the sake of her own individuation. Therefore, women who have been dutiful wives and mothers and want to divorce in their late forties and fifties are facing a more serious challenge than empty-nest syndrome. Their midlife crisis in this sense is no different from that of men: for both, it is the challenge to find the authentic Self.

Nancy, a married woman of fifty-six, came to therapy because of persistent headaches that no amount of medication seemed to abate. Her doctors, after a thorough battery of tests, found no organic cause for her symptom and suggested psychotherapy.

Although a housewife, Nancy dealt with everything in her life like a logical businessman, with what she called "structural understanding" of a problem. Every life situation was a problem to be solved. She was at a loss because she could not solve this "disgusting and nagging headache," nor could her highly trained doctors.

It took more than three years for Nancy to admit that, despite her well-preserved persona of a happy wife/mother, she was very unhappy with herself. But she could not figure out why, and that made her even more unhappy. Surprisingly, this admission was followed by a gradual remission of her headaches. It took another year before she could see the symbolic connection between her headaches and her rational control of every life problem.

Nancy's dreams often had images of men with head injuries. In one, a young man was beheaded in a ritual setting. In another, a severed head of a woman rolled down the kitchen floor. She began to realize that some sort of sacrifice of her habitial thinking had to happen. Eventually new feminine figures began to emerge. Some were very primitive and sexy, the kind of women she looked down upon. She had great resistance to recognizing these figures as parts of herself. Her rational understanding could not help her at all. This period of analysis was a painful journey. Many hours of tears of shame and humility finally made her accept her repressed sexual and more primitive side, her unlived potential. Her final dream before leaving analysis after five years was quite illuminative.

I'm walking on a narrow path on the edge of an unknown town. I seem to be following a woman who walks a few yards ahead of me. She guides me to a dark house and I go inside. Here she faces me, and to my shock I see an old classmate from high school days who was notorious for her sexual escapades and had to drop out because of some scandal. In the dream she comes very close to my face and touches my temples gently. Her fingers feel cool and healing. I wake up with a peaceful sensation.

She connected this figure in the form of the high school dropout with the healing part of herself. For Nancy, her animus-identification had to dissolve before she could connect with her healing feminine side.

The painful and shameful emotions that Nancy had to experience before she could reconnect with her sexuality are essential for any psychological transformation. Contemporary women who emulate the heroic journey of the separation from the mother have the hardest time entering their emotions, especially the painful ones. How, then, can these women return to a more conscious femininity?

The answer is complex because different women may take different routes, depending on personality and psychological history. Some, like Nancy, must do it individually with the help of a guide. More extroverted women may join support groups or the women's movement to benefit from others' experiences.

THE ROLE OF FEMINISM

While conventional marriage is an ancient institution that serves a stage of anima/animus development, women's movements are fairly recent innovations. Today's feminism had its earlier versions in the suffragettes and political organizations that tried to achieve legal and economic rights for women.

In the 1960s the feminist movement offered a support system for women who lived in the shadow of men. For the first time in years, women in this country belonged to a sisterhood based on cooperation rather than competition. Housewives and nonprofessional women could express themselves more freely and began to feel confident in themselves. They learned to exist without so much masculine approval.

However, this confidence, at least in some women, soon degenerated into an animus stand, and some feminists began to spend their energy in fighting against the patriarchy. The radical branch of the movement especially took on an Amazonian approach, fighting men with men's weapons. Psychologically, they might as well have been fighting the tyrannical animus within. Some of the sensitive leaders eventually realized that getting the government to pass a few bills in their favor did not seem to satisfy their deeper needs.

The real need of women of the 1980s and '90s is to be free of animus-identification and to reconnect with their repressed and wounded femininity. Now that they have succeeded in competing with men in the outer world, they need to return home—the inner home—to nurture the woman within. What Nancy had to do in midlife, more and more women are beginning to feel even in their early thirties.

Janice came to therapy because her lesbian partner suddenly left her for a man. This devastated Janice; her partner's act, as she put it, was not only a betrayal of their relationship but also of the ideal they stood for. They had embraced the feminist cause of developing intimacy with other women. It took Janice more than two years before she could realize that she was hurt because she lost a nurturing sister—a mother she never had. Through analyzing many dreams and gradually admitting her inner needs, Janice saw how desperately her inner feminine self was asking for attention. So far, she had offered this through her relationship with her lover. The loss of her partner, therefore, offered her an opportunity to return to herself.

The self-acclaimed feminist, more than others, runs the risk of not seeing the inner picture because she can easily justify her extroverted activities by commitment to worthwhile political causes. The less radical branch of the feminist movement intuitively knows that the problem is not only an outer one. Its members are more interested in feminine consciousness than in usurping the masculine rule. Some are scholars and writers; some are activists who march silently to protest nuclear bombs and the pollution of the earth. These symbolic and pacifist means of protest against the political decisions that could destroy the ecology and psychology of humanity can be emotionally effective. They touch a deeper chord of feeling that manifests itself in the Feminine archetype, where internal processes are defined by natural balance and cyclical movement.

RECONSTRUCTING A BALANCE

I have tried to assess the social, cultural, and psychological conditions that led women to take the journey toward a new consciousness. Given the strong values placed on the masculine style in this culture, women who found their mothers' models of femininity denigrating had little choice but to follow the masculine style of rationality. To counterbalance the very personal, subjective, and totally dependent existence of their mothers, they embraced the collective model of economic independence through an unconscious identification with the professional animus. While the rational and active animus was lived, the negative animus in its tyrannical and controlling aspect still remained unconscious and was, therefore, projected out onto the outer world. At the same time, these women lacked the feminine instinct to guide them back to themselves.

Because of the limits of the masculine consciousness, however, women recently began to question their lives and to register their dissatisfactions more honestly than the generation before them. Already initiated to action, they are also more prepared to do something about their deeper needs. Women of this generation know that a woman's journey to consciousness must be different from that of a man, whose myth of killing the dragon (i.e., separation from the Mother) is now obsolete. The dangerous dragon or the negative aspect of the Feminine archetype cannot be annihilated; it lurks inside all women and all men, although in different ways.

If not consciously accepted, this repressed destruction within the psyche of women and men would devastate our civilization with such vengeance that no hero would be able to stop it. The only way to appease the dragon is to acknowledge that we are part of its nature. And we must relate to that part rather than trying to fight and control it.

In the case of individual women (like Nancy and Janice described earlier), this acknowledgment is painful because it begins with the shame of admission that the dark and angry Feminine archetype within has been neglected too long. Yet, this must be done. Because without the help of her feminine nature, a woman's well-developed animus cannot function as a guide to her sexual, creative, and spiritual fulfillment.

In actual life, a woman can discern the approaching balance between the two archetypes within herself when she is no longer "driven" to action or speech or upholding a collective ideal before first realizing what she really values for herself. When her feminine nature is not overriden by her animus, she will feel a sense of peace and intimacy with herself. Even outward relationships may not be that essential at this point, because she may no longer need to project her animus or her femininity outside herself.

If, indeed, it is the repressed and violated Feminine that is about to strike back at our one-sided civilization, women carry a grave responsibility to help men in reconstructing a balance. I believe a woman knows more about true balance than a man does. First, however, she has to be a woman in her body and soul and in her social and cultural roles. Moreover, she needs to acknowledge that her power can both create and destroy. Only then can she have a meaningful relationship with her animus and with men and society. Then the animus, in its turn, will be released from its controlling position to be free to serve her feminine ego, so that a woman can fulfill her individuality and destiny by creating the birth of a new consciousness.

12 · THE BREAKDOWN OF ANIMUS IDENTIFICATION IN FINDING THE FEMININE

. . . .

JANE WHEELWRIGHT

Eminent Jungian analyst Jane Wheelwright echoes Manisha Roy when she points out that only the woman who is not dominated by her animus can have a healing effect on society. To achieve this psychological development, women need to reclaim the "biological female ego" and offer the animus a supporting role.

However, there are few models of this Conscious Femininity to inspire us today. Many women get stuck in the animus-woman role, with the unconscious Masculine reigning as an inner tyrant, re-creating society's patriarchal drama. Wheelwright calls this "living a lie." Or we live out the anima-woman role, with the unconscious Feminine carrying the stereotyped projections of men—Madonna or whore. Given these extremes, there is little room for a conscious, chosen style of femininity that includes the inner Masculine in its proper place.

For this reason, Wheelwright says, some kind of breakdown often needs to occur for a woman to shift realities. Her body may react with psychosomatic symptoms, or she may suffer post-partum psychosis following childbirth. Perhaps she will experience long-term difficulties in relating intimately with men. Any of these personal problems can bring her to therapy, which eventually helps her to take the next developmental step.

Wheelwright discusses the advantages of working with a woman analyst or psychotherapist under these circumstances. Most men, she says, would reinforce those patterns the client is trying to overcome and would be unable to help her uncover her buried female ego. During this time, a woman therapist or mentor who is conscious of her own internal Masculine and Feminine can be a gift to any woman seeking a more harmonious inner balance.

Jane Wheelwright is a practicing analyst who worked with Carl Jung in the 1930s. She is a founding member of the C. G. Jung Institute of San Francisco and the author of Death of a Woman *and* Ranch Papers.

I believe that only the uncontaminated Feminine—a woman not dominated by the animus—can balance the overly masculine element in today's society.

The word *patriarchy* derives from the word *patriarch*, which in turn is associated, according to the Oxford Dictionary, primarily with religious groups. It refers to the ideal of the venerable, wise old man. He is our society's most revered figure. For most Westerners, he is God.

A baby girl born into a society that believes in this ideal, even if only implied, will inevitably be affected by it. If people are imprinted at birth as animals are, the baby girl will have little to say about her development. Her future will depend on masculine influence.

According to Jungian analyst Florence Wiedemann, many young women under the age of thirty-five who come to therapy are, in their dreams, victimized by male figures. If this is generally so, and I believe it is, we must ask ourselves why the positive ideal of patriarchal influence, the venerable old man, is to this extent negative and what, if anything, can be done about it.

These women, who are internally damaged and feel inferior, nevertheless may be the lucky ones because they will be forced to uncover their inherited female potentials, such as with the help of analysis. The only hope for women in this predicament, if they are to lose their sense of inferiority, is to fight back with feminine strengths. It is the only way they can put their male dream figures or imagined figures in their places—namely, in the service of the biological female ego.

By biological female ego I am referring to the individual woman's center of consciousness, as opposed to what sometimes passes as the center but actually is society's ideal of what a woman should be. It also differs from the female ego that is contaminated by an inner masculine component that is out of place. In short, the normal biological female ego has its roots in the female self. The woman who speaks or acts out of her own convictions and does not hesitate to contradict, as a woman, what seems to her lacking or wrong about the male-dominated society (or psychology or religion or any other field of interest) is functioning out of her true female center of consciousness. My definition of biological female ego also is inclusive of, but goes beyond, woman's physical reproductive potential. It can be concerned with intellectual, spiritual, or artistic creativity that often, if not always, manifests in the pattern of the physical. Therefore, the modern mature woman, to find herself, has to proceed on the basis that she is innately different from men but capable, because of support from her inner male component, of achieving as well as—and sometimes even better than—her male associates. Her achievements, however, will be more humane in quality.

These achievements, if made under the direction of a woman's inner male attribute, her animus, will be inhuman. If the female ego does not lead the male figure in her psyche, she will be taken over by the impersonal male component and lose her pro-human orientation.

Our efforts to erase the differences between women and men by the concept of androgyny are questionable. If we are ever to counteract the world's dilemma, we need women to be different from men. If men cannot stop our headlong race to destruction, how can women, subscribing to male behavior and male thinking, make any difference?

Because of the phenomenon of imprinting, we must suspect that problems derived from patriarchal thinking are widespread. Women who seem to get along well enough are as normal as society expects them to be. But not being crippled enough to seek help, they go unnoticed in the first half of life. They are the young women who, permitted to live the role of father's daughter, look as though they function adequately until they reach age thirty-five or so. After that, they may find themselves too old for the daughter role and for the first time in a quandary about themselves.

Sooner or later they also may find that their work life, designed to fit male standards, has appealed to only one-half or less of their psychic potential, namely their masculine archetypal component. The other, more important, psychic part, their biological female ego, normally rooted in the female aspect of the self and ideally fostered by a positive experience of the mother or mother surrogate, has had little to say about how they should live and work. These women almost have to find out they have been living a lie, and that for the first time they have a chance to experience their true basic identity. More important, however, they will have acquired invaluable skills in imitation of the men they have admired.

The mother's daughter, on the other hand, may find herself in no hurry to get married. She may feel out of step because most women, following patriarchal guidelines, concentrate early on the relationship to men. Mothers' daughters, if they choose, can stand alone. Best of all, having had the backing of their mothers, they can, if they believe in themselves, spearhead the modern woman's effort to know herself. But, unless sooner or later they live out the experience of the father or father surrogate, they may find themselves at a disadvantage with men.

The young girl's tomboy stages, when not interfered with too much, may help women muster the energy to instinctively fulfill masculine demands. As girls in competition and companionship with boys their own age, they stand a better chance to recognize their basic talents. They even may acquire a taste for independence. Whatever their experiences of the Masculine later in life, by risking themselves in the patriarchal man's world (or what's left of it) they are sometimes the ones who find themselves in the worst predicament.

If such women seek help from a therapist, they tend to choose a man. His understanding of the woman, with the help of his anima, only postpones the patient's confrontation with a woman who could fill in the missing experience of the mother. A respected colleague of mine mentioned that men analysts can "mother" female clients. But, he added, a man cannot be womanly. For me, that means that a man cannot help with the uncovering of the instinctive female ego. Ego development requires at least temporary identification. A man is the wrong gender for that.

These women, for perhaps two-thirds of their lifetime or more, entrenched in male activities, have remained oblivious of the basic wrong in their attitudes: they have not found their female ego strengths. The inner male component, supported by society's bias, is no longer the achiever it was originally and, without the female ego strength to challenge it, becomes instead the tyrant.

Women, by being bright and capable, sometimes athletic, more often mentally endowed to compete with men in our institutions, have proceeded under false impressions of themselves. They may find themselves stuck for life in an inner patriarchal system of their own. For the first time, in spite of being successful according to society's masculine standards, even in work that suits her, a woman might stop after midlife (if not sooner) to ask herself why she is not happy with her success. My answer would be that someone else did her achieving for her—namely her male component.

These women do not realize sufficiently that overall they have developed mostly along their achieving lines—some of them to the point of becoming identified with their achievements. They are unaware that the strain on them is equivalent to the strain on a man who spends most of his time and energy socializing. The social collective bias, however, keeps men on the whole from falling into this lopsided trap. For women there is no equivalent guideline.

This woman may develop threatening physical symptoms and be referred by her medical doctor to an analyst. Or she might find an older woman friend who, from her wider experience, sees what is happening. The female body, home of the female potential, will retaliate when the woman is mentally overactive. Her male work-self, concentrated in her head and in her will, must be understood for what it is and be put in its place.

If this woman should marry in spite of her masculine orientation and have a baby before she is wise to herself, she may run the risk of being contaminated by the still-unconscious, instinctual archetype of birth when the time for delivery comes. If she has concentrated mostly on achieving in the world of men and in competition with them, she will not have sufficiently honored her female instincts that know about giving birth.

Instinct and archetype are, after all, two aspects of the same phenomenon. The contents of the birth archetype, if not expressed bit by bit throughout a woman's life and with the help of a trusted mother relationship, will gain power over her when she gives birth. If she has looked forward throughout her youth to the expression someday of her reproductive potential, she will have drained off enough content to depotentiate the archetype as a threat.

If her energies, on the other hand, are too focused on professional ambitions, the neglected reproductive archetypal energy will gather overwhelming force in the unconscious and blot out her biological ego, which has been underdeveloped because of the lack of mothering in her own childhood. Once her ego has been eliminated by the birth archetypal impact, the unlived and other unconscious material pours out in a disordered flow.

In other words, the woman succumbs to a post-partum psychosis. Erupting forces have been triggered by an outer situation that corresponds to an inner pressure.

I know a woman who is a good example of the problem just posited. When her baby was born she was overdue for a major inner change in attitude. The twofold pressure inside and outside became overwhelming, and she plunged into the unconscious for a brief period.

This woman's warning dream, the first indication she had of living a lopsided life, was of an invisible man leaving behind him only his footprints. She woke in terror. But there was no one around to explain that her animus, her inner male figure, was invisible, totally independent of her, and, like a thief, could do her in. It had become a split-off part of her psyche. She would have to make its acquaintance to avoid disaster.

Even if there had been someone available to tell her about the animus, she might not have listened. When the animus is in power, the female ego is likely to be too suppressed to take advice from others. Besides, the animus when it is on the loose avoids detection. Only by seeing the animus for what it is, good and bad, can a woman entice it over to her side to help her, not harm her.

This woman, admiring powerful men and having no positive woman around to impress her, found the man's world appealing and challenging to the natural adventurousness she was born with. Men of influence had always captured her attention because of her unusual achieving potentials —to such an extent that her ideals became more and more masculine. Finally, as her outer contacts were less of a mystery, these ideals activated and developed her inner male potentials as though they had been incorporated from the outside. In her psyche, a more powerful male force evolved, which a human man could not approximate. The changeover happened so gradually that she was totally oblivious of what had been going on. Her main symptom, one she could not understand, was that she had trouble connecting with men of her own age. She had become too competitive, knew too much, generalized to such an extent that mature men around her avoided her. She finally married a man who eventually helped her, but at first he seemed to her only a second choice. Children were next, and the devastating episode already mentioned overtook her. She developed a post-partum psychosis.

In the psychotic episode the animus once more was the central figure. When she began to spontaneously recover, she told her analyst about a dream: *She was standing in a row of late-teenage girls. In reality she was about thirty years old. A man also around thirty, carrying a rifle, passed along the line of schoolgirls aiming his gun until he came to the dreamer. He fired. The bullet entered her forehead and she turned into a ghost.*

She recalled how amazed she was at how much of her was left even though she was dead. It was the first time she realized that once her head, the symbol and seat of the animus, was put out of commission, there was a whole human woman left. In this episode the animus was both destructive and constructive. The animus, according to the dream, although forcing her into the unconscious by shooting her in the forehead and killing her, also knocked itself out of its dominating position. The breakdown seemed to be nature's way of bringing about a balance in the woman's psyche.

To sum up: the animus in a male-dominated society, when it is not tied in with the woman's psyche in a helpful way, overexaggerates its despotic rule until, left to itself, it disposes of itself.

So drastic an approach might have been ideally mitigated by a woman analyst or a female friend with whom this woman could identify, who understood the problem of the masculine component. If the patient was prejudiced against women, she could also have been helped by a man who understood that her unconscious expected him not to dominate her female ego. But the male analyst needs to know that the woman must get insight into the animus that she unconsciously sees in him. For the sake of the preservation of her ego, he will have to be humble enough not to be inflated by her powerful male projection on him.

To keep a right connection with her, the male analyst would have to make her aware of his own lacks. He would have to help her sort out the discrepancies in her too heroic view of him. In other words, he would have to counteract the patriarchal influences under which she had grown up. Sooner or later, perhaps, she would find her way to a woman analyst or friend with whom she could at least safely identify. At any rate, in the very long run and given enough perseverance, the woman client with the help of this enlightened male analyst could realize that her expectations are not human, that they are instead contaminated by a power of her own that resides in her psyche. By recognizing the power she attributed to the analyst as her own, she could eventually have available her independence and her own inspirations. She would be able to go it alone and not be a dependent woman or a poor imitation of a man. By then she might also have her first chance to make a satisfactory relationship to flesh-and-blood men.

In the actual experience of the woman who suffered post-partum psychosis, her male analyst set out to help her fill the hole made into her unconscious so that she would not be vulnerable to more eruptions. Because of her stage of development, and because of society's lopsidedness, she developed a tremendous transference to him. It was the first time she had come into close contact with a man older than herself who had achieved beyond her own potential. This man, she thought, could more than fulfill and represent her highest masculine aspirations. Inevitably her transference was monumental. The analyst, in a way, was God to her.

Much later she had an affair with a man who rarely wrote letters during their long separations. Desperate to hear from him, she began to wonder why she cared so much. Suddenly she realized that her pressure was similar to that of people who pray to God. And God never answers. In a flash she realized she had projected the male God onto this ordinary man. The potency of the animus was thus revealed. It was, in fact, a manifestation of the male aspect of the self.

As the analysis progressed, she dreamed of being carried down a spi-raling passage deep into the earth. She was clinging to the shoulders of an elderly, distinguished religious educator—the headmaster of a boys' school she had met years before. Religious education seemed to be the objective of her descent to the unconscious. Once more, according to the dream, her animus was older and larger and more accomplished than she was. It was in charge.

Later, another dream appeared. It was of a huge black-bearded giant sunk up to his middle in the earth. The analyst, looking very small, stood there dwarfed by the giant—in fact, very much dominated by him. Pointing to the giant, the analyst said, "He is your genius, not I." Her unconscious, knowing best, was trying to tell her and her analyst that he must give back to this woman her autonomy. But the analyst's prominence, high quality, and age, coupled with society's prejudice, had taken their toll. She decided to become an analyst herself and proceeded to prepare for the role. Having had little formal education, she had to work hard. Once more she pursued her achiever life to the neglect of her true female nature.

Ultimately, the young woman found her "femininity" in relation to the analyst. She had not found, however, her true self as separate from his idea of what a woman should be. Although she fit better into society than she had before, she was still not able to stand alone. This woman built up a psychoanalytic practice and did as well as other women in the profession. But she could not present her findings for others to benefit from. She was blocked.

She dreamed, years later, that her parents were blocking the way for her and a group of Jungians. In this dream, her mother was a negative, dominating, heavy-handed, thinking woman more than life size, and her father was a pink-cheeked, feeling but ineffectual man, who was also larger than life size. The dream mother as an intellectual could be associated with her actual mother, who had died years before. Otherwise, these dream parents were totally strange to her. The juxtaposition of these two figures, however, fit the woman's early experience of the parental relationship: the revengeful, disillusioned mother and the compliant father. In the dream, the daughter blasphemed the mother and got her out of her own and the group's way. In so doing she was able to proceed with a paper she wanted to write on women.

Because she had been contained in the transference to her analyst and in a sense living out his anima ideal, the young woman had never been confronted by the negative archetypal figures behind her parents. Her mother problem had been solved by the psychosis, but otherwise, and in a deeper sense, she could not get on with her life.

Before this dream, which finally unlocked her creativity, she had an earlier experience that gave her an inkling of her plight. Her analyst, long after her analysis, had come to her in a dream and made it clear that his women followers were not important to him. Only then did she begin to question her analysis. Long before that, he had confessed in her presence that he knew nothing about women, but somehow she could not hear him. The transference had deafened her. The man had been her ideal and even, in a way, her salvation. Rejection from him, even though appearing only in her dream, had forced her out of her bondage to him, without her quite realizing it. One could say he voluntarily abdicated, like the gunman who knocked himself out in her dream of psychosis. From then on her own original views of how women really function began to take form.

None of this lifelong experience of being in thrall to the man's world need have happened if our young woman had had the luck to be the daughter of an enlightened mother. She might have been encouraged to use her initiative to try herself out on her environment any way she saw fit, until she found her true niche. Standing by her, her mother would have counteracted the male social prejudices that otherwise might have driven her into channels of activity that had nothing to do with her real self.

On the other hand, with a less ideal mother, she might have had trouble with a nagging, interfering animus and gone for help to an older woman who at least understood the woman's male complex. With the understanding and respect of a woman conscious of her own masculinity, this young woman could have found her true self in a reasonable length of time.

Men, if they are to be helpful, need to know that the patriarchy is virtually over, and the sooner they understand their fear and anger at the imprinting, unfulfilled, unconscious, revengeful mother, the better. They might benefit from also knowing that mothers with opportunities to develop and challenge the world will before long be revealed as ordinary human beings.

Women must realize and explain to men that, no matter how much the ideal of androgyny is promoted, the man's way of functioning, thinking, creating, is not their way. They need to believe that when women are convinced of their uniqueness, men and women both will gain.

13 · RETHINKING FEMINISM, THE ANIMUS, AND THE FEMININE

· · · · · · ·

POLLY YOUNG-EISENDRATH

Now that we've shed some light on the subject of the Masculine element in women, let's turn to Philadelphia analyst and feminist Polly Young-Eisendrath to throw a monkey wrench into the system. In her bold attempt to blend the internal symbolic world of Jungian psychology with the sociopolitical realities of feminism, Young-Eisendrath makes a provocative critique.

She seeks to redefine the archetypes of the Feminine and the animus by pointing to their origins in a dated, patriarchal belief system. Rather than seeing them as archetypal or innate universal structures of the human psyche, she proposes, through the lens of feminism, that they are acquired by individuals in a given culture via subjective experiences. In her book co-authored with Florence Wiedemann, Female Authority: Empowering Women Through Psychotherapy, *Young-Eisendrath no longer refers to the animus as an archetype; rather, she calls it a "complex," a set of ideas and images that is absorbed from personal experience. And she outlines stages of increasing consciousness of the animus in women.*

Furthermore, with the help of feminist scholarship concerning gender differences, Young-Eisendrath points out that both the Feminine and the animus were defined (primarily by men) in relation to men and the Masculine. For this reason, the Feminine seems forever to lack what the Masculine symbolizes (intelligence and objectivity, or logos), and to be overloaded with its opposite (feeling and relatedness, or eros). At the same time, the animus has gotten a bad reputation by providing for women those qualities that make them over in the image of men.

The dilemma for women becomes how to imagine and live an authentic femininity and, at the same time, develop as strong, independent individuals. Young-Eisendrath might call this a "feminist femininity."

Polly Young-Eisendrath, Ph.D., is a Jungian analyst, chief psychologist at Clinical Associates West in Philadelphia, and senior research psychologist at the

Institute of Pennsylvania Hospital. She is author of Hags and Heroes: A Feminist Approach to Jungian Psychotherapy with Couples *(1984),* Female Authority: Empowering Women Through Psychotherapy *(1987), and* Jung's Self Psychology *(with James Hall, 1990) and is a national lecturer on Jungian psychology, developmental psychology, and feminism.*

Being a Jungian analyst and an avowed feminist may seem to be a path to healthy self-awareness, but more often it has been a struggle with alienation. Many of my Jungian colleagues are reluctant to accept feminism as psychological theory, even perhaps to accept *any* serious concern with the social or cultural meanings of being female. In turn, many of my feminist colleagues are sternly critical of the misogynist or patronizing biases of Jungian psychology.

My identity as a Jungian feminist has often seemed a vexing reflection of my own dividedness. For some years I hid my dividedness; I was a "closet feminist" among Jungians and a "closet Jungian" among feminists. Some time ago, however, I pledged to myself that I would no longer silence my political and social beliefs when writing or speaking about Jungian psychology, or hide my Jungian psychological ideas in speaking with feminist colleagues and friends.

FEMINISM AND WOMEN'S NARRATIVE

Feminism, as a cultural movement and a personal meaning system, has been basic and fundamental to my discovery of myself as a female person. Prior to my acquaintance with feminism—prior to about 1976—I was nonetheless a happy, enthusiastic person fully engaged in life. I lacked (although I only "knew" it was lacking by the unspoken discomfort it perturbed) a form of discourse that included with precision my experiences as daughter, student, wife, mother, author, professional, and person. The only genuinely female form of discourse that was available to me was gossip, in which I wholeheartedly engaged. Gossip, though, was disparaged by others; even, alas, by me at times. Ultimately I classed it as trivial.

Many of my concerns, in fact, seemed trivial, including such subjects as my love life, my reproductive system and its vagaries, my particular perspective on Western philosophy, my relationships with my mother and other women, my desire to describe the details of kitchen work or housework, and many others. As I reflect back on my darkest pre-feminist hours, perhaps most poignant were the dreadful times I spent in remorse and shame, afraid of my enraged, sometimes murderous feelings toward my two delightful and beautiful babies. These feelings would overwhelm me at times, especially at night when I would drag myself from bedroom to bedroom, attempting to soothe, nurture, and contain what was troubling my children. At one point, when I was about three years into mothering, I thought I would go berserk. I knew I had intensely conflicting feelings about the existence of my children, but I could find no reference to these feelings in any text or manual on infant care (and I had many). On the absolute brink of desperation, I encountered a copy of Adrienne Rich's 1976 book *Of Woman Born* and had my first feminist experience.

Although I had been politically active in the women's movement before 1976, even having given a lecture in 1974 on "Jungian Psychology and Women Today," I had not previously had the experience of discovering a new narrative, a form of discourse in which my own experiences were validated. Reading *Of Woman Born* was liberating in a way I had never known. What I discovered was a woman's narrative of her *experience* of mothering and its contrast with the *institution* of motherhood. My eyes were opened for the first time to the possibility that my own experiences were not alien, isolating, or even perhaps unique, but rather that they had not been *recorded* and that they fell outside of institutional truths.

That was the beginning of my search into feminism. My own definition of feminism shares its principal themes with many others. Feminism is a discipline of thought and action that aims to enhance mutuality and trust among all people; to reveal the meanings of gender differences, especially as these might interfere with reciprocity and trust among people; and to oppose all models and methods of dominance-submission for relationships among people. What feminism has revealed, in its many forms from theology to literary criticism to psychology and philosophy, is that the silencing and trivializing of women and their ideas affect all of us all of the time in the way that we expect the world and ourselves to be.

Feminism has awakened an appreciation for the fact that our beliefs influence our perceptions, and that whatever we take to be real—what we assume to be "really true" of ourselves and others—*is* true from our vantage point at that moment. We do not discover some reality that is "out there," but rather we invent our reality from our beliefs. Our knowledge is primarily pattern-matching, and we all search for the best fit with the patterns or expectations that we hold. These expectations function as biases in the way we expect things to be.

We come to our biases largely through influences from family and society, especially through language—what we are told. Feminist psychologists Rachel Hare-Mustin and Jeanne Marecek have written that "language highlights certain features of the objects it represents, certain meanings of the situations it describes. Once designations in language become accepted, one is constrained by them. . . . Throughout history, men have had greater influence over language than women."[1] This is not to say that women have made no contribution to patriarchal language and culture, but rather that men—primarily Caucasian men—have had privileged status at all levels of cultural participation from education (and literacy) to leadership, decision-making, writing, and publication.

I believe that we are just now entering a period in which women are beginning to take control of their own belief systems. Perhaps for the first time in recorded history, "enough" female people have now entered the cultural record to open an avenue for female discourse, which is barely open and needs protection. In the United States, the 1970s and '80s produced an outpouring of female voices on every level of discourse, from reports of sexual abuse and battering to accounts of philosophical and theological theory-making. We seem to be in the midst of constructing a feminist epistemology—a feminist theory of the nature and grounds of knowledge (how female people come to know and recognize themselves and the world). It is my belief that this epistemological project is an essential, if not the most essential, aspect of contemporary feminism, given the sociopolitical limitations of current patriarchy. A study of the nature and grounds of our knowledge will permit female people to develop narratives of strong and complete women.

At this moment, we are still in the position of being dominated by gender stereotypes that function to limit our experiences, expressions, and expectations of the lives we live. We all necessarily participate in everyday conversations in which the given worldview includes assumptions of female inferiority, inadequacy, and weakness. Inevitably all female people arrive at adulthood with feelings and significant beliefs about their own inferiority. As I have written elsewhere,[2] female persons must identify in some way with the theory of female inferiority in order to survive. Attributions about women's inadequacy and weakness, about their lack of competence and objectivity, are sustained in ongoing conversations in which both verbal and nonverbal communications are structured by the hard-core belief that female persons lack something. Inevitably all female people develop individual theories of themselves, their families of origin, their bodies, their intelligence, their competence, their nurturance, or the like, that indicate to themselves and others, "Something is wrong with me."

Until a woman is offered a feminist explanation of her felt condition of personal inadequacy, from a theory that accounts for the function of gender stereotypes and the reality of female experiences, she is necessarily in a double bind about her own strengths and authority. If she behaves "as a woman" she will be taken to be childlike, incomplete, or perhaps even worse (mentally ill). If she behaves as a "healthy adult" she will be considered unwomanly and to be compensating for some inherent lack—of intelligence, objectivity, worth, a penis, a man, money, or children. If she insists forcefully that she is an authority, she will inevitably encounter many situations in which her right to occupy time and space, and to engage in ongoing conversations, will be questioned. Necessarily she will be threatened and then tend to accept an explanation that she has been doing something wrong—she is too controlling, masculine, dominating, intellectual, emotional, abstract, or concrete.

What we painfully lack as a patriarchal culture are accounts of complete and strong women. These accounts are necessarily different from any inherited version of heroines, goddesses, or idealized female figures that have been created principally from men's imaginations. Feminist writer Carolyn Heilbrun wrote:

How can we find narratives of female plots, stories, that will affect other stories and, eventually lives, that will cause us neither to bury Shakespeare's sister nor to throw up our hands in describing George Sand because we are unwilling to call her either a woman (under the old plot) or a man when she isn't one?[3]

French writer George Sand (1804–1876) is a perfect illustration of the problem I am trying to describe. As Heilbrun says, Sand was an enigma for her biographers and her friends because she lived thoroughly as a woman in a manner that was not permitted for a woman. Although Sand was quite comfortable with the womanly activities of running a hospitable home, delighting in her grandchildren and her garden, she also relished the possibility of social revolution. She had many lovers, usually younger men whom she treated well. She refused to live by the gender stereotypes of her day and took a man's name and dress in order to move freely about the cities in her youth. One of her biographers, Ellen Moers, expresses the dilemma about Sand when she says, "She was a woman who was a great man."[4] The point is made explicitly by Heilbrun throughout *Writing a Woman's Life*; it is simply that we have no narrative, no plot, no paradigm for the life of a strong, adventurous *woman*. We always speak about such women as masculine or male-identified rather than as wholly women. If a woman refuses the plot that most women live—that is, either explicitly in the family or distinctly out of the family (as a celibate, for instance)—then she would be hard put to answer the question of where she is going or what she wants.

Feminism has taught me to examine the implications of gender, and of difference in general, to help me and others see the ways in which people are "expected" to be, and to differentiate these from how they are and how they would like to be. This is an exercise in awareness, a bringing to consciousness of the underlying structures I use to create a woman or a man from my beliefs and imagination. I have come to be alert to how my prejudices may silence, eliminate, or destroy another's or my own subjectivity—the ability to go on being a self-recognized unity of intentions, desires, and identity.

WOMEN, THE FEMININE, AND THE ANIMUS

In a paper I published in 1987, I said of myself and other Jungian analysts, "I believe that some of our archetyping of styles and standards of living, some of our typing of racial and gender differences according to [our] ideal models, and some of our theorizing about psychological types have become stereotypes with unexamined assumptions."[5] I would like to bring to awareness here the functions of gender stereotypes as they appear to hamper our ability to understand female people, both ourselves and others, in applying Jungian psychology.

On many occasions I have written and spoken about the great disservice done to feminists, and to women in general, through the Jungian stereotype of the "animus-possessed" woman. Fundamentally, the Jungian theory of animus is that female people gradually form a somewhat repressed sub-personality of a male or masculine sort. This repressed personality, the animus, lives a life of its own, as it were, as the female identifies with being female and then sees male persons as not-I. (The female sub-personality of the male is the anima.) Jung and some Jungians have used the concept of animus in a biased and psychologically damaging manner when they apply it to indicate a lack of objectivity in women and girls.

The assumption here is that a universal principle of Masculinity exists, of which both male people and the female animus are aspects. This arche-typal Masculine is the opposite of the archetypal Feminine. The archetypal Masculine is described as logos: its contents are rational, logical, intentional, and objective. Because females are not structured by this archetypal Mas-culine, they are *by nature* less rational than males. Because the unconscious personality of the female is organized by the Masculine principle, a woman has the possibility of developing these qualities, but only through struggling with her naturally less objective tendencies. In practice, then, any insistent woman is "strident" and merely attacking without reason, because she is relying on her animus (her inferior objectivity).

The idea that the animus is an archetype that has a universal meaning of inferior objectivity (until it is integrated with the Feminine nature) is a stereotype based on a culturally relative notion of masculinity that Jungians have called universal. If a woman accepts this stereotype, of course she must assume that she is by nature inferior in her capacity for thought, reasoning, intelligence, and factual evidence; if she rejects it, a Jungian therapist might label her as unconscious; if she rejects it vehemently, she would be under-stood as both unconscious and a victim of animus-possession. Exactly a double bind.

When I was first acquainted with Jungian psychology and read the literature on animus, I was disappointed because I did not find my own experiences there. The idea that the animus was both masculine and rational, and was the guide or "psychopomp" for the female unconscious, was en-tirely alien to me. My childhood experiences were replete with women who were astute and competent organizers of the domestic scene and the class-room. On the other hand, my knowledge of boys and men led me to conclude that they were emotionally dependent, given over to periodic and inexplicable fits and rages, and unable to be objective. My prototypical masculine complex was alien, irrational, threatening, and unstable. (That *was* a description of my animus.)

When Florence Wiedemann and I began working on our model of animus development, published in *Female Authority: Empowering Women through Psychotherapy* in 1987, we believed that animus theory was poten-tially useful but too narrow and rife with harmful stereotypes about women. The problem seemed to lie in the connection of the animus with a universal Masculine principle, rather than with the experiences of women and girls in terms of their own beliefs and constructions of men and masculinity.

If we assumed, as Jungian theory generally did, that animus functioning was archetypal—an aspect of a universal Masculine principle—then we would have to predicate the model on a given meaning of masculinity. If, on the other hand, we assumed that female masculinity was constructed from women's experiences of men, males, and masculine institutions, then we could connect the animus with the masculine themes that we discovered in women's dreams, relationships, fantasies, and ideals.

We decided to define the animus as a psychological complex (rather than an archetype) of ideas, images, affects, and habits that accrues around the archetypal core of the "Not-I" or Other, the archetype of self-conscious emotions. Rather than assume in advance that the animus is a positive or negative guide or critic (as earlier Jungians typically had done), we collected thousands of dreams from our women clients and examined them for themes that seemed to characterize different images of men, boys, and masculinity. We discovered five clusters or motifs that we have called stages of animus development. These motifs seem to depict a developmental sequence for female people in our society: from a first stage of Alien Outsider to a final one of Androgyny (or integration of all human potentials). It is likely that these images would be different for women who have grown up in cultures different from ours.

For some time now I have ceased to speak in terms of the archetypal Feminine or the Feminine principle along the lines that I theorized in *Hags and Heroes: A Feminist Approach to Jungian Psychotherapy with Couples* (1984). At the time I wrote that book, I was so grateful to be able to grasp and articulate a new narrative—one involving attachment, empathy, and trust —that I saw this narrative as an inherently Feminine principle or ethic. In gathering the data for *Female Authority*, I gradually began to recognize the enormous difficulty of permitting women to speak from their own experiences about what it means to be feminine or masculine.

I began to recognize the burden of living in a culture that promotes men's images of their feminine experiences—of the anima in Jungian terms—as though these were the images of women. Magazines, movies, TV, novels, and poetry are full of anima images masquerading as accounts of female lives. In order to differentiate the female person, in her own subjectivity, from the male person's object of desire and fear, we must begin with women themselves. Women's ideals, reports, dreams, fears, wishes, and narratives form the foundations for categories of female psychology that can be compared and contrasted with the images of anima generated by men.

Demaris Wehr and Andrew Samuels are two Jungian theorists who share with me a critique of universal principles of Masculine and Feminine.[6] The central problem here is with two assumptions: one is that it is both right and natural for women and men to fit into proscribed roles and categories, and the other is that the archetype of the Feminine encompasses both female psychology and the male anima, and that the archetype of the Masculine includes both male psychology and the female animus.

First, the notion of a universal gender principle is offensive to me. I have been opposing all forms of reductionism and determinism for a long time. Reductionism and determinism are methods that lead us to believe in "simple truths" that serve the purposes of some dominant group, whether they are scientists or psychologists or politicians. When someone promotes a particular idea about the "real nature" of human differences (e.g., that African-Americans are less intelligent than Caucasian-Americans), I am skeptical. What are the motivations of the promoter? In terms of gender differences, I certainly believe there are significant differences in the lives of women and men in all known cultures, but what these are and what they mean is still largely unknown. We do not know what is masculine or feminine except in relation to context; and we will not know until women's experiences are clearly recorded and integrated into our mind-sets.

Also, the legacy of the Feminine in Jungian psychology is androcentric, even though the concept has been worked out in part by women. The Feminine in Jungian psychology centralizes men's experiences of women and their relationships to women. As Wehr points out, the characterizations of the four personality types of the Feminine (from the models of Jungian theorists Ann Ulanov and Toni Wolf) all include a manner of relating to men.[7] This seems to be good evidence that they are derived in part from male psychology. Great trouble and sadness can arise for female people in importing male meanings and imaginings—men's fears and fantasies about women and mothers, for instance—into the central holding place of female psychology. The result is what I have called Pandora psychology, or the construction of a "female" from men's experiences (as Eve, who was fashioned from Adam's rib; and Pandora, who was designed by Hephaestus under Zeus's command). Such a female being is fundamentally inadequate because she is not a man.

I think of gender differences as cultural inscriptions on a universal condition of sexual difference. If we talk about gender as archetypal, then we hold that its content is always the same (e.g., logos as masculine and eros as feminine), and we assume that we already know what the particular patterns of healthy functioning should be. If instead we talk about gender in terms of psychological complex, then we can incorporate the particular images and meanings that derive from cultural and familial context.

As a Jungian analyst, I like to be clear about what I understand *archetype* to mean in any case. It is a primary organizing tendency to form unified, sustained, and coherent images around a core of emotional arousal. Two examples are the archetypes of Great Mother and Terrible Mother; these are tendencies to form sustained images of states of attachment and fear in infancy, not simply experiences of actual women. Archetypes are universal because certain human emotions are ubiquitous and function to organize human relationships that sustain our selves throughout life.

The tendency to form an image of a self is universal and occurs *after* the development of self-conscious emotions, such as pride, shame, guilt, and envy. These emotions organize the archetype of self into self- and other-images. Gendered self is one occasion of such organization. Biological differences in sexual structure determine the placing of an infant into a gender group; when these structures are ambiguous, the ambiguity is resolved (by surgery or decision) and the infant is placed into one gender group or the other. Gender groups are mutually exclusive in all major cultures. Membership in one guarantees that a person will organize an image of the other as an outsider. The particular meanings associated with each gender are flexible and relative to cultural and familial contexts; the assignment into a gender group and the biological structure of the body are not flexible. Gender membership lasts from birth to death; it is perhaps the *most different* difference in human life, but its meaning is relative to context and culture.

To put this into a practical context, I turn to something I have written about extensively: cross-gender relationships. Jungian psychology assists me in understanding the fundamental envy between the genders—the belief that the Other possesses richness and power that oneself cannot have. The initial organization of animus (in the female) or anima (in the male) takes place in childhood, beginning between two and three years, often around the theme of envy. We arrive in adulthood with a fairly well-organized and defended contrasexual complex. That complex then tends to be projected onto the intimate (or potentially intimate) Other of the opposite sex. If the Other identifies with the projected complex, both people suffer miserably from lack of differentiation. They are caught up in a web of "you don't understand me," "you don't see, hear, know me." Only the development of mature empathy can help untangle the mess of fantasy and reality. Mature empathy is the ability to recognize and hold one's own point of view while being able to infer another's. It is an ability that depends on differentiation and trust, that blends objectivity and subjectivity.

I believe that a psychology of gender difference is basically useful and that the Jungian concept of a repressed gender complex adds a necessary level of meaning in understanding the experiences of women and men. This concept allows us especially to chart a path of gender differentiation between male and female persons in relationship. That means each person becomes conscious of the meaning of her/his beliefs and expectations connected to animus/anima. Thus, in order to pay attention to me, you must be able to differentiate from me. Otherwise you will simply silence me, imagine me, or refute me according to your beliefs and expectations, without being influenced by me.

To return to the dilemma of women, in order for us to differentiate we must claim the legitimacy of our own experience. We must recognize how and why we construct our experiences as female. This is where feminism assists us psychologically, in discovering our own narratives and discriminating our experiences from patriarchal institutions, such as marriage and motherhood.

Feminism assists us in both deconstructing and reconstructing our life meanings. Feminist deconstruction offers a critique of inherited cultural and psychological assumptions of inadequacy of female self and triviality of female ideas and work. French feminists have especially assisted us in this area. Many of them assume that when women speak and write, they cannot possibly represent themselves because they have to enter into the domain of man-made language. They encourage us to investigate ourselves through the blind spots, the gaps, and the deficits that hide our being in the texts we have inherited. In order to do this we must become subversive readers of patriarchal texts. Philosopher Luce Irigaray recommends the metaphor of the speculum for turning an examining mirror back onto the originators of our theories, to pose questions about where and why female subjectivity has been disguised.[8]

American feminists invite us to believe in reconstruction, in our ability to wrest our own experiences out of the forms we possess. We are invited, for example, to believe in matrifocal and goddess-based cultures of the past. Relational theorist Riane Eisler, for one, constructs a vision of the past that "reads" history differently, subversively. She invites us to claim a past in which women and men already lived as equals. In that society, people worshipped the regenerative principle of life that is close to the reproductive cycle of the female body. Eisler is saying we don't need to invent or discover ideal forms for female narratives; we only need to remember them.[9]

The reconstructive aspect of feminist epistemology is a vision quest for inspirations and articulations of female experiences. Two major beliefs stand in the way of women directly claiming the worth and wisdom of their own gender, as sociologist Jean Lipman-Blumen has shown in her analysis of gender and power: (1) the belief that men control the knowledge necessary to direct our daily lives; and (2) the belief that men control the major resources on which we all depend.[10] Feminist analyses of resources, vitality, agency, and ideals of female persons provide a persuasive counterposition to these beliefs. Feminist theologians assist us in training our minds to spot new ideals and ideal images of female authority.[11] Feminist psychologists invite us to think differently about our resources and our knowledge system—to investigate our selves, voices, and minds.[12]

When I look at the massive work of contemporary feminism, I like to think that women are working on a large-scale "paradigm shift" in the sense meant by Kuhn.[13] The feminism of the 1970s introduced and advocated subjectivism ("gut feelings") in contrast to scientific objectivism. In the early 1980s we witnessed the development of relativism in terms of a feminist awareness of gender differences as constituting essential human differences. In the late 1980s we have seen the formulation of feminist constructivism (and deconstruction) in terms of the influence of context and pattern-matching on reality-making. I believe that feminism has vastly influenced culture-making, moving us away from reductive arguments about the universal nature of human difference and toward an appreciation of reciprocal valuing of difference.

The reciprocal valuing of difference leads to the possibility for mutual self-revelation, the joining of knowledge and desire, in ongoing conversations from different points of view, different persons. In order for this kind of dialogue to take place between men and women, we must learn about our repressed gender meanings. Jungian psychology can help us, provided we revise the psychology to bring it up to date with relativism and constructivism.

We also must learn to overcome the silence and silencing of female persons. Having ideals, images, visions, narratives, and life histories on record is a major move toward "real talk" in women's voices. When feminism informs psychology, it reveals the gaps, blind spots, and deficits that color female subjectivity within the history of patriarchy. When feminism is incorporated into psychology, it serves to liberate descriptions, narratives, accounts, and ideals of female persons.

Although feminism is not a spiritual practice, or a promise of relief from human suffering, it serves a spiritual goal. Releasing girls and women to speak, vitalizing their artistic and creative practices (from the ordinary tasks of housework and personal decoration to the extraordinary contributions to literature, art, philosophy, and religion), permitting the possibility of dialogue between the genders, revealing new paradigms of thought, and appreciating compassion as a primary human impulse—feminism is a vision quest on the boundaries of patriarchal worlds.

· · · · · · ·

RESACRALIZING THE FEMALE BODY: HEALING OUR RELATIONSHIPS WITH RHYTHMS, INSTINCTS, AND DESIRES

The root words for "knowing"—*kennen* and *konnen* ("being able to") in German; *ken* in Gaelic; *gnosis* ("knowledge," "wisdom") in Greek; and *gnosco* in Latin—are the same ones we find in such words as *genus, gender, genital,* and *engender*.

Knowledge and creativity are sexual as well as spiritual. When the Bible tells us that Adam "knew" his wife, it likewise expresses this experiential, creative meaning of knowing that includes the body.

The subsequent devaluation—indeed the abhorrence—of the body and bodily experience which took place during the reign of the patriarchy was part of the rejection of the magical and feminine dimensions. It culminated in the Cartesian mind-body dichotomy . . . and was the starting point for psychology and psychoanalysis and effectively severed our conscious mind from awareness of the magical transformative dimension. . . . Ritual gradually and increasingly became ineffective and meaningless.

EDWARD C. WHITMONT
Return of the Goddess

In ancient times, before the Feminine was banished and women were robbed of all powers, the mysteries of our bodies were celebrated with ritual. Menstruation, sexuality, childbirth, menopause, and death were seen as passages of great import, transitions between worlds, to be honored in the realms within and the realms without. And the female body was the vehicle for this passage.

In our times the rites of passage are lost, and so is our reverence for the mysteries. We are cut off from our bodies as we are cut off from the earth, orphaned within "skin-encapsulated egos." Therefore these special times of ceremony can become instead times of great personal difficulty, and the opportunity for spiritual breakthrough can turn into spiritual breakdown.

Recently, a revival of ritual has appeared. Small groups of women interested in various forms of feminine spirituality gather to celebrate occasions of transition in the natural world, such as full moons, solstices, and equinoxes. Others studying shamanism and native cultures create dance and musical ceremony or healing ceremony for occasions of personal transition, such as births, birthdays, weddings, illnesses, and deaths.

The following articles serve to reconnect us in ceremonial imagination to an era before the patriarchy had stolen the awesome beauty of the Goddess and rendered her sterile. They point the way back in order to point the way forward.

Betty De Shong Meador details a ceremony of menstruation in which the cycles of the female body are tied to the cycles of nature. Deena Metzger portrays sexual initiation as a means to renewal, with the female body the doorway to the Divine. And Elizabeth S. Strahan re-creates the rite of menopause as a way for women to consciously reclaim their power after the childbearing years.

14 · THESMOPHORIA: A WOMEN'S FERTILITY RITUAL

. . . .

BETTY DE SHONG MEADOR

The first of the women's mysteries we confront in our own bodies is menstruation. Most women I have known have not experienced their first periods, or any there-after, as magical events; rather, we have been taught to see them as physiological events, even mechanical ones, in which the body sheds our substance as an alternative to fertilization.

While our mothers typically knew nothing about the coming of menstruation (and often thought, with the first blood, that they were in danger of losing their lives), we were prepared with up-to-date scientific explanations and with tools and medications to enable us to act as if nothing were happening. The ideal, then, was to be able to ignore the bleeding.

Berkeley, California, Jungian analyst Betty De Shong Meador harkens back to the Thesmophoria, a pre-patriarchal fertility ceremony that linked the seeds of the harvest to the seeds in women's bodies. The ritual involved purification, descent, sacrifice, and an encounter with Snake, the underworld deity of fertility. You may notice that many of the elements of this descent resemble those described by Sylvia Brinton Perera and Elizabeth S. Strahan. They are the universals of female initiation.

This piece is reprinted with permission from the Los Angeles Jungian journal Psychological Perspectives, *volume 17, number 1, 1986.*

Betty De Shong Meador is a Jungian analyst in Berkeley, California. She is on the faculty of the C. G. Jung Institute of San Francisco and is a co-founder of the Lavender Rose Women's Mystery School. She has written numerous articles on the dark Goddess and translated the myth of the goddess Inanna.

You dream of menstruation. You dream of hemorrhaging, of flooding, of staining your clothes, of spotting. You dream of having your period with your friends, with your mother, with your daughters. You dream of other women flowing, staining, hemorrhaging. You dream of welcoming the flow, of hating it, of being embarrassed, of hiding.

You gather memories of menstruation. You remember seeing blood in the toilet, but you cannot remember what your mother said about it. You remember she called the red sheet stain fingernail polish.

You remember Jean Ann, Grady, Nancy, and Jo Ellen bending over the dictionary on the den floor at Charlotte's house. They are looking up the *word*. You think its starts with an "a," "administration." They laugh. "No! Menstruation!" They are talking about something you have never heard of, something as dirty as fucking.

You are the last one to start your period. You have taped a toilet paper pad on your bride doll. You feel your face, your groin flush when you play this game with her.

Your period starts. You are in the pink bathroom. Your mother is outside hanging sheets on the clothesline. You tell her you think you have started your period. Neither of you has ever spoken that word between you.

She comes inside with you. She does not say much. She says, "Sometimes it is a relief when it starts." You wonder what she is talking about.

You are walking home from school with Jean Ann. She has on her red teddy bear coat. Something drops. "Look over there," she says. She picks the something up. You do not see what it is because you were looking where she pointed. Later she tells you her Kotex fell off.

You menstruate for thirty-four years. After you have stopped menstruating, you hear your friends talking about having their periods. You realize you are now set apart from them. You dream that you need to make a ritual marking the passage from having periods to their ceasing. You cannot think what to do.

You begin to see yourself as a non-menstruating woman. Walking down the street, you notice the women who still menstruate. In cafés you watch them. You sense the cycle going on in their bodies. You sense the trembling edge of their fertility. Your body begins to tingle. You feel tears pressing behind your eyes. You feel a surge of caring for them. You have an urge to protect them in their vulnerability.

You hear that Northwest Indian women menstruate sitting on the ground on soft moss. Carol says she was at a cabin alone once and wanted to menstruate into the earth. She could not bring herself to do it. You hear of a woman who owns a beaded African gourd used to collect menstrual blood. Judy says she would like to collect her menstrual blood, but she does not know what she would do with it. Nyla says the blood is good for plants. She knows a woman who puts menstrual blood on her plants, and the plants flourish.

You hear that in the past women's ritual centered around the mystery of the blood. You learn that women celebrated the connection between the fertility cycle in their bodies and the fertility cycle of the earth. You learn that the women honored their menstrual cycles as a gift from the deity. You learn that women fiercely protected the sacredness of their fertility. You feel the power of a ritual gathering of women, articulating and celebrating the mystery we carry in our bodies. You want to know more about the sacred ritual we have lost.

The fields belong to woman. In her body woman carries the secret knowledge of fertility and growing. Woman is like the field. The field and the woman both caress the seed. The seed is at home in her body and in the earth's body. The seed feeds off the moist nurturing food her blood carries and the earth carries. Her body naturally harbors the seed in her womb. The seed grows. The mystery astounds her. And she is the mystery. Wisely, the fields belong to woman.

Long before the Olympians came to power, led by the great patriarch, Zeus, the women in Greece celebrated the Thesmophoria. Each year at the time of planting, the women gathered to remember the sacred mystery of the seed in the earth and the seed in their bodies. No one knows the ritual's beginning. Votive remains, similar to those used in the Thesmophoria, have been found in all parts of Old Europe dating from 6000 B.C.

The ritual is of immemorial antiquity. From the time women discovered that wild seeds gathered could be saved, could be buried in the earth, could grow, they began to bless the seeds with blood and flesh. They celebrate the ritual which in Greece became the Thesmophoria.

Women who take part in the Thesmophoria have reached the age of the beginning of their menstrual cycle. They have blossomed, have borne or can bear children. They share the common bond in their bodies of the ripe pear of a womb filling and shedding blood with the moon. Or they have passed beyond the menses. They have survived childbirth, disease, miscarriage, hardship, famine, sorrow, turmoil. They have passed the climacteric, and the memory of the bleeding, the blood memory, mixes with time to form wisdom.

For the young girls who do not yet menstruate, the Greeks hold a separate rite called the Arretophoria. Girls between the ages of seven and eleven participate. In the Arretophoria the girls enact parts of the ritual drama of the Thesmophoria, but the mystery is carefully hidden. Four girls of noble birth lodge during the festival in the temple of the goddess. On one of the nights the girls carry sacred objects which cannot be named and cannot be seen. Women place objects in baskets which the four girls carry on their heads. They walk down a natural underground passage. At the bottom of the descent they exchange the sacred objects for something else which is wrapped and hidden. This they bring back to the temple. Thus the young girls begin their preparation for the central mystery of their lives which they will later celebrate in the festival in the Thesmophoria.

The ritual of the Thesmophoria begins with nine days of preparation, during which the women observe rites of purification. For nine preparatory days and nights the women abstain from sexual intercourse. Thus they begin their withdrawal from men. In their houses the women sleep alone. They prepare cots on which to sleep away from the marriage bed. The women begin to work and walk alone. They begin to enter wholly into the femaleness of themselves. They eat garlic to repel the men by the unappetizing smell of their breath. They carefully place a garlic supper for Hecate on her piles of stones at crossroads.

At dusk on each of the nine preparatory days, the women gather at the chosen fields. There they build the huts in which they will sleep during the nights of the ritual. There they prepare the great altar.

Each woman constructs her own hut where she will sleep. She brings from the countryside great branches of the wild fig, the tree which in Greece designates the entrance to the underworld. She covers her shelter with branches of the wild fig. Inside her hut she prepares a couch for herself of grasses and soft piles of leaves.

Over the hut and on the couch she strews the lygos plant. She weaves its twigs around the hut's opening. She secures its leaves and flowers into the walls over her couch. In a ceremony after the work is finished each evening, the women gather and sip a cooling drink of crushed lygos leaves.

The women tell many stories about the lygos plant. They say lygos flowers in three colors by the river Imbrasos, or Parthenios. They say lygos grows on the island of Samos, or Parthenia, Island of the Virgin. They say lygos grows profusely on the sandy flats of the riverbank, its blue, white, and pale red flowers appearing in countless numbers. Here among the lygos Hera would come to pass her katamenia, her menstrual period. Here the women of Samos would bring each month the statue of Hera from her temple, would pass with her the katamenia. Afterward, the women would bathe Hera and return with her to the temple, virginal.

In preparation for the Thesmophoria the women drink the lygos drink to urge on the menses. The leaves of the lygos plant tremble on the branches at the door of the hut, a sign of the impending flow. The droplets of blood begin to loosen in the walls of the women's wombs, begin to gather in silent streams. From the first show of the blood, the women are sanctified for the great Thesmophoria. They tie a red band around their arms telling the others they are ready, flowing, set apart, untouchable because sacred. The flow of this month of sowing, Pyanepsion, is holy, belonging to the deities who rule the Thesmophoria.

The day of the festival arrives. The women gather at the sacred field. Only the women gather. Not even a male dog is allowed. The women guard the area with sacrificing knives, roasting-spits, and torches. Once, women with blood-smeared faces castrated a man caught spying.

The first day of the three-day festival is called both Kathodos and Anodos, Downgoing and Uprising. The women, purified in the nine days of purification, carry down into a chasm newborn suckling pigs. Squealing and wiggling, the piglets struggle in the strong arms of the women. Together they descend into the chasm.

The same day, the women climb out of the chasm carrying great heaps of rotted pig's flesh. The sacred nature of this ritual silenced any report of what actually happened down below. That the women killed the pigs is certain. The source of the rotted flesh, which they carried out the same day, is unknown. Some say the flesh remained from the pig slaughter the year before. Some say the rotted flesh belonged to pigs sacrificed during the spring threshing ritual. Some say the transformation of the sweet flesh to rotten meat is a mystery.

The little pigs, they say, were food for the great underground primal deities, the snakes. The Snake deity carries life itself under the earth, rules the mystery of the deep earth. The women bring food to the great Snake deity, little piglets with their fat and fertile propensity.

The women bow before great Snake in wonder. They are inexorably bound to Snake, even when they do not know it or do not acknowledge it, for Snake is the power in the earth, in the field, and the power in the bodies of the women.

The women honor Snake with sacrifice. Each woman descends into the chasm with a pig for Snake. The pig is a promise to Snake, a promise which yearly seals the bond between Snake and woman. Snake does not need to be reminded of Her power, but the women! Ah! They tend to forget. When life is going well in the village and the storehouse is full, the women might say, "How clever we are! How well we provide for our people!" They might forget that the power of life belongs to Snake. To remember this, they celebrate the Thesmophoria.

The women are fond of the little pigs with creamy pink skin soft as a baby's. Each woman brings her pick of the litter, the feistiest, healthiest, roundest little pig, takes it to Snake at the Thesmophoria. At the bottom of the chasm, near the sacred abode of Snake, the women kill the pigs. They slit open the pigs' bellies. It is hard for the women to do and pains them. The little pigs become part of them. The women say to Snake, "Here! Here is little pig! She is a part of me! She with her ripening cunt, her estrus, her great belly waiting for seeds! Here she is! Now, Snake, I give her to you! She belongs to you anyway. It is you who stir life in our wombs. At this moment I know the life you sustain in my body. Great Snake! Mystery! Eat!"

They say the snakes eat almost all of the pig flesh.

The women climb out of the chasm carrying baskets of the rotted flesh of pigs. The rattling and hissing sounds a snake makes accompany the women climbing. They carry in baskets the transformed food of Snake. They make the sounds of Snake. The women have become Snake. Snake enlivens the women, incarnates in the women. Snake is alive and emerges into the upper world inside the bodies of the women.

The second day of the Thesmophoria is called Nesteia, the Middle Day, the day of the solemn fast. The only substance eaten is the red-fleshed seed of the pomegranate. Should a seed drop on the ground, it remains there for the dead. Silence and gloom pervade the atmosphere.

On this middle day the women mix the rotten pigs' flesh with seed corn. They place the mixture on the great altar. There it remains in the sacred place throughout the day.

In bringing up from the chasm a portion of the rotten flesh, the women have taken food from Snake. As compensation for this removal, they now carry down a substitute. They make sacred images whose names may not be spoken. They form the images from cereal paste and carry them down in baskets into the chasm. The *sacra* whose names may not be spoken look like penises and scrota or like coiled snakes.

The remainder of the day the women fast seated on the ground. They say the women imitate the ancient way of life. They move into the primitive way their grandmothers knew. They sit upon the ground. They sit in ritual silence in the sacred fields.

Silently their own blood flows into the fields. They sit cunt to earth, kiss the sweet soil of the fields. The blood of the women flows into the field. The soil of the field drinks the rich blood of the women. In solemn silence the women give to the earth their own substance. Snake moves through the women in the blood flow. Snake carries the fertilizing blood richness into the earth's body. The women are one with the earth. The life of the earth and the life of the women co-mingle, an open exchange, a bond of kin, revitalized by the mysterious power of Snake.

The fast is broken at sunset. In a ritual gathering the women eat sacred cakes. The cakes are replicas of the great pudenda which sits on the altar. The silence is broken. The women begin to joke and to laugh as they pass to one another the little cakes the shape of a cunt, a slender crescent, a half moon.

In the evening the women gather around the fire. The jovial mood which began after the fast was broken now swells to hilarity. The presence of Snake in the women sweeps away the boundaries of ordinary life. Gone are the daily concerns which bind the women to the life of the village: the care of children, lovers, husbands, gossip, struggle. The women have severed their ties to daily life and begin to see with the pitiless eyes of Snake.

The vision loosens their tongues. They tell what they see. Passion stirs and rises. They begin to shout at each other. What has been tolerated, ignored, hidden, is exposed. They hurl scurrilous remarks, scathing, burning, descriptions of imagined acts of utmost privacy. No one is spared, not the women, not their parents, relatives, husbands, lovers, friends. They laugh. They jeer. The one who is shouting vies to outdo the last. They rage. They cry. They fight, hurl clods or stones.

No one is spared. Secrets, grudges, hatreds, envies, jealousies, all are exposed. A woman cannot avoid seeing her secret self made public, her dark and hidden passions flung in the air by the voices of the shouting women. The shouting exposes secrets, shatters pride, levels the women to a common ground.

The women are mortified. They are stripped of pride, shaken, and leveled. The tongue of Snake cuts away foolish pride, foolish desire. They acknowledge all belongs to Snake, and no one of them creates, loves, works, builds, plays outside the life-sustaining embrace of Snake.

One by one they begin to walk toward their huts. Each goes to her own hut to sleep. Each carefully strews lygos over her couch. The lygos which brings on the blood flow is said to be hostile to reptiles. Each woman knows that the intimate contact with Snake is double-edged. Snake's gifts of sight and fecundity are only a thin line removed from Her powers of wild possession and madness. The women protect themselves with the lygos at night when their heightened daytime alertness fades into sleep. They ask great Snake to guard them from madness and possession, acknowledging that madness, too, is in Her power.

The third day of the festival is called Kallegeneia, Fair Born or Fair Birth. The women awake singing. They have survived the great trials of the Thesmophoria.

They have dared to enter the abode of Snake. They have sacrificed before Her. They have participated in a ritual death in Her presence. Snake has filled them. The deity Herself has risen from the depths in the bodies of the women. Her awesome power possessed them. She loosened the boundaries of ordinary life and shook the women.

Now the day of the Fair Born arrives. Snake returns to Her chasm. Now the women move about, sensing Her withdrawal. The air is clear. The air is no longer shaking. Snake has departed.

The old hierarchy returns. The older women approach the altar, the honored ones who have slept many years on the lygos. The women gather around them. The old ones speak of Snake's departure. We are left with Her memory, they say. They lift the baskets of seed-flesh off of the altar and pass among the women. Each woman takes a portion of the mixture and follows the basket carriers into the field. There the women bury the seed-flesh in the sanctified soil. When all the seeds are planted, the women stand in the plowed rows. Softly they begin to sing. Whatever name they give to great Snake deity, they sing Her praise. From time immemorial they sing to Her. She has had many names. Few have survived to us. In ancient Sumer she was called Ereshkigal.

Where in modern life can women find a place to praise the great Snake deity? She is lost here. There is no place for Her. We have not received memory of Her from our mothers. We have forgotten how to pass knowledge of Her to our daughters. No sacred festival honors the central mystery of our lives. Our mothers are ashamed to speak of it.

Our tradition is gone. The memory is shattered. We gather only broken pieces. We have forgotten which pieces belong together. We have forgotten that the same deity rules the descent to the underworld and the mysterious cycle in our bodies. We have forgotten that descent must have its sacrifice. We have forgotten that the rotten substance of the sacrifice is a gift of fecundity.

In the festival of the Thesmophoria menstruating women open themselves to the Snake deity through sacrifice. Each tears a piglet from a sow, kills it before Snake. To perform these acts, a woman sacrifices her natural nurturing ways. She sacrifices the claim of family, children, village. She acts out of a vision beyond the habits of caring, the safe structures of society. She places herself outside the claims of civilization and descends to the deity who exists prior to civilization's achievements. She acknowledges that her roots as woman extend to the great below, that life in her body with its natural cycle is sustained by a mystery deep in the underworld. She acknowledges the claim of the underworld deity. She hears Her call even in the midst of ordinary life. . . .

Before a woman of our time can bring fertility to the field and to herself, before she can realize her creative powers, she must participate in the Downgoing. She must gather herself together. She must remove herself from the ongoingness of her daily life. She must descend into the chasm, go deep into the earth, under the ground. She must take with her an offering for that which sustains life, Snake. She must remind herself of her inexorable bond to Snake through her body, renew her bond with a promise. She must give to Snake a little pig, or her valued possessions, or even her life. She must give her sacrifice to the underlying, sustaining mystery and then wait while her gift rots. She is naked now and bowed low. The snakes dance around her and around her gift and are pleased. They eat the rotting flesh. They accept the woman's gift. When the time comes, they bless their bond with the woman, load her baskets with the transformed stinking flesh, send her away. She returns to the upper world with the substance of her own creativity.

The mystery of Thesmophoria tells us that woman's creativity comes from below. To receive the gift, she must go down. There in the dark dwelling place of primal life, she encounters an older sister, One who lives prior to herself, One who supports the fragile structure of civilization. The encounter shakes her narrow beliefs. Her beliefs fall before the claim of the primacy of life itself. She returns enlarged, expanded. She returns with gifts of understanding, with praise.

15 · RE-VAMPING THE WORLD: ON THE RETURN OF THE HOLY PROSTITUTE

· · · · · · ·

DEENA METZGER

Among some Native American tribes, there is a woman who is trained in the sexual arts to initiate boys at puberty into the ways of a woman's body. This "Fire Woman" and her counterpart, the "Fire Man," who initiates girls, are revered as teachers of the sacred. They undergo extensive training, and their initiates are permitted to make love with them for as long as they like. In the context of Quodoushka, *as this native sacred sexuality is called, lovemaking is a spiritual practice and sexual healing, ideally, should be made available to all.*

Los Angeles psychotherapist, poet, and author Deena Metzger tells us that the Fire Woman has a forebear in ancient times, the Quedishtu, *or Holy Prostitute. Before the apocryphal split between sinful and sacred, priestess and priest, body and mind; before the Feminine was disgraced and abandoned and the Masculine became the sole province of power, the Holy Prostitute offered access to the divine. As an embodiment of the Goddess, She guided men to reconnect with what is holy in them, and with what is holy in Her. As the story goes, every woman served this function at the temple, sometimes for as long as a year.*

Today, of course, this idea is not only shocking, it is such heresy that it is difficult to comprehend. The split between sexuality and spirituality is entrenched. Our natural sexuality has been disowned, our instincts repressed, while our sense of the sacred has been banished to an afterlife. As Metzger points out, in a sacred universe, She is holy; in a secular universe, She is a whore.

The consequences have been devastating: Men face a split projection of the Feminine archetype, and seek nurturing and caring from one source (a mother figure, or madonna), excitement and eroticism from another (a mistress, lover, or whore). As women living under the burden of these projections, we have lost the connection to our own sexuality, which was once, long ago, a means of joy and self-expression and a link to the sacred in our own bodies.

Metzger's original and provocative piece is, as we used to say in the 1960s, a call to loving arms: she demands that we make love as a political act . . . and that we make love as a spiritual act. She calls for the resacralization of our bodies and our loins.

Deena Metzger is a Los Angeles poet, novelist, playwright, and psychotherapist. Her books include Dark Milk; The Axis Mundi Poems; Skin: Shadows/ Silence; The Woman Who Slept with Men to Take the War Out of Them; Tree; Looking for the Faces of God; *and* What Dinah Thought. *She is currently working on* Writing for Your Life: Creativity, Imagination and Healing. *She is married to Michael Ortiz Hill, has two grown sons, and lives at the end of a dirt road with her wolf, Timber.*

Once upon a time, in Sumeria, in Mesopotamia, in Egypt, in Greece, there were no whorehouses, no brothels. In that time, in those countries, there were instead the Temples of the Sacred Prostitutes. In these temples, men were cleansed, not sullied; morality was restored, not desecrated; sexuality was not perverted, but divine.

The original whore was a priestess, the conduit to the divine, the one through whose body one entered the sacred arena and was restored. Warriors, soldiers, soiled by combat within the world of men, came to the Holy Prostitute, the *Quedishtu,* literally meaning "the undefiled one," in order to be cleansed and reunited with the gods. The *Quedishtu* or *Quadesh* is associated with a variety of goddesses, including Hathor, Ishtar, Anath, Astarte, and Asherah. It is interesting to note, according to Patricia Monaghan in *The Book of Goddesses and Heroines,* that Astarte originally meant "She of the Womb" but appears in the Old Testament as Ashtoreth, meaning "Shameful thing."

Despite scripture and orthodox thought, war was seen as separating men from the gods, and one had to be reconnected in order to be able to re-enter society. The body, the sexual act, was the means for re-entry. As the body was the means, so inevitably pleasure was an accompaniment, but the essential attribute of sexuality, in this context, was prayer.

In Pergamon, Turkey, I saw the remains of the Temple of the Holy Prostitutes on the Sacred Way, alongside the other temples, palaces, and public buildings. Whatever rites we imagine took place in these other buildings, it is common—whether we elevate them as do neo-pagans or condemn them as do Judeo-Christians—to associate the Holy Prostitutes with orgies and debauchery. But it is possible that neither view is correct, as each tends to inflate the physical activity and ignore or impugn the spiritual component. Our materialist preoccupation with form blinds us to the content.

But it is no wonder that from the beginning, the first patriarchs, the priests of Judea and Israel, the prophets of Jehovah, all condemned the Holy Prostitutes and the worship of Asherah, Astarte, Anath, and the other goddesses. Until the time of the priests, the women were one doorway to the divine. If the priests wished to insert themselves between the people and the divine, they had to remove women from that role. So it was not that sexuality was originally considered sinful per se, or that women's sexuality threatened property and progeny; it was that in order for the priests to have power, women had to be replaced as a road to the divine —this gate had to be closed. It was, we can speculate, to this end that the terrible misogyny that we all suffer was instituted.

Women had been the essential link to the three worlds. Through the mother one came into this world; through the Mysteries, the rites of Demeter or Isis, one entered the underworld; and through the Holy Prostitute one came to the divine. Access was personal and unconditional. It was not sufficient for a new priesthood to supplant the women. In the days of the *Quedishtu* every woman served the gods as Holy Prostitute, often for as long as a year. This was contradictory to the hegemony that a priesthood required.

For the sake of power, it is often necessary to set the world upside down. Therefore the priests asserted that the sacred was depraved, that the way to the divine was the way to perdition. Reversals such as this are not uncommon. Incoming religions often co-opt, then reverse, existing spiritual beliefs and practices. So Hades, the spiritual center of Greek paganism, became Hell. The descent into Hades, the core of the Eleusinian mysteries and a spiritually required initiation for anyone who was concerned with soul, was likened to suffering and perdition. Where once Pindar had written, "Thrice blessed are those who have seen these Mysteries for they know the end of life and the beginning," later Dante was to inscribe, "Abandon all hope, ye who enter here." Similarly, Dionysus, the life god, became Satan; Adonis, the consort of Aphrodite, became Christ. Mary Magdalene, the Holy Prostitute, was converted and transformed; Aphrodite became Eve became the Virgin Mary. The reversals were complete. Psyche's (soul's) journey toward individuation became almost impossible as Aphrodite, the mother of Eros, no longer existed to beckon the Self.

Three of the essential roads to the three worlds were blocked or debased. The gods did not die in Nietzsche's time, but centuries earlier with the subversion of the priestesses and the secularization and degradation of the holy body.

This article is about seduction, about vamping, about eros; about an attempt to restore a tradition, to reinstitute a way of seeing the world. It is not only about restoring practices, it is first about restoring the consciousness from which those practices may derive.

What was the impact of the suppression of the Holy Prostitute on the world? We are not concerned here with the suppression of certain rites but rather with the deprivation of consciousness implicit in that suppression. All the practices that honored the way of the woman ceased. The Eleusinian mysteries, which had provided immortality, were suppressed; the mysteries of the Cabeiri, designed specifically to redeem those with blood on their hands, were suppressed; procreation was infused with anxiety and guilt; fertility festivals that had provided a link between earth and spirit were condemned. When the priests separated the body from the gods, they separated the divine from nature and thereby created the mind-body split. The world was secularized. We can only speculate as to the consequences, though we must assume there were consequences when men returned from war without the ability to clean the blood from their hands, when the physical, quotidian community between the gods and the people was not reconvened. It was not woman per se who was attacked, but the gods who were exiled. Perhaps the world as we have come to know it—impersonal, abstract, detached, brutish—was engendered in that division.

In a sacred universe, the prostitute is a holy woman, a priestess. In a secular universe, the prostitute is a whore. In this distinction is the agony of our lives.

The question is: How do we relate to this today, as women, as feminists? Is there a way we can resanctify society, become the priestesses again, put ourselves in the service of the gods and eros? As we re-vision, can we re-vamp as well?

Vamp: A woman who sets out to charm or captivate by the use of sexual attractiveness.

Re-vamp: To mend, repair, renovate, refurbish, or restore.

In 1978, I wrote a novel, *The Woman Who Slept with Men to Take the War Out of Them*, about Holy Prostitutes. In the novel a woman whose name is Ada walks down the street of an occupied village from the cemetery, passing her own house to the General's house, which she enters without a word to lie down unashamed on his bed. She does this with the full cognizance that she is committing a political act. Later in the novel, Grace, a prostitute in an old-age home, reminisces:

> Still so sweet the men who came. We didn't allow whips. No rough stuff. And when they left—little lambs. Do you think the wives sent us a basket at Christmas time with a little homemade jam, for thanks?
>
> Always used to say those men would have torn the entire town apart on Saturday night if not for us. I thought we should have gotten a commendation from the marshall's office. I told that to the chief of police straight out. We were the best investment in law and order they ever made.

What does it mean to re-vamp a society? It means that we must become vamps again, sexual-spiritual beings, that we must act out of eros. This means that we must first alter ourselves in the most fundamental ways. We cannot become the means for the resanctification of society unless we are willing to become the priestesses once more who serve the gods not in theory and empty practice, but from our very nature. It means that we must identify with eros no matter what the seeming consequences to ourselves. Even if it seems foolish, inexpedient, even if it makes us vulnerable. It means that we cannot be distracted from this task by pleasure, power, lusts, or anger. It requires a sincere rededication.

It is, however, exactly this rededication to the principles of the Feminine that is so problematic. The Feminine has been so devalued and degraded, has so little power in the world, we have suffered so much loss of opportunity, have been so oppressed, that it is difficult if not sometimes seemingly impossible to continue to enact the Feminine in the world without feeling as if we are opening ourselves to further violation. So we are caught in a terrible paradox. To feel powerful, to acquire some gain, we must learn the very masculine modes that oppress us and that are about to destroy the world. In either case we seem to participate in our own destruction. But if we utilize the Feminine, it is possible that the planet will survive, and also the species, and that eventually we will thrive. Without the Feminine and eros, everything is irretrievably lost.

And so let us consider becoming Holy Prostitutes again.

When contemporary feminism was established sufficiently to offer real hope and possibility, women who had formerly considered themselves atheists turned to spiritual matters. The Goddess and goddesses were reinvoked. There was an extraordinary interest in spirituality, myth, rite, ceremony. The spiritual instinct buried in a secular universe erupted.

As part of this new spiritual order, we must engage in two heresies. The second is to re-sanctify the body; the first, even more difficult task is to return to the very early, neolithic, pagan, matriarchal perception of the sacred universe itself. But to overthrow secular thought may be the heretical act of the century. That is why we are in so much psychic pain.

Susan Griffin writes the following in the last chapter, entitled "Eros," of *Pornography and Silence*:

> The psychic is simply world. *And if I let myself love, let myself touch, enter my own pleasure and longing, enter the body of another, the darkness, let the dark parts of my body speak, tongue into mouth, in the body's language, as I enter a part of me I believed was real begins to die, I descend into matter, I know I am at the heart of myself, I cry out in ecstasy.* For in love, we surrender our uniqueness and become world.

If we become world through love, then love is essentially a political act. If we become world reaching to the gods, then love is essentially a spiritual act that redeems the world.

How then do we become Holy Prostitutes? How do we materialize without literalizing the Holy Prostitute? How do we bring her essence into being? How do we restore the temple? How do we change not only behavior but our consciousness as well?

To become the Holy Prostitute is to be willing to endure the agony of consciousness required of the heretic. It is the willingness and ability to hold one worldview when the majority holds another. It is to commit oneself to eros, bonding, connection, when the world values thanatos, separation, detachment. The Holy Prostitute was Everywoman, and she made herself available in the service of the gods, especially to those outside the province of the gods. The contemporary Holy Prostitute must be willing to try to bring the sacred to the one who is defiled; she must be the one who will take in "the other"—the one who makes love with "the other" in order for him to be reconnected to the community. She carries the belief that "the other" does not want to remain an outsider.

These ideas are old and familiar, easy to say, so difficult to enact. Yet when they are transformed from idea to belief within ourselves, transformation outside ourselves follows.

I have done some work called personal disarmament. I ask individuals to consider themselves a nation-state and to impose upon themselves those conditions they would like to impose upon the country. In this exercise they must identify their enemies, their armies, defense and offense systems, secret weapons, and so on. Then after this self-scrutiny, I ask them to publicly commit at least a single act of personal disarmament to initiate the change to a peaceful world. It seems to me that our militarism and defensiveness are signs of our inner fear and aggression. I believe that ultimately it will be easier for us to disarm as a nation if we are disarmed as individuals.

The same scrutiny is essential to the issue at hand. If we built brothel adjuncts to our temples and sent our young girls there at eighteen, it would be ludicrous, it would change nothing; nothing can change as long as we devalue the Feminine, denigrate the body, and disbelieve in a sacred universe. Certainly the sexual revolution has proven this, for it has changed nothing. So it is not sex we are after at all, but something far deeper.

The task is to accept the body as spiritual, and sexuality and erotic love as spiritual disciplines; to believe that eros is pragmatic; to honor the Feminine even where it is dishonored or disadvantaged. These, then, are some of the questions I think it is appropriate for us to ask ourselves:

Whom do I close myself against?

When do I not have time for love or eros?

When do I find eros inconvenient, burdensome, or inexpedient?

When do I find eros dangerous to me?

When do I indulge the erotic charge of guilt?

Where do I respond to, accept, provoke the idea of sin?

When do I use sexuality to distract rather than to commune?

When do I reject eros because I am rejected?

When do I abuse the body?

How do I reinforce the mind/body split?

When and how do I denigrate the Feminine?

When do I refuse the gods? When do I pretend to believe in them?

How often do I acquiesce to the "real world"?

In a guided meditation, I was confronted by a large, luminous woman, approximately eight feet tall, clearly an image of a goddess, though I had never encountered a goddess figure in any of my own meditations. Her hair was light itself. As she came close to me, I was filled both with awe at her beauty and terror at her presence. If I were to take her into me, I knew my life would be altered, I would have to give up many of the masculine modes I had adopted in order to negotiate successfully in the world. The woman was powerful, but her power was of receptivity, resonance, magnetism, radiance. She had the power of eros; she drew me to her.

As she appeared, I was reminded of a statement by a friend. "When it comes to the bell," Dianna Linden said, "we all want to be the clapper, we don't want to be the body; but it is the body which sings." Still, when she appeared, I consciously experienced the terror of the Feminine I had so often read and heard about. I was afraid of my own nature. At that moment, I committed myself to risking heresy, to converting, whatever the personal cost, to the Feminine.

So, though I have written about it, thought about it, tried to act accordingly, I must admit that I have not been able to fully put on the role of the Holy Prostitute. This fills me with sadness, also awe at the difficulty of the task. But I do commit myself; she is the woman I aspire to be.

16 · BEYOND BLOOD: WOMEN OF THAT CERTAIN AGE

· · · · · · ·

ELIZABETH S. STRAHAN

In an elegant ritual of imagination, Southern California Jungian analyst Elizabeth S. Strahan unveils a bit of the esoteric mystery of menopause, the final cycle in a woman's life in which her body ceases its monthly rhythm, rendering her no longer able to bear children. But, Strahan tells us, the pause in the menarche signifies even more than bodily change; it invites us to shed old ways and open to new life once again.

Drawing on both history and fantasy, Strahan imagines that in ancient times, with the onset of menopause, a woman retreats alone to a Dionysian cult in which she is initiated by priestesses and offered a meeting with the phallus, the impersonal source of generative sexual power. Like the snake, the phallus contains the fertile, creative juices of nature. Embodied as the god Dionysus, wild, chaotic, and divinely mad, he is both alluring and terrifying.

In her trance state, the participant cannot tell whether certain events actually transpire—whether she, like the men who are renewed by the sacred prostitute, also receives a sexual healing from the god, or whether these images came alive only in her fantasy. It matters not, for she has rediscovered the power of her femininity independent of her relationship to husband, family, or children, and independent of her youthful beauty. She has entered this stage of her life consciously, willing to bear the mystery of the moment.

Elizabeth S. Strahan is a Jungian analyst in private practice in Fullerton, California. She was trained at the C. G. Jung Institute in Los Angeles and has served as chairperson of its certifying board and as president. She has been married for twenty-eight years and has two grown sons. She gives lectures and seminars on women's issues and also loves to dance, cook, and create beautiful spaces in her house and garden.

I turned fifty this year. The idea of it took hold of me at least six months before the event. The number itself seemed so big, so archetypally significant. I would be driving along, going about my life in the ordinary way, and break out in laughter at the ludicrous thought that I, who would be a very grown-up nineteen forever . . . I would be fifty years old.

Age had never mattered to me, except a mild crying spell at my thirtieth birthday lunch. I never thought about myself as a "middle-aged" woman, but fifty is bound to be somewhere near the middle. Along with the conceptual consciousness of aging was the very present physical reality of my body changing: gaining weight without eating more, crepeing skin, hot flashes, tiredness, heart palpitations, and so on. I also was finding myself crying often and deeply about very small things. This must be menopause, I thought.

What is the meaning of all of this change? What do the headaches, depressions, fears, and emptiness of women at this age suggest? What is life asking of us?

Little is actually written about women and menopause. Only recently have women lived long enough to tell about it. At the turn of the century the life expectancy in women was fifty, and menopause occurred in the mid-to-late forties. Now 20 percent of the female population in the United States is over fifty-five, and the life expectancy is seventy-six.[1] Most of us will live twenty-five or more years after menopause.

A woman's life might well be divided into three stages: birth to menarche, menarche to menopause, and menopause to death. Where and when I grew up, there was an equal amount of secrecy and fear around menopause as around the beginning of menstruation. A woman is the passive recipient of these bodily rites of initiation. She does not choose if or when; the events choose her in their own time. Attitudes toward menstruation range from "it's nothing, you are no different, go on about your life as if there were no change," to "it's all over, the curse is upon you." These attitudes toward the menarche reflect basic attitudes toward being a woman and toward the Feminine itself, with its ever-changing reality.

Menstruation was a secret shared by the primordial woman and the serpent. Ancient belief systems held that the onset of menses was caused by copulation with a supernatural snake. The holy "blood of life" was feminine and real in matriarchal cultures. Blood, especially menstrual blood, has always held great power. It has been regarded with both dread and numinosity; it was thought to have the power to kill and the power to create new life. Men who so much as looked upon a menstruating woman could die. In some cultures human life was thought to have been created out of a mixture of menstrual blood and dirt. Religious rites were often presided over by old women, due to the ancient belief that post-menopausal women were the wisest mortals because they permanently retained their "wise blood."[2]

Recently women have begun to talk to each other about their personal experiences and to look for guiding images from antiquity, when women had community rituals to help them through life's changes. Rites of passage are needed to integrate the personal and the transpersonal, to make social our individual crises, and to find validation for our experience. Mircea Eliade expresses the need for rituals: "Every human life is made up of a series of ordeals, of deaths and of resurrections. Initiation lies at the core of any genuine human life."[3] Jung said, "The second half of life must have a significance of its own and cannot be merely a pitiful appendage."[4] He saw middle age as a time to work inwardly and symbolically.

An ancient ritual for midlife women is suggested by the frescoes on the walls of the Villa Dei Mysterii near Pompeii. The villa was excavated about seventy-five years ago and is about a mile north of the ruins of the city of Pompeii, just past the cemetery. Remarkably intact, it houses intriguing and artistically beautiful frescoes. It is obviously not a family home but a group house. Not much is known about what actually happened there. I imagine that those pictures are about a ritual for proper Roman women seeking renewal and initiation into the last third of their lives. I will take mythopoetical license . . . a weaving of history and my imagination . . . in telling what I imagine to have happened there.

The villa was maintained by a group of women who belonged to an Orphic cult serving Dionysus. He is the Greek god of ecstasy, of surrendering to the spirit in Nature with wine and song. He is also the god of death and the underworld. According to Orphic tradition, he was able to take on the form of several animals (snake, deer, kid, and bull) when he was pursued. Even so, he was torn apart and eaten by the Titans, who were then burned to ashes by great Zeus. It is from these ashes that human life was formed, imbued with the guilt of the Titans and the fullness of the life/death of Dionysus.

This was a secret society, and the villa was as self-contained as possible, with its own wells and gardens, pastures for cows and goats, vineyards, wine storage vaults, ovens for baking bread, and many individual rooms. The intricately detailed friezes and designs throughout the house suggest the care and artistic awareness of the inhabitants. There is a large courtyard with a beautifully proportioned bath at its center and surrounded by inner and outer porticoes of fine-fluted columns. There are many small rooms with various mythological designs on the walls: griffins, winged and crowned dragons, ibis, quail, doves, all in pairs, interspersed with delicate renderings of Queen Nerfertiti and her lover Horus. A common design theme is an orderly, stylized Greek frieze at the top of the room topped by an organic and colorful watery design, perhaps suggesting the movement from geometric to organic order inherent in the rites held here. The main chamber is about twenty by thirty feet, with all four walls richly painted with frescoes that tell the story of what went on at the villa. The background of the paintings is a fine, deep rouge red; there are ten panels. The pictures titillate the imagination and please the eye.

A Roman woman knew that when her life in the community had dried up, when her blood no longer flowed, when her spirit had abandoned her, it was time to go to the villa. Knowledge of the villa and its mysterious healing was passed from woman to woman in careful secrecy. Participation in the rites of the retreat offered the promise of hope and renewal. But there was also the fear of what one might encounter there. There was the threat that one could lose everything . . . all the accomplishments, the financial security, the orderly world of the known—even one's mind.

On the appointed day, a woman would be welcomed to the villa by the women who lived there. She would arrive in all her finery—layer upon layer of rich fabric draped about her and covering her head, wearing proper shoes, well-coiffed hair, wedding band intact—having learned and performed well the way of life of accomplished wife, household manager, social dame, and mother. She would be appropriately dressed and appropriately mannered but with no sparkle in her eyes . . . tired, exhausted, dead in her tracks. To her left as she enters the main chamber she finds a portrait of a matronly woman, just like herself, reminding her that she is not alone: this is the way of woman.

The priestesses at the villa welcome her with a fine meal and wine. Then a young prepubescent boy, nude except for his sandals, reads the procedure for a stay at the villa in solemn voice, his woman guide at his side with a similar scroll in her hand. A beguiling pregnant woman then leads the initiate to a throne-like stool, where she is invited to disrobe. She is offered some sweet cakes to eat with her wine and then given a laurel twig to chew, deepening the intoxication begun by the wine and the caring setting. Another priestess leads her to a warm bath in the center of the house, where she gently massages her hands and feet with oil.

As the initiate falls more and more under the spell of the laurel twig, she is led to her own room, where figures of satyrs and maidens, griffins and winged snakes, grace the walls. She begins to hear music and can no longer tell whether she is asleep or awake. She sees old Silenus, the drunken teacher of Dionysus, beckoning her with music from his lyre. He is accompanied by goat-eared fauns dancing around him, one playing a wooden flute. She sees a female faun nursing a baby goat from her breast while a black goat stares straight at the initiate, reminding her that she is about to have a stark confrontation with nature. She awakes in horror, wanting to run back to safety but tempted to go deeper into the unknown. What has she done? What does it mean to be initiated into a cult of Dionysus?

She remembers: Dionysus is the god of boundaries . . . of crossing boundaries . . . he is the great Loosener . . . Dionysus was raised by nymphs on the Isle of Naxos, disguised by Ino as a girl, taught by Silenus the secrets of nature. He had been an initiate into the mysteries of the goddess Rhea. It was she who dressed him in fawn skin, dropped a band of vine leaves on his head, and sent him out to teach her intoxication. He is the god of wine and trails his rapture through the vineyards. He is known for his divine madness, his love of nature, his dissolving of boundaries. He has an ivy-twined staff topped with a pine cone. He is accompanied by maenads (frenzied women) and satyrs (part human, part goat).[5] Perhaps, she muses, these half-human creatures stay attached to Dionysus because they have not

been able to complete this initiation. They are stuck in these perverse forms
. . . stuck in the border region . . . women who cannot integrate their
madness and men who cannot integrate their goatness.

Dionysus often wears a panther skin, and there is wild dancing and
exciting music around him. Where is Dionysus?

The Roman woman has glimpsed the depths and the unknown world
of the unconscious where Dionysus rules. Does she turn and run back to
the life of light and order, or does she continue her descent? Her drugged,
heavy eyelids and her desire to know pull her farther under. She sees Silenus
laughing wickedly while he raises a silver bowl over which a faun holds a
mask of Dionysus for reflection. The faun must see his own face and the
mask reflected together in the bowl. Would she see her face with the god's
face? she wondered. Was the god coming? Was she dying?

Falling into deep sleep, she is (or dreams herself to be) Ariadne, the
bride of Dionysus, seated on a throne with the god languishing at her feet,
spent from lovemaking. Has Dionysus made love to her? Or has she dreamed
that? Ariadne was part human, part divine; her parents were born of the
union of a god and a human. She had the dark underworld character of
Persephone and the passionate capacity of Aphrodite, the goddess of love.
She fell in love with the hero Theseus on the Isle of Crete and helped him
kill the Minotaur in the labyrinth. She led Theseus out with a ball of thread.
But he deserted her on Naxos, where Ariadne either killed herself or was
killed by the goddess Artemis in a jealous rage. Dionysus came there to get
her. He gave her a crown of gold, a symbol of wholeness, and they were
united in a mystical marriage.

Has the Roman woman, like Ariadne, been abandoned by all her heroic,
civilized efforts and left to die? Is she wed to the wild god Dionysus, the
Bull-roarer? Filled with awe and enlivened, half-conscious, half-asleep, she
imagines herself so empowered. She dreams that she is crowned with a
smooth saffron-yellow cap and veiled in the same yellow. She kneels before
a large winnowing basket. With her left hand, as if by magic, she lifts high
the purple veil covering the basket, while her right hand brings up a huge,
erect penis from the basket. Enthralled at her newly found power, she is
stunned to see a grand, dark-winged female angel coming at her from the
sky with ferocious threat. "Stop!" the angel commands. She is awakened
from her dream state by the blows of a leather whip across her shoulders.

A kind woman holds her, wet with sweat and tears, while the even
kinder angel whips her out of the trance and back into reality. Comforted
and bathed, she brushes her glowing hair and smiles at herself as she puts
on her new gold earrings and bracelets. Crowned with a myrtle wreath,
she is given a new gossamer drape and finger cymbals and invited to join
the dance with the other initiates. She is given a mirror in which she sees
her flowing and brilliant self. Happy and wondering about her mysterious
experience, she prepares to go home, not forgetting that over her left shoulder she could just catch a glimpse of impish Cupid, smiling at her with his
bow at rest.

Did the Roman women have actual sex with young men masked as Dionysus at the villa? Was it a place to facilitate intercourse with the god himself? The mystery insists on each woman finding her own experience. The mystery keeps the drama alive and forces the experience back on the initiate.

In this ritual, there are three main threads of particular importance to menopausal women: going away alone, submission to being initiated by other women, and an encounter with impersonal phallic power, Dionysus and the phallus itself.

Going away alone. Women tend to be instinctively and culturally driven toward relationship. Often that instinctive eros force becomes unconscious entanglement, and a woman becomes so merged with the people in her life that she forgets herself and depends on others for her sense of self. Many women get their sense of identity from their husbands and children. Their own house and familiar surroundings invite too much of their native relatedness. "Going away" frees the woman to experience herself as an individual. The experience of the unknown that she finds in travel breaks her away from a solid sense of knowingness and appropriateness. She submits to the anxiety and excitement of a new place, and its demands awaken in her a sense of responding to what is, rather than her ordinary concerns about how things ought to be. This surrender to what is is the surrender to Dionysus.

Many women find that they cannot create anything more profound than a good meal at their home with its endless scream of things to be done. Being away stimulates the woman's creative thinking and a new way of seeing things, a sense that she is somebody in her own right. Disentangled from all the mergers in her life, she may find that, indeed, she knows who she is. She can hear herself. She just hadn't been able to hear her own voice in the midst of the clatter of all that Otherness.

Submitting to the care and initiation of other women. There has been a deep sense of distrust and devaluing of women and of the Feminine in us, inherited from our mothers and reexperienced in our lack of connectedness with them. Many of us have felt a natural guardedness with other women, self-protection against the devourer or cold rejector we imagine to be hiding in their offerings. However, in the past ten or fifteen years women have begun to trust each other. Women therapists, women friends, and women's groups have become the source of healing for individuals in times of crisis and/or change.

There is a risk and a reward in submitting to the care of other women. The energy is so powerful that it is often colored with erotic excitement, sometimes homoerotic fantasies and dreams. Being with other women stimulates a woman's awareness of her own body. The reward is that she can experience the relaxation and affirmation of being mirrored, being truly seen (if she is lucky) in a way that she did not get from her mother. There is also a freedom to explore and extend the boundaries of ideas and ways of behaving with one's own kind. Women can work together in a most effective way, in a kind of unconscious cooperation in which tasks are accomplished without any need to delineate responsibility. Women can play together joyfully. The dancing and singing and reveling in our bodies that belonged to us when we were girls can be recovered or discovered for the first time.

Contact with phallic power. After an exhilarating bout of writing imaginally, one woman dreamed: "I awaken in a strange bed with a huge, erect penis in my right hand. It is terrifyingly warm and big and glowing. I turn over and try to put it on my husband. It is ludicrous. In no way can I fit it on him. It is far too big." Often we try to "put it on our husbands" with great disappointment and great frustration. Husbands chafe under the weight of such a burdensome projection.

What to do with this snake, this pulsating creative power? The disembodied phallus is a form of Dionysus. In the frescoes at Villa Dei Mysterii, he appears as an erect phallus in a winnowing basket. (And in front of the villa at the souvenir stand, disembodied penises with wings were sold . . . lest one get too esoteric.) This woman was visited by a god . . . the god of spirit in nature, wild abandon, imagining, drunken, unknowable, uncontrollable, unpredictable, dismembering, celebrating. How is a woman to handle such energies when they appear in her hand?

There are no answers; each woman must find her own way. But the appearance of that phallic power, which cannot be projected onto the men in her life, enlivens her and requires her attention. To have the phallus in her right hand means that perhaps the very hand with which she was writing attracts that energy in this woman. She is free to be fully woman and has the gift of penetrating, creative energy in her hand.

The ancient rituals and our personal dreams instruct us about how to integrate spontaneous images in such a way that our lives become enriched and enlivened. The beginning of menopause is one of those very powerful in-between spaces in a lifetime: the woman is not a young woman anymore, nor is she one of the old wise ones. She is truly middle-aged. Such in-between spaces have great power; senses are heightened, emotions intensified, experiences peaked, both positively and negatively. Everything seems in stark relief.

In his book about midlife, Murray Stein speaks about the quality of this space as "liminality." Liminal space is the space in-between. The death of what has been and the preparation for what will be coexist. There is a sensation of floating, of being neither here nor there. There is an internal experience of loss. Dreams and waking life are often not so differentiated. There is an altered sense of time. "At midlife through the experience of liminality, the soul is freed from self-delusion and awakens to a level that endures beyond the ego's defeat and death."[6]

Stein points out that this is a time for a return of the repressed. The repressed shadow creeps out around the corners of our existence: "nice" girls acting out in sexual frenzy, irritation at our mates with whom we have too closely identified, bizarre spending patterns for frugal people, kleptomania in well-behaved middle-aged women who have given away too much. The neglected gods demand our attention.

Menopause invites our importune ghosts to come forward. It demands a more fundamental confrontation with our dark side. It is a period for coming to terms with the shadow. It is a neutral zone in which a woman might acknowledge the distance between her ideals and what is. She can acknowledge what in her is incomplete, fearful, and wounded. It is a time to weep the tears that are still unshed: the tears for what was, the tears for what might have been, and the tears for what will not be.

An encounter with Dionysus can break one out of the old structures of the appropriate and the expected. One woman dreamed that she was in a very large, old, fine building and the walls began to shake and the thing crumbled around her, almost trapping her between some fallen, giant, heavy, wooden beams. She saw a small opening in the rubble and crawled through to bright light on the other side. She felt mysteriously "saved" and grateful to be able to begin again in a new place.

Such dreams point toward the renewal that is possible through sacrifice, even when forced. The loss or the sacrifice removes a woman from the worn-out structures in her life: the rules, the "shoulds," the necessities, the established order. Through Dionysus, we learn to trust Nature. Dionysus brings a new kind of order: order by nature replaces the old order by principles. We are able to approach each situation with wonder, as if for the first time. We can encounter others with curiosity, noticing their part in the drama of reality, without preconceived notions of what they ought to be doing or not doing. At such times we can rest in a kind of quiet acceptance of what is, of the actual, no longer focusing on the potential. Such a way of life is rather anonymous, unstoried, plotless perhaps. It is not about accomplishment and visible success. It focuses on the holiness of the mundane and familiar. Meaning and magic are found in the small, ordinary events of the day. It can teach us to see the numinous in the everyday and the trivial.

And the paradox appears: While entertaining dreams and fantasies authored by the Great Loosener and Binder, Dionysus, who can lead us into ecstatic wildness, we find contentment and comfort in our own lives.

PART 5

. . . .

REAWAKENING THE DIVINE FEMININE: HEALING OUR RELATIONSHIPS WITH THE GODDESS ARCHETYPES

Do not be ignorant of me.
For I am the first and the last.
I am the honored one and the scorned one.
I am the whore and the holy one.
I am the wife and the virgin.
I am the mother and the daughter.
I am the members of my mother.
I am the barren and many are her sons.
I am she whose wedding is great
    and I have not taken a husband.
I am the silence that is incomprehensible
    and the idea whose remembrance is
      frequent.
I am the voice whose wound is manifold
    and the word whose appearance is
      multiple.
I am the utterance of my name.
I am shame and boldness.
I am shameless; I am ashamed.
I am strength and I am fear.
I am war and peace.
Give heed to me.
I am the one who is disgraced and the
    great one.

UNKNOWN AUTHOR

Growing up as young girls, we are told by adults that we were made in the image of God. Yet, in our newly forming imaginations, the face of God looks more like a smiling, kind, white-haired grandpa or a stern, finger-wagging old patriarch than the face we see in the mirror. As a result, God is something Other, outside of ourselves—and boys and men have a closer link to Him than we do.

However, at a mythological level, we *are* truly made in the image and likeness of our gods. That is, we are what we imagine. The form we give to our divine ancestors in our collective and personal imaginations is the form we aspire to become. If we imagine Him as perfect and all-powerful, we hold these qualities as ideal. If we imagine Her as bountiful and all-giving, *these* qualities become exalted.

For millennia, the many faces of the divine previously known to cultures the world over have been reduced to a one-dimensional snapshot. For women, this singular God with male gender has been a terrible loss; our imaginations have been impoverished, our abilities to identify with the divine diminished. Ultimately, life under the rule of "God the Father" came to mean that much which had been valued in the female experience during an earlier time—such as sexuality, menstruation, birth, mothering, menopause, aging, ritual, and female power—lost its meaning and its sacred authority.

In her essay "Why Women Need the Goddess," published in the book *Womanspirit Rising*, Carol P. Christ points out that symbols, including symbols of the divine, have both psychological and political effects because they create those inner attitudes and feelings that lead people to accept social and political arrangements that correspond to the symbol system. She says: "Religions centered on the worship of a male God create moods and motivations that keep women in a state of psychological dependence on men and male authority, while at the same time legitimating the *political* and *social* authority of fathers and sons in the institutions of society."

Ultimately, "female power" becomes an oxymoron; a woman can identify with God only by denying her own identity. That means, to be a woman is not to participate in the Divine.

Just as the male spiritual or religious hierarchy supports the interests of men in a patriarchal society, Goddess symbolism supports the interests and imaginations of women. Whether we conceive of the Goddess as a single transcendent figure, or we imagine many Goddesses within us as metaphors for the energies of life, She brings us a vision of Woman that stands outside the walls of the patriarchy. And She affirms our bodies, minds, hearts, powers, and sisterhood.

To imagine the Divine Feminine is to meet a deeply felt need. It is also to turn our priorities topsy-turvy. Christine Downing, in her book *The Goddess*, explains it this way:

> To be fed only male images of the divine is to be badly malnourished. We are starved for images which recognize the sacredness of the Feminine and the complexity, richness, and nurturing power of female energy. . . . We seek images that affirm that the love women receive from women, from mother, sister, daughter, lover, friend, reaches as deep and is as trustworthy, necessary, and sustaining as is the love symbolized by father, brother, son, or husband. We long for images which name as authentically feminine courage, creativity, loyalty, self-confidence, resilience, steadfastness, capacity for clear insight, inclination for solitude, and the intensity for passion.

For me, as a father's daughter and an Athena-type woman, it has been painfully difficult to open this gateway to the Conscious Feminine. For a long time, I did not feel the need for the Goddesses in my life; it seemed to me regressive to call upon such ancient images from a time before women could have had much opportunity for personal development. Later, when I understood their archetypal value, I did not know how to let them in without feeling as if the ground I stood on was moving.

Eventually, I began to perceive the Goddesses as impersonal patterns of feeling and behavior that can reveal hidden dynamics both within and between people. For instance, I could see a Goddess at work if I felt abused, like a victim in relation to a man. She would lift me out of the emotional turmoil, the anger and blame, by showing me the larger pattern of behavior, thus freeing me from too personal a perspective.

This is one of the gifts of consciousness from the Goddesses. They do not represent a secret formula by which we can become an ideal Hera/wife, Aphrodite/lover, or Athena/independent woman. They should not remain fixed, archaic images to be acted out like theatrical roles. Rather, they represent dynamic potentials with a capacity to ignite our imaginations and free us from gender prisons.

Today's Goddesses, as mirrors of the Conscious Feminine, have come primarily from two sources: pre-patriarchal cultures, such as those described earlier by Riane Eisler and in this section by Sylvia Brinton Perera; and the Greek culture, which, as a patriarchy, has more clearly differentiated Goddess archetypes, as described here by Jean Shinoda Bolen (and by Robert Stein in Part 1). The Western religious tradition, especially in its esoteric forms, also has feminine faces of God that have been lost to us. Sophia, retrieved here by June Singer, is the goddess of wisdom from the Gnostic tradition.

With this section on the Divine Feminine, we come full circle back to Part 1, the loss and abandonment of the Feminine in human history. What was lost now has been found, and its power to heal has turned out to be tremendous. The Goddess can bring sustenance to the transpersonal realm, to a spiritual life devoid of female models. And She can help to re-mother us, healing us from the wounds and limitations of our personal mothers.

Finally, our reclaiming of the lost Feminine archetype is a boon to Her. Without us, She is lost in the corridors of time. Alive in our imaginations, She returns home.

Eminent Greek novelist Nikos Kazantzakis wrote a small, elegant book called *The Saviors of God.* I quote him:

> It is not God who will save us—it is we who will save God, by battling, by creating, and by transmuting matter into spirit.
>
> But all our struggle may go lost. If we tire, if we grow faint of spirit, if we fall into panic, then the entire Universe becomes imperiled.
>
> Life is a crusade in the service of God. Whether we wished to or not, we set out as crusaders to free that God buried in matter and in our souls.

17 · THE GIFTS
FROM
RECLAIMING
GODDESS
HISTORY

· · · · · · ·

MERLIN STONE

Merlin Stone has made a major contribution to the developing field of women's spirituality. In When God Was a Woman, *Stone revealed a crucial link between women's social status and widespread reverence for the deity as female. In* Ancient Mirrors of Womanhood: A Treasury of Goddess and Heroine Lore, *she unearthed a mother lode of ancient feminine images that had been buried in pre-patriarchal cultures. (The Goddess references here can be found in that book.)*

Her findings reveal that these early Goddesses had many attributes that we do not think of today as feminine; therefore, our current categories of description are severely limited. It may be, she implies, that all of the powerful characteristics inherently belong to both genders. For example, we cannot correctly state that women are healers and men are violators; nor can we say the opposite, for women have a capacity to destroy and men to nurture.

Therefore, developing the Conscious Feminine, for Stone, means releasing our preconceived notions about containing the Feminine in certain spheres of influence (e.g., nurturing, passivity, receptivity) and denying it in others (assertiveness, creativity, daringness). To reevaluate these very basic definitions and to allow them to change our lives is to heal the wound of the patriarchy.

Unlike most of the other contributors to this book, Stone's field is not psychology. She is more concerned with the historical reality of these figures and their relevance as models for women today, as well as how patriarchal religions have affected women's status. In contrast to the archetypal psychologists, she explicitly links the Feminine to females, the Masculine to men; yet her research truly deepens and enriches the meaning of what is feminine.

Merlin Stone is the author of When God Was a Woman *and* Ancient Mirrors of Womanhood: A Treasury of Goddess and Heroine Lore from Around the World. *She has spent many years of research at numerous museums and goddess sites in the Near and Middle East and is currently at work on a play about the Sibyl of Delphi with Olympia Dukakis.*

Since the start of the women's movement in the late 1960s, the subject of what is truly natural and specific to the female gender has been the focus of intense discussion and study. Whatever conclusions various researchers and writers have drawn, the one common effect of our exploration is that we have become more conscious of the questions to ask—as well as of the problems involved in determining answers.

One of the greatest problems encountered in consideration of this subject is the vast diversity and complexity of the personalities of the billions of women all over the world, past and present. Can we make statements about what is intrinsically feminine that correlate with all women, or at least nearly all? Another major problem is that it is close to impossible to separate natural behavior from social conditioning. How do we extricate what is truly inherent in the female gender from the multiple layers of patterning absorbed from a society?

The word *feminine* is derived from the Latin *femina*, meaning woman; according to most dictionaries, its primary definition is "characteristic of women." Over the last few centuries the word *feminine* became identified with an assemblage of very specific attributes and diverse subtle implications, often reflecting nineteenth-century European customs, somewhat Victorian ideals, middle- or upper-class behavior, and male perceptions of females. In turn, an assumption that these attributes and implications were universally true led to the development of this assemblage into an abstracted principle, "the Feminine." The acceptance of this abstract principle as an established truth further led to theories that were constructed upon it. Divorced from its primary meaning, the Feminine no longer referred only to the female gender, but could supposedly be found in males as well.

It is time to observe the ethnocentricity and chronocentricity in many of the current ideas about what is feminine. This must be done before the Feminine can be put forth as a sound and reliable principle, and certainly before theories can be built upon this principle. Metaphorically, we may have been formulating our view of the world by extrapolating only from what we know of our own neighborhood. It is time to travel, geographically and chronologically.

One area that is of immense value and interest in a search for the intrinsic Feminine is the massive body of historical evidence about Goddess worship in ancient cultures, as well as in later cultures in which Goddess worship existed or still exists. By becoming familiar with the multitude and diversity of Goddess figures throughout history and prehistory and their accompanying legends, rituals, and belief systems, we discover perceptions of the Feminine that would not otherwise be available to us.

I always had been extremely interested in studying the religious beliefs of ancient civilizations throughout the twenty years of my education and teaching of art history. I had read a multitude of prayers, epic legends, and other ancient texts about various Goddess figures and the sites where they were worshipped. But it was only at the dawning of the women's movement that I decided to devote myself to the even more intensive research on Goddess history that resulted in my writing *When God Was a Woman*. At the time (1969) when I decided to gather my research into a book, the historical evidence of Goddess worship had been ignored in general education and, except for a smattering of Homer and Greek "mythology," this was an unfamiliar, often unknown, subject to most people in our society. But as we were beginning to be more conscious of our status as women, and as I realized how little was known about ancient Goddess reverence, I felt it was vital for women to know more about Goddess history, and how the suppression of Goddess reverence had affected us.

Now, fourteen years after its publication in 1976, I have had the joy not only of contributing to the very beginnings of Goddess reclamation and to the women's spirituality movement but also of observing and participating in the rapid and widespread expansion of this knowledge. Goddess history is finally making inroads into the general culture. It is this history that provides us with images of the Feminine that cut across many temporal and spatial boundary lines.

Upon learning about Goddess images, many contemporary women began to use this knowledge in a rich variety of ways. They have been incorporating various Goddess figures into the visual arts, literature, music, dance, drama, film, ecology, history, women's studies, ethnic studies, psychology, sociology, philosophy, theology, and other areas of study and creative expression. This ongoing process of gradually developing a comprehensive body of culture that contains a knowledge of Goddess history continually raises our consciousness of the Feminine, even as it continually revalues and redefines it.

As we consider the Feminine here, a knowledge of Goddess figures from diverse periods and cultures will provide us with two primary areas of exploration. First we will look at traits and belief systems associated with Goddess figures that our society generally identifies with the Feminine. Although some of these characteristics and belief systems have been devalued or trivialized in contemporary society, discovering them to be attributes of ancient female divinities has encouraged us to reevaluate them. This in turn has led to a conscious consideration of our attitudes about these characteristics and belief systems as they may exist within ourselves.

Secondly, we will discover that some characteristics of Goddess figures differ quite markedly from the usual views of the Feminine today. As these traits emerge in the visually or verbally described natures of many specific Goddess figures, they challenge some of our most basic ideas about the nature of the Feminine and lead us into deeper considerations of what we define as feminine. They encourage us to become aware of the wide and often unacknowledged diversity of aspects of the quintessential female, the Goddess, ranging from the explosive Hawaiian Pele to the Egyptian goddess of architecture, Seshat, to the compassionate Chinese Kuan Yin—and eventually to the marvelous diversity of ourselves. Most important, our discovery of Goddess attributes that may not have been previously defined as feminine leads us to the liberating realization that consciousness often includes the element of choice. Recognizing a characteristic that is generally designated as masculine today, but was an attribute of a Goddess several millennia ago, helps us to understand that this characteristic *may not be gender specific at all*.

In this exploration some readers may find that they hold certain intellectual or religious preconceptions about Goddess reverence. One major factor influencing the perception of Goddess figures is that of viewing them as mythology. Regarding the historical accounts of Goddess figures as mythology tends to lessen our comprehension of the degree of sanctity and social importance they possessed within their own cultures. As we examine the specific traits and characteristics of Goddess figures, it is vital to be conscious of the reality that what is so often referred to as mythology is the collection of images, symbols, and narratives from historically recorded religions, respected and revered by large numbers of people, much as the images and symbols of mainstream religions are respected and revered by many people today. Realizing that certain characteristics were known to be associated with a female deity by large populations of women and men for thousands of years, as contrasted with thinking of Goddess images tucked away in the depths of the human psyche, conveys a different understanding of how these figures affected popular perceptions. As we explore the Conscious Feminine, whether or not the reader wishes to consider these figures as archetypes of the human psyche, please be aware of the actual historicity of the religious worship of each of the Goddess images and the widespread public knowledge of them when and where they were worshipped.

One familiar refrain we hear in any discussion of the Feminine is about the trait of nurturing. "The hand that rocks the cradle" has been romanticized and praised, while at the same time it has been belittled and taken for granted. We see the characteristic of nurturing depicted in the images of Goddess figures such as Anath in Ugarit and Isis in Egypt and Rome, nursing one or even two children. The familiar portrayal of the Goddess offering her breasts also conveys the idea of nurture. The outspread wings of Isis protecting Osiris, and the wings of the Goddess Nut sheltering and comforting those who have died, also may be seen as images of protective nurturing, as are the breasts and wings in accounts of Simurgh in ancient Iran. The African Goddess Songi is said to have taught the Bantu women who revered Her to file notches in their teeth to signify that they would be the recipients of Her abundance and protection. The Chinese Goddess Kuan Yin is still regarded as the embodiment of nurturing mercy and compassion; numerous Chinese writings tell of people calling upon Her when they were in trouble. Akkadian prayers to Ishtar read: "You care for the oppressed and mistreated, every day offering them your help . . ." and "It is Ishtar who changes destiny, making what is bad become good . . . at Her left side is goodness, from Her sides emanate life and well-being."

Women have nearly always been viewed as the nurturing gender, surely as the result of being able to give birth, to nurse, and to take most or all of the responsibility for child care. But today the value of the trait of nurturing is seen from divergent points of view. On one hand, we may regard the characteristic as beautiful and desirable, but we can also see that devoting one's life to nurturing others can place a woman's own needs and wishes in a secondary position. All too often this desire to be nurturing has led women to deny themselves any right to a fulfilling or satisfying life, especially if they believe that trying to achieve their own goals might in any way decrease their nurturing of those around them.

As we consider nurturing, we begin to see it as a trait that is in need of greater respect and acknowledgment. In addition, it would better serve society to encourage this trait in males as well as females. Perhaps most important is the growing consciousness that we can—perhaps must—remember to nurture ourselves, taking our lead from the accounts of such Goddess figures as Macha of Ireland, Lia of Australia, and Skadi of Scandinavia, all of whom acted assertively to take care of themselves in difficult situations.

Many Goddess figures have been described as divinities of healing which may be seen as a form of nurturing. The Egyptian Isis was known as the Divine Physician, as was the Sumerian Goddess Gula. The Mayan Moon Goddess Ix Chel, especially honored at Cozumel, was invoked along with recipes of herbal remedies for the ill, for those in labor, and for those wanting to become pregnant. The Celtic Goddess Brigit was known as a miraculous healer of vision, impotence, and leprosy through the water of Her sacred wells or by the mere touch of Her hand. Although healing has been associated with women for millennia, recent centuries relegated female healers to a second-class status. Only very recently have we been able to break through the idea that all doctors are male and all nurses are female. In light of our knowledge of Goddess history, this attitude requires a much more careful consideration of contemporary society's gender stereotyping of the healing professions.

We often hear it said that women have a better understanding of the cycles of life because of our menstrual cycles, especially because those cycles are temporally related to the cycles of the moon. The ethnological evidence of Changing Woman shows this sacred female figure of the Navajos to be the very embodiment of the cycles of life. The Sun Goddess Akewa from the Toba people of Argentina is portrayed as young and lively when the days are short, old and walking with a cane when the days are long, and then young again as the days grow shorter—conveying the sense of an ever-repeating cycle. Narratives about the Greek Goddess of agriculture, Demeter, and Her daughter, Kore/Persephone, were annually enacted within the mysteries of Eleusis. These rituals commemorated the cycles of the seasons as well as the round of life and death, as each year Kore descended into the underworld of Hades for several months and the grieving mother, Demeter, held back the growth of the crops until Kore returned. Much earlier archaeological evidence from Sumer and Egypt indicates there were sowing and harvesting rituals associated with the Goddess revered as the one who first gave the gift of agriculture, such as the Sumerian Ninlil and the Egyptian Isis. In Mexico, yearly planting and harvesting rituals were celebrated for the Corn Goddess Chicomecoatl. Participation in these agricultural Goddess rituals experientially provided people with a sense of the continuous cycles of seasonal change.

The perception of growth and life as cyclical patterns encompasses aging and death as part of the natural cycles. It affords a view that is quite different from our society's discomfort with these realities. The honoring of older women as "wise old crones" in many women's spirituality groups today and performing special rituals for women at menopause have been a direct outgrowth of this renewed celebration of life cycle, just as many of these groups have been enacting celebratory rituals at the time of the new moon, the full moon, and the solstices and equinoxes of the sun.

One of the most interesting views of the Feminine is the idea that women are more closely related to nature in general. The title Mother Nature suggests that God (as male) is on high, while Mother Nature is here on the ground. Unfortunately, this connection has all too often led to regarding women as exploitable, as nature is regarded as exploitable—a connection first pointed out and described brilliantly by Susan Griffin in *Women and Nature* (1978).

The symbols associated with various Goddess figures do suggest a deep connection to various aspects of nature, as does the symbolism associated with certain male deities such as Pan. The Finnish Goddess Mielikki, known as Mistress of the Forest, was portrayed as the very spirit of the woods, her "clothing" changing with the seasons. Upon studying the accounts of the animal transformation and shape-shifting capabilities of the Welsh Goddess figures Rhiannon and Cerridwen and the Irish Morrigan, we can see how various animals would be viewed as possible embodiments of the Goddess. This is also noticeable in ancient Egypt, where we find worship of the Goddess Sekhmet as a lioness, the Goddess Hathor as a heifer, and the Goddess Bastet as a cat. Peruvians revered the Goddess Mamacocha as a great whale. In Greece, Demeter was at times described as a horse, while Artemis was regarded as the protector of the animals of the woods in which she lived.

To the Greeks, dryads were female spirits who lived within trees, wielding axes to protect them; naiads were female spirits who lived in the fresh waters; and nereids were female spirits who lived in the salty seas. Such beliefs reveal an inherent sense of sanctity about these aspects of nature. In Sumer, the symbol for the ocean was the pre-cuneiform symbol for the Goddess Nammu, who was elsewhere described as "the mother who gave birth to heaven and earth." The Canaanite Goddess Asherah was known as Lady of the Sea, while the Goddess Yemaya (Iamanja), originally of Yoruban origin, is still regarded as the ocean in Central and South American ritual. The Celts revered the Danube River as the essence of the Goddess Danu and the Seine as the Goddess Sequana. The Indian Goddess Parvati was identified as a specific mountain in the Himalayas, while the Polynesian Goddess figures of Pele and Mahuea were linked to volcanic mountains. Throughout the Mediterranean, serpents and trees were closely associated with ancient Goddess worship. The Greek Goddess Gaia was revered as the entire Earth.

Recovering information about Goddess reverence provides us with evidence that people in other times viewed the sacred as existing within all life. This concept is known as *immanence*. It offers us a very different view of existence and reality than the concept of *transcendence*, the belief that a deity is above us—i.e., up in heaven. Yet, most mainstream religions today still regard divinity as transcendent.

The image of a transcendent deity appears to be closely connected to societies that developed structured systems of hierarchy, accepting the idea of an invisible, omnipotent potentate who moves everything and everyone around like pawns on a chessboard. The concept of immanence reveals an entirely different view of the world. Regarding both genders, other races, other species, plant life, even rivers and oceans as sacred creates quite different attitudes and feelings about life. When spiritual beliefs lead us to the perception of all life on earth as sacred, pollution of the environment is viewed not only as antisocial or illegal but also as blasphemy. A knowledge of Goddess history not only gives us a more positive sense of ourselves as women but also offers a personally experienced comprehension of ecology with a view of the natural environment as the manifestation of the divine.

The idea of immanence has been embraced and experienced by many (perhaps most) of the women reclaiming Goddess reverence today, while Gaia is now being popularized in theories concerning the planet as a living entity in and of itself (or Herself). As a result, the name Mother Nature takes on a much greater depth of meaning.

Another trait closely associated with the Feminine is that of intuition, which has inspired both admiring awe and negative criticism. Whatever intuition actually is—perhaps something as simple as really paying attention to all that is going on around us—evidence of Goddess shrines reveals a special faith in women as oracular priestesses, those who "knew" the future. Throughout the Near and Middle East, many Goddess shrines and temples were widely respected as oracular sites. Two of the titles of the Goddess Ishtar were the Prophetess of Kua and the Lady of Vision, while Akkadian tablets reveal the names of several of the priestess/prophetesses who heard and announced messages from Ishtar: Sinkisha Amur, Belit Abi Sha, and Ishtar Bel Daini, among others. One of the most famous shrines of oracular divination was that of the Greek Delphi, which was originally an oracle of Gaia. The Pythia priestess who gave the oracles at Delphi was regarded as hearing the voice of Gaia, until the time when the shrine was changed into a temple of Apollo. Even when the wisdom was said to be received from Apollo, it was heard and spoken by a woman. An oracular shrine on the Delta of Egypt in Buto was originally a place of worship of the Cobra Goddess Ua Zit, whose symbol appeared as the cobra on the headdresses of Egyptian deities and royalty. The positioning of the Egyptian cobra in the location of the Third Eye—the eye of spiritual wisdom as it has been known in various cultures—may reveal a connection between Ua Zit and the concept of the Kundalini serpent at the sixth chakra of Indian yoga. The shrine at Buto was later known as an oracle of the Greek Goddess Lato, whose generally unrecognized importance may be revealed in the fact that she was regarded as the mother of the moon (Artemis) and the sun (Apollo).

There has been a growing tendency among women interested in women's spirituality to trust intuition as a viable means of access to information. The advantages of this may be challenged by those who prefer the results of empirical studies, yet the revival of honoring intuition has encouraged many women to develop a greater trust in their own judgment and opinions. And, as I mentioned previously, intuitive knowing may well be the result of being able to recognize and register (consciously or subconsciously) many forms of information that are generally ignored.

The Feminine also has been described as dark and mysterious. Association of caves with wombs is almost universal. But rather than regarding this cavelike darkness as possessing birth-giving powers, many writings of the last few centuries have associated symbolism of the dark and mysterious with fear and death. These interpretations may well be the result of a male view of women's sexuality, or even reveal white attitudes toward darker people. With a renewed honoring of the dark Goddess figures such as the Indian Kali, the Anatolian/Greek Hecate, the Greek Nikta (Night), the Black Madonnas of Europe and Central and South America, and the Colchian priestess of Hecate, Medea, many women have been redefining this mysterious darkness not only as comfortable and positive but as being filled with female power and strength. This honoring of the dark and mysterious also includes the ancient evidence of sacred black stones that were symbolic of the worship of Kybele in Anatolia and Rome, Astarte in Canaan, and the Goddess of the Amazons in Colchis. In pre-Islamic periods the famous black stone of the Ka'aba was identified with the Arabic Goddess Al Uzza in Mecca. According to texts from Byblos, the black stone associated with Astarte held the souls of all people and whispered the future to those who were capable of hearing it. Drawing upon the evidence of these dark Goddess figures and symbols, women do not reject the dark and mysterious as aspects of the Feminine but redefine attitudes about them, to the point of regarding them as a source of female power.

Some of the most noticeable information found in Goddess research reveals the sanctity of the physical body and bodily processes of the Goddess. In Akkadian Babylon, a prayer to Ishtar tells us that on the twenty-eighth day in the month of Tammuz, a vulva of lapis lazuli was placed upon the altar of Ishtar's temple. Thousands of small sacred Goddess statues from the ancient Near and Middle East show a nude woman, Her hands under Her breasts as if offering Her sacred milk to worshippers. The menstrual blood of the Indian Goddess Shakti at Kamrupa was known as kula nectar and considered to be a sacred drink at rituals enacted at the time of the dark of the moon. Far across the waters, rituals of the Cuna Indians in Panama, who revered the Goddess Mu Olokukurtilisop, Great Blue Butterfly Lady, included a passage rite for young women as they reached their menarche. In this ritual, as the young woman was given her secret name and welcomed into the society of adult women, she was painted with the red juice of the sacred saptur tree, which was considered to be the menstrual blood of the Goddess.

Recovering the right to define our own bodies may be the first and most basic step in the development of a consciousness of what "feminine" truly is. Because "feminine" means characteristic of the female, there is certainly nothing more feminine, more specifically female, than the female body. Yet today's attitudes toward women's bodies and bodily processes have most often been defined and stereotyped from a male point of view. This has caused many women to feel more "feminine" when they fit the stereotypes, and ashamed, embarrassed, and even less "feminine" when they do not. Those stereotypes of our physical selves as women are gradually being challenged by an ever-increasing familiarity with Goddess history, as well as a consciousness of what we can learn from it. Knowing about the visual and verbal imagery of the physical body and bodily processes of Goddess figures has freed many women to enjoy and honor their own bodies, just as they are. Without benefit of any written texts, simply the knowledge of the existence of the small statues of the very rounded bodies of the Paleolithic Venus of Willendorf, and the nearly 8,000-year-old enthroned Goddess from Catal Huyuk, has brought a new pride to women who were previously uncomfortable about their weight. With a knowledge of Goddess history we arrive at the perhaps surprising, yet obvious, conclusion that all female bodies and female bodily processes are central within the realm of the Feminine.

The aspects of Goddesses mentioned above are in alignment with the conventional definitions or perceptions of the Feminine. But we also find certain Goddess attributes that have not generally been regarded as Feminine. These raise important questions about definitions of the Feminine and what is inherently natural to us as women.

Assertiveness has most often been regarded as a masculine characteristic, while passivity is usually listed as feminine. Just how much have the gender assignments of these traits been the result of social conditioning? Goddess figures, such as the Irish Macha, who successfully defied and shamed the men of Ulster; the Scandinavian Skadi, who made a pair of skis from the headboard of Her marriage bed and used them to ski away from an incompatible marriage; and the Australian Lia, who led a group of abused women to a better life, provide us with images of woman as courageous and independent, acting in ways that are far from passive.

Just as certain ancient Goddess images challenge the idea of a natural female passivity, attitudes about sexual passivity as a feminine characteristic must also be reconsidered, in light of the evidence of the overt sexuality in the narratives and rituals of various Goddess figures. All the way from Anatolia to Greece, women enacted sacred sexual rituals within Goddess temples, such as those of Inanna of Sumer, Ishtar of Akkad, Astarte of Canaan, Anahita of Iran, and Aphrodite of Cyprus and Greece. One of the most ancient titles of these women was *qadishtu*, literally meaning "holy or sanctified women." Modern-day translation of *qadishtu* as "prostitutes" reveals an ethnocentric subjectivity that entirely distorts the actual role of these women as participants in religious rituals. Detailed descriptions in ancient texts of the *hieros gamos*, the sacred marriage, as it was enacted in Sumer and Akkad, also help us to understand that in the worship of ancient Goddess figures, women's assertive sexuality was regarded as sacred. Accounts from Sumer reveal Inanna as the initiator of sexual encounter with Damuzi, as accounts from Akkad tell of Ishtar's sexual invitations to Tammuz and to Gilgamesh. The Celtic Goddess Morrigan proposed a sexual liaison to Cu Chulainn.

The double bind that many contemporary women have experienced, that of wanting to be "a good girl" and simultaneously wanting to be sexually appealing, has been challenged by a knowledge of Goddess history. We know now that much of the double standard applied to women's sexuality, as compared to that of men, originated in later efforts to institute and maintain patrilineal descent patterns that required male control of women's reproductive capacities to insure unquestionable paternal identity for every child. Thus the freedom women achieve upon realizing from this evidence that an overt sexuality and spirituality are not in opposition, but in ancient and traditional coalition, has been another gift from learning about the Goddess.

Conventional views of feminine creativity are usually limited to ceramics, weaving, interior decor, floral arrangements, sewing, and cooking, the so-called lesser arts and crafts. It is most often the male artists who are thought of as the great painters and sculptors, the composers of great music, the authors of great literature. The efforts of the last twenty years have wrought some changes in this attitude. On one hand, there has been a deeper consideration and affirmation of the unique beauty and value of these so-called lesser arts and crafts. Simultaneously, we have retrieved and reevaluated the works of some extremely talented women artists and writers of the past. Yet the general attitude toward creativity, which includes being inventive, innovative, and daring, is that these are masculine attributes.

In light of this attitude toward creativity, one of the most interesting bodies of evidence forms around accounts of the Goddess as creator. Images of Her as the embodiment of ultimate creativity appear repeatedly in ancient texts, not only in the role of the mother of all life but also as the creator of the entire universe.

The African Goddess Mawu of Dahomey created the Earth and all of the astral bodies. The Sumerian Goddess Nammu "gave birth to heaven and earth." The Hopi Spider Woman spun a web in the great void and thus created everything in the universe (with the help of Her two daughters).

The Finnish Goddess Ilmatar moved about in a cosmic ocean and, by the mere touch of Her fingers and toes, created the Earth. Gaia, revered as the entire Earth, gave birth to heaven, Uranus. The Mexican Goddess Coatlicue, the Akkadian Goddess Mami Aruru, the Chinese Goddess Nu Kwa, and the Sumerian Goddess Ninmah (with the help of Nammu) were each credited with creating the first people. It is interesting to note that Nu Kwa and Mami Aruru were described not as giving birth to the first people but as forming them out of clay.

Perhaps because most of the above information is not widely known, innovative creativity is still generally regarded as masculine. An outgrowth of this view is a widespread belief that the initial developments of the earliest civilizations must have been by males. We find a duality in contemporary thought that associates the Feminine with nature, and the Masculine with culture and civilization. Yet just as men are actually as much a part of nature as women are, feminine creativity is as much a part of the development of culture as masculine creativity.

Agriculture was the initial development that allowed cultures to settle in one place long enough for other forms of culture to be invented and put to use. Most of the available evidence suggests that it was women who initially developed agriculture as an outgrowth of food-gathering activities. Goddess figures such as Ninlil, Nanshe, Isis, Demeter, Ceres, and Chicomecoatl, among others, were revered for having invented agriculture and for having given this gift to their people. Subsequent developments such as architecture, mathematics, writing, even legal systems were for the most part made possible by the discovery and use of agriculture, because a greater control of the food supply allowed previously nomadic food gatherers to stabilize in one area. Although agriculture has at times been associated with the Feminine, these other developments of early civilization have seldom been identified with female creativity.

However, attributes of various Goddess figures suggest that this attitude should be questioned. The Canaanite Asherah was revered as the tutelary deity of both carpentry and masonry, while the Egyptian Seshat (Sefchet) was called the Divine Architect and was shown using a cord rule to measure off lengths of ground as She prepared to build a temple. The earliest tutelary deities of written language occur in the areas that reveal the earliest developments of writing. These were the Sumerian Goddess Nidaba, the Indian Goddess Sarasvati, and the Egyptian Goddess Seshat. Several Goddess figures were described as the developers and presenters of the basic law of the tribe or community. Demeter, Isis, Nidaba, and the Goddess Ala, who was revered among the Ibo people of Nigeria, were each celebrated as the one who created the laws that civilized their people. The Egyptian Goddess Maat and the Greek Goddess Themis were both portrayed holding the scales of justice and described as judges of the law. These cultural attributes of Goddess figures suggest that the duality of feminine/nature versus masculine/culture needs to be examined much more carefully.

Although the idea of intuiting or divining the future has been associated with the Feminine, the capacity to affect or create the future has not. Planning the future and blazing new trails are generally viewed as masculine pursuits. Yet the ability to create the future emerges in the symbolism of several Goddess figures. The Akkadian Ishtar and the Sumerian Inanna were each described as the one who decreed destiny. The Scandinavian Norns and the Greek Fates were each seen as groups of three sisters who had control of destiny. Seven Hathors were said to assemble at the birth of a child to decree its future. The Scandinavian Goddess Frigga was portrayed as sitting at Her wheel and loom, spinning and weaving the future. Although the acts of spinning and weaving may be in perfect alignment with usual views of the Feminine, what shall we make of ancient evidence that proffers the powerful suggestion that it was woman who was thought of as creator of the future?

Whether intelligence is a factor of creativity, or creativity a factor of intelligence, the attribute of intelligence is seldom associated with the Feminine. Yet the ability to use logic and to reach conclusions through reasoning and deduction appears as an attribute of Goddess figures in legends of Isis, Morrigan, Loy Yi Lung, Lia, and Seshat. But beyond the ability to think logically or possession of an intuitive intelligence that has been granted to the Feminine—albeit along with aspersions of quirkiness or unreliability— I would like to consider the intelligence associated with an enduring and consistent wisdom. Wisdom has for so long been claimed to be a masculine attribute that nearly all of our images of gurus, wise elders, even philosophers, have automatically been drawn as male. But various Goddess figures, such as the Greek Athena and Roman Minerva, were each known as the Goddess of Wisdom. Ishtar was called upon for Her counsel and wisdom. Although not presented as a Goddess, the divine Hebrew figure of Hokhmah was literally known as Wisdom. Most interesting is the Greek Goddess Metis, whom Hesiod called "the wisest of all." The story goes that Zeus swallowed Metis when She was pregnant, hoping to receive Her counsel from inside his belly; but the child Athena was then born from his head. This strange story may reveal the patriarchal effort to appropriate both wisdom and pregnancy and childbirth as male capabilities.

Wisdom is perhaps one of the most difficult traits for women, even today, to believe we might own. Ironically, it is generally associated with very young children or with great age. Images of old men as wise are familiar. Images of old women have been terribly distorted, probably to a great extent by the paranoia created during centuries of witch-hunts and witch-burnings. Until we can erase the false but ubiquitous images of "foolish old women" or "crazy old ladies" and completely grasp the possibility of a woman being truly wise, reclaiming wisdom as a feminine or non–gender-specific trait will be one of the most difficult obstacles in our drive toward wholeness.

But it is perhaps the tendency toward wholeness itself, the desire to gather together, to patch things up, to unify seemingly disparate factors, that manifests as some of the most interesting and powerful Goddess imagery and suggests itself as a major characteristic of the Feminine. This idea arises in various forms. It first occurred to me as I was collecting accounts of journeys as they appear in Goddess history. Each of the following major Goddess figures undertakes an important journey: Isis, the Tibetan Tara, the Hebrew Shekhina,[1] Nu Kwa, and Demeter. Unlike most journey narratives in spiritual literature, none of these journeys was undertaken to find an answer or to seek a source of wisdom. They were taken to gather something together.

Isis traveled throughout Egypt to gather the scattered body parts of her brother/consort Osiris, whom She reassembled. Tara travels in Her Boat of Salvation to rescue souls shipwrecked on the Ocean of Life and brings them back to safe shores. The Shekhina travels about the lands to gather up the Jewish souls in exile and helps to bring them home. Nu Kwa traveled throughout the world after a universal holocaust, repairing and restoring the shattered columns that hold up heaven; She then patched the torn heavens together again. Demeter searched far and wide for Her daughter Kore/Persephone, to reunite their family. Underlying each of these accounts is the motivation to restore what has been separated to unified wholeness. There is the theme and perception of an overall pattern, along with a consciousness of the specific parts that must be included.

Theologically, we may see this tendency toward wholeness in the evidence of the sanctity of the physical body and bodily processes of Goddesses. We may compare this evidence to the later concept of duality inherent in the religious schism of body and soul. The split between soul as sacred and body as secular, along with the judgment placed upon soul as being of greater sacred value than body, is a far different view of body/soul than the intrinsically unified imagery in the texts and artifacts of ancient Goddess worship.

A tendency toward wholeness as a trait of the Feminine may even be anatomically explained by recent research showing greater physical connections in women between the right and left hemispheres of the brain, through parts of the central corpus callosum.

As I gather together the various characteristics that seem to belong to the Feminine or that appear to be non–gender-specific, I must include a mention of the political event of the women's movement of the last twenty years. It has raised our consciousness of being female. Without it, I doubt that we would have reached this point of considering the birth of the Conscious Feminine.

Whatever our opinions about specific aspects of the Feminine, we are able to comprehend that the characteristics of Goddess figures, or of human women, are exactly that—characteristics. As I mentioned before, becoming conscious about something often includes the element of choice. Thus we may be able to accept, develop, or reject many characteristics as our individual differences motivate us. The freedom to choose, a familiar slogan among women, may eventually reveal a feminine nature that is more multifaceted than we have yet been able to imagine. At that point we may find that "the Feminine" has become synonymous with "the human."

Many of the women reclaiming the Goddess today join in circles to celebrate life. As we chant or sing or dance or meditate, there is often the intuitive feeling that it is actually the Goddess, with Her thousand names and guises, gathering us together—to help each of us understand the fullness and richness of who and what we truly are.

18 · ATHENA, ARTEMIS, APHRODITE, AND INITIATION INTO THE CONSCIOUS FEMININE

· · · · · · ·

JEAN SHINODA BOLEN

In her best-selling book Goddesses in Everywoman, *San Francisco Jungian analyst Jean Shinoda Bolen, M.D., introduced a wide audience to seven mythological patterns of the Feminine derived from the Greek goddesses. As feminism had revealed oppressive stereotypes in women's roles, Bolen and others revealed potentially oppressive archetypes lying hidden in women's psyches and secretly ruling our behaviors.*

If these patterns remain unconscious and we live out their destinies (such as Hera, who places greatest value on finding a husband and being married; or Athena, who values primarily the logical life of the mind), our lives become one-dimensional and lose the vast richness of psychological possibilities. Jungian psychologists refer to this as possession by an archetype.

However, Bolen proposes that we can gain consciousness through naming these archetypes and detecting them in ourselves, eventually learning to choose which to befriend and which to banish. The task of dancing the archetypes consciously in this way is not an easy one; it takes a vigilant awareness to be able to perceive the universal stream running through us and to contain and release it in such a way that it takes on a unique form. But this is a potent practice that can lead to the emergence of the Conscious Feminine.

Bolen elaborates this idea by pointing out that a dominant Goddess archetype may help determine which gateway to the Conscious Feminine will be open. Artemis women, for example, are drawn to feminism, while Athena types, who easily become successful as "fathers' daughters," typically feel no need to identify themselves as feminist and may require a deeper spiritual initiation.

In this piece, written for this volume, Bolen's personal reflection on the experience of childbirth as a time between realms, which mirrors our collective passage from one realm into another, speaks to that place in each of us that is always giving birth.

Jean Shinoda Bolen, M.D., is a psychiatrist, Jungian analyst, and clinical professor of psychiatry at the University of California Medical Center, San Francisco. She is a faculty member of the C. G. Jung Institute of San Francisco and is the author of Tao of Psychology; Goddesses in Everywoman; *and* Gods in Everyman. *She is involved in exploring and linking the archetypal and spiritual dimensions of the women's movement, nuclear disarmament, and concern for the Earth.*

As a Jungian analyst who looks at myths as shards of earlier psychological and historical times, I find that one particular myth speaks to me about what happened to feminine consciousness in the past and suggests a metaphor for what is happening now. This is the story of Metis, who was a pre-Olympian goddess of wisdom. She was the first consort of the sky god, Zeus. He tricked her into becoming small and swallowed her when she was pregnant with Athena. Only after Athena had grown to adulthood did she emerge from her father's head, and then with no knowledge that she had a mother at all.

Like Metis, the matriarchy and its values were historically swallowed by the patriarchy. Evidence shows us that Europe was inhabited for 25,000 years by peaceful, matrilinear, goddess-worshipping, agricultural, and artisan peoples who were defeated and absorbed by sky-god–worshipping warrior tribes. This finding emerged only recently, as documented by archaeologist Marija Gimbutas in *The Goddesses and Gods of Old Europe*, which was first published in 1972. It was clear, when I listened to Gimbutas speak about her life and work, that it took a self-determined woman with a specific interest that could be called feminist to pursue and prove the existence of a female-centered culture when it had been dismissed as fantasy by male scholars.

Also lost in history was the perspective of the early Gnostic Christians, who trusted individual gnosis, or intuitively experienced awareness of divinity, unmediated by a priest. Gnosticism was a Christianity that included a feminine divinity, Sophia or Feminine Wisdom. Our awareness of the beliefs held by early Gnostic Christians came through the discovery and translation of the Nag Hammadi scrolls found sealed in jars in the Sinai desert.

The significance of the feminine mode of perception and the presence of a feminine divinity might not have been treated as significant had the scrolls been found at an earlier time, before feminism. It seems synchronistic that they came to light when there were women theology scholars, such as Elaine Pagels, author of *Gnostic Gospels*, to understand them, as well as scientific means to preserve and translate them.

The women's movement enabled us to become conscious of what was formerly invisible: we became aware that we lived in a patriarchal culture and began to understand what this might mean to us personally and collectively. We could understand that feminine attributes were belittled: like Metis, women and feminine wisdom had been tricked into becoming small and had disappeared from view, swallowed so to speak by the patriarchy. The process through which we began to liberate ourselves from the psychological limitations and institutional oppression of patriarchal assumptions was appropriately called "consciousness raising." Ideas that had been voiced earlier in the century about women's equality and rights caught on, and a change in the status of women became an idea whose time had come.

As a result, the 1970s were considered the decade of the women's movement in the United States. Doors were opened to women to enter academic, business, and professional fields, where they could use their intellects, exercise power, and compete successfully with men. It was a liberation of the Athena archetype in women—a competent and impersonal mind that could strategize and use power. Like the goddess Athena's emergence out of Zeus's head, women who had Athena's abilities became visible and were recognized and validated by the Father culture. Like Athena herself, however, most successful Athena women were fathers' daughters who did not consider themselves feminists. With male mentors and plentiful opportunities, they usually had not felt oppressed; they maintained an allegiance to Zeus principles and had no conscious connection to Metis as feminine wisdom.

While the initial beneficiaries of the women's movement resembled Athena, the movement itself was led by women who were archetypally Artemis, the Greek goddess of the hunt and moon, the only goddess who came to the aid of her mother, had women companions, and preferred to be in the wilderness. Women in childbirth prayed to her for aid. Artemis personified the archetype of the sister, who like the goddess felt a deep bond of sisterhood with other women and with Mother Nature. The women's movement was thus an expression of the Artemis archetype, as is concern for ecology, the wilderness, and Mother Earth.

For women who develop Athena's qualities, as well as men who rely only on proven scientific data, knowledge of an inarticulate, intuitively known, or physically felt feminine wisdom would come later, if at all, through an initiation experience, such as participating in a birth, having a near-death experience, or having an ecstatic spiritual epiphany that changes consciousness.

When we are moved by a profound experience of love and beauty, which so often accompanies these kinds of experiences, it's as if Aphrodite has emerged from the unconscious as an awesome, revered presence. We become aware of the missing feminine aspect of divinity that heals the split between spirit and matter (which comes from the word *mother*), when divinity is experienced as an aspect of our humanity and of the physical universe. The ability to articulate this kind of initiatory experience, to witness what is happening and reflect upon it afterward, takes it out of an unconscious matrix (or mother) realm, into a conscious awareness that is feminine.

Musing upon the birth of the Conscious Feminine stimulated my thinking about the difference between the abstract idea of the birth experience, which I anticipated during medical school in obstetrics courses, and the direct experience of giving birth. I was better prepared for the actuality, having been briefed about what to expect, but there were worlds of difference between a description and the real thing.

I was reminded, too, that the physical experience of childbirth evoked and stimulated a shift in consciousness in me then: as a consequence, I had felt deeply linked to all women who had ever given birth. For me, childbirth was an initiation into a sisterhood of women that made me a feminist, and the beginning of the dawning awareness of the physical, psychological, and spiritual demands and gifts that arrive with becoming a mother.

I did not appreciate until later the fact that childbirth also is an experience akin to living a myth (which occurs whenever we have an archetypal experience). And only now do I also see that the birth experience can serve as a metaphor to describe the birth of the Conscious Feminine in individuals and in the culture; here, as in the delivery room, *how* one learns about a subject and *what* is learned are intimately connected. When this is so, knowledge comes through an initiatory experience, which changes us deeply.

The transition to a new birth occurs all along the way but is most dramatic just before delivery. The labor pains are the longest and most intense as the baby comes through the cervix into the foreshortened birth canal, passing under the mother's pubic bone to emerge into the world. Similarly, transition periods are times when we are in between our former lives and the next stage of growth. That time in between one realm and the next, one state of consciousness and another, is experienced as "liminal," from *limen*, a Latin word for the horizontal beam of a doorframe, under which we pass. In liminal times, we are in the process of change and are exceedingly vulnerable. Transformation and growth or destruction and regression are often equally possible at such times.

I believe that we are collectively in a liminal time of major transition, during which a Conscious Feminine is emerging into the world as an evolutionary step of consciousness. This shift grows out of the same matrix as the women's movement. The longing to find a new identity comes in many forms—women's spirituality, creation-centered spirituality, a return of the Goddess, global awareness, ecological concern, a new appreciation for Gnostic and Celtic Christianity, to name a few of its expressions.

This evolution also comes into our awareness through the highest development of the cognitive mind, via the accomplishments of space-age technology, which brought humankind the experience of seeing the earth from outer space. Many people are moved by the awesome beauty of the earth into a new consciousness: we become aware of our dependency upon the planet, of her fragility, and of the miracle that makes life possible. We shift from being like children who expect that Mother Earth can and will provide for us forever, to being appreciative adults who know that she could be destroyed by nuclear holocaust or by simple human neglect.

The knowledge that we are living at a time of major change provides us with a sense of structure, even purpose. My premise, shared by many others, is that what is coming into form and ushering in a new age is feminine, personal, and planetary in scope, at once deeply sacred and simultaneously the stuff of ordinary life.

This growing feminine edge of consciousness is known through intuition, archetypal or mythic consciousness, body perceptions, images and imagination, or ritual expression. It calls upon the soul/psyche to participate and to be emotionally and spiritually affected by the experience through which it knows more, which is different from the impersonal detachment in which the mind works best—as different as those functions ascribed to the right brain are from those ascribed to the left; as different as reading about a baby is from giving birth to one.

19 · FINDING THE LOST FEMININE IN THE JUDEO-CHRISTIAN TRADITION

· · · · · · ·

JUNE SINGER

June Singer, Palo Alto, California Jungian analyst and author, traces the wide-ranging effects of the apocalyptic split of the Feminine from the Masculine in Judeo-Christian culture. While Riane Eisler (chapter 2) examines the effects of this split in the ancient world on the social realm, Singer focuses on the spiritual domain.

She is seeking to uncover those moments in the biblical tradition when the Feminine or the Goddess was rejected, abandoned, and ultimately banished to the lower worlds. She sees the divine divorced from nature and the human body, placed on a pedestal in the form of a wise old man. For this reason, she points to religion rather than patriarchal society as a whole as a source of oppression. We observe the long-term results of this shift in today's institutional religion, which still claims that women cannot have a direct relationship with the divine; it must be mediated through a priest or husband.

Singer also ties other long-term effects of this split to contemporary problems: confusion about archetypal distinctions between Masculine and Feminine; confusion about interpersonal roles for men and women; and a disrespect for the fragile ecology of the earth, the Great Mother, which calls out for the nurturing feminine qualities of us all.

Like the other contributors in this section, Singer offers us a form of the Divine Feminine from another time and place—Sophia, the Gnostic goddess of wisdom, who reminds us that she can be seen as our source, course, and goal.

June Singer, Ph.D., is a Jungian analyst practicing in Palo Alto, California. She is the author of Love's Energies; Boundaries of the Soul; The Unholy Bible; Androgyny: The Opposites Within; *and coauthor of the* Singer-Loomis Inventory of Personality. *In her latest book,* Seeing Through the Visible World, *she explores the Gnostic roots of Jung's psychology. While not pondering serious matters, she enjoys puttering in her garden or flying to faraway places.*

An emerging feminine consciousness is bringing an awareness that certain basic problems we now face are not problems of today alone. They are our heritage from ages past—the long-postponed consequence of the alienation of the patriarchal culture from the Feminine principle.

These problems exist on five different levels:

(1) On an archetypal level, the distinctions between the sexes, while biologically based, have led to a splitting of gender roles. What is considered masculine or feminine may differ from society to society, but the essential point is that there is always a difference.

It is difficult to determine whether what we perceive as masculine or feminine is a direct consequence of our experience in the world, or whether these are images that we carry with us into the world as archaic lenses through which we view the present. Contemporary depth psychology, especially that work influenced by C. G. Jung, has led us back to the archetypal forces in the human psyche that generate images, attitudes, and, eventually, behavior. The god-images of ancient times, including the images of goddesses, have served as inner psychological templates that have generated sexual stereotypes, which in turn appear to us to be objective—that is, coming from the phenomenal world.

Surely it is not a case of either/or, for we are neither wholly activated and propelled through life by the circumstances of our environment, nor are we altogether able to transcend our individual, cultural, and phylogenetic inheritance. Recognizing the importance of both nature and nurture, I will take the often overlooked position that we must consider some of the major issues of our day in the light of their archetypal foundations.

(2) On an interpersonal level, men and women react to one another based on their own internal value systems, which may be determined in part by archetypal factors. How do we view ourselves? Do we have power, control, authority, self-esteem? How do we view the opposite sex? Are "they" to be trusted to help, support, and further us? Or do we see them as adversaries, competing with us for recognition, threatening to undermine our own autonomy or expecting us to behave in ways that are not compatible with our personal value systems? Do we view society as favoring our goals and values or as opposing them? In situations viewed as non-threatening, women and men tend to cooperate and support one another. In the opposite kind of situation, it is each person for himself or herself. Most of us find ourselves in a variety of circumstances, some helpful, some hurtful. Inevitably these circumstances, plus our own values and expectations, play an influential role as we determine the nature of our interpersonal relationships.

(3) On the level of society, the split between masculine and feminine roles is an issue that includes differences in power and authority. In which institutions do men prevail and in which do women make most decisions? Let us not fail to realize that some of the issues on which women are often the most vocal are not solely women's issues—for example, abortion. What is at stake here is the perceived welfare of the fetus, and not necessarily that

of the woman whose body contains it. How successful are we in bringing the interests of both sexes to bear on the decision-making process in our society?

(4) On the environmental level, the rape of the earth is an outcome of the elements in our society that seek domination and control over nature —the so-called Masculine principle in both men and women. Nor do the inhabitants of our cities, which we call home, escape overcrowding, pollution of air and water, and lack of good education and care for those of our children who need it most. These are visible symptoms of the alienation of the Feminine principle from the whole.

(5) On the spiritual level, there is a rift as well—between the temporal and the infinite realms. Bringing this down to the proportions of the everyday, the problem is that too many people of power and influence are more concerned with immediate gains than they are with an overall evolutionary view of humankind and its welfare. We are unable, as Jung often said, to view our lives "under the aspect of eternity." Too many of us remain unaware of the possibilities for spiritual renewal of the here and now. We settle for immediate gratification as if there were no tomorrow.

I hope to show, through a sampling of a body of myth that belongs to the Judeo-Christian culture but was excluded from the Bible, how the historic alienation of the Feminine from the Masculine has contributed to some of these contemporary problems.

THE GODDESS MYTH AND THE HERO MYTH

In our time, when women have been able to adapt more and more effectively to the exigencies of the modern world and increasingly to assume positions of respect and importance, an interesting phenomenon has arisen. An old-new myth, the myth of the Goddess, has been reawakened—to such a degree that it has nearly replaced the myth of the hero that was so characteristic of the ideals of the early part of the twentieth century.

Perhaps this has happened because the hero myth, with all its attendant and supporting gods, has not succeeded in bringing about the peaceful and harmonious world that most of us seek. The hero represents the individual who by strength or wit has prospered—often at the expense of less ambitious, weaker, or more socially conscious individuals. Only a minute portion of the population resembles the hero, while the vast majority must struggle individually or collectively to survive economically, socially, and spiritually.

I think it not too bold a generalization to say that the hero archetype is one with which men historically have tended to identify either as an ideal or as a standard by which they judge themselves, while the Goddess represents a vital and life-giving aspect of the Feminine with which women can more easily identify. This image has been devalued, rejected, and denied in the Judeo-Christian culture. Only today, when both men and women have begun to realize that the mythology of the ancient past speaks the language of the soul in symbolic terms, have we started to wonder where the Goddess went while we were paying homage to the hero.

The hero myth in modern culture expresses itself in the growth of great corporations, conceived and developed by dedicated individuals who let nothing stand in the way of their accomplishments. Lesser men would serve their heroes and bask in their reflected glory; but the secret wish implanted within little boys by their mothers, that any man could be president of the United States, has never been entirely forgotten. This myth is lived out vicariously as men cheer for their athletic heroes, insist on the right to carry deadly weapons, or proclaim, "My country right or wrong!"

On the other hand, the repressed Goddess myth speaks of the particular power of the Feminine. It is not the power of physical strength that characterizes the Goddess, but the power of creativity. The womb is only one aspect of this. But it is through the womb that men have always been able to perpetuate themselves through their seed, just as it has been in the fertile trough in the earth that men could plant and, with the help of rain from the sky, provide the food they and their families needed for sustenance.

Yet the hunger that man feels, and that can only be filled by woman, goes beyond any physical or sexual need. It is that connection with the spirit, with the wholly Other, that men seek in the Feminine, for she is all that a man is not. If she is loving and compassionate, she is also to be respected and feared. She is that huge Mother who towers above the man, as she has since he was an infant, the one who can either grant his wishes or deny them, either hold him to her bosom or abandon him. To become a man, the boy must wrest his freedom from the mother.

This buried trace-memory from the past transmogrifies into the secret power of the Goddess. It is little wonder, then, that the patriarchal Judeo-Christian culture has rejected her. As a consequence, the Masculine has been separated from the Feminine for a long time. The alienation between them has led to a one-sided consciousness and a dark, shadowy unconsciousness.

Rejected or not, the Goddess has not completely disappeared. She has been in hiding, awaiting a propitious time to reemerge, a time when the world had need of her and might be willing to pay attention to her. It appears that the time for her second coming has arrived.

RECASTING THE OLD MYTHS

Today we are seeing a renascence of the old myths, but we do not rest merely with their retelling. We are recasting them in terms of their archetypal meaning. In the mysterious tales of long ago, we are seeking common themes that describe and characterize the development of ego-consciousness out of its matrix in the primitive group-participation of earlier times. We are looking into these myths for indications of the obstacles that have interfered with this development and thrown us backward into archaic states of consciousness. We are learning to recognize the eternally recurring patterns of thought and behavior in the myths that have come to dominate our Western Judeo-Christian culture—and to detect where the Feminine got rejected and eventually lost.

For example, let us consider the holiday of Easter in the Christian calendar. It is, of course, commonly associated with the resurrection of Jesus Christ. In how many churches on Easter Sunday is mention made of the fact that the very name of the holiday comes from Astarte, the Sumerian fertility goddess who was worshipped in the Near East as the embodiment of the Feminine Earth as long ago as two thousand years before the time of Christ? Astarte was only one goddess; there were also the Babylonian Ishtar, the Persian Anahita, the Egyptian Isis and Hathor, the Lydian Cybele, the Greek Aphrodite, and the Roman Venus—each feared and revered as the Great Goddess, Holy Mother, Sacred Prostitute, or Source of Wisdom.

Contrary to popular opinion, the Goddess was not worshipped *instead* of the God. Rather, the Feminine was seen always in relation to the Masculine, with full recognition that a relationship was required in order to insure the fertility of the earth and of humankind. Interestingly enough, traces of the Goddess remain in the Hebrew Bible, as in the story of Esther (derived from Ishtar?) who became the wife of the Persian god-king Ahasuerus and succeeded in saving her people, Israel, by intervening in their behalf against her husband's intention to destroy them.

Findings such as these have led many scholars to wonder why the Goddess was removed from her throne at the command of the Hebrew God, whose patriarchal presence dominated the Hebrew religion and, later, its daughter religions, Christianity and Islam. Biblical history tells us that when the nomadic Hebrews arrived in Egypt they were a troublesome lot, unwilling to worship the gods and goddesses of that agriculturally based country. When they threw off the yoke of slavery and returned to their nomadic ways, they followed their own patriarchal tribal-god into the wilderness and eventually into the Promised Land. Along the way they were given the Law of Moses, which included the history of this people from the time of creation, as well as specific instructions and commandments as to how to conduct themselves with respect to their God, to each other, and to the rest of humanity. This history and these rules, along with subsequently acquired documents, became the Holy Scripture by which the Hebrew people were to be governed and the standards by which their faith and behavior were to be measured.

Upon their return to the land of their ancestors, the Hebrews found the entrenched local inhabitants worshipping fertility goddesses, goddesses of love, and sometimes goddesses of wisdom. In their gentler expressions, these earth-mothers embodied compassion and nurturing, but in their fiercer personifications they engaged in human sacrifice and all manner of rituals that seemed lewd and lascivious to the moralistic Hebrews. Nevertheless, these rites must have held temptation for some, for the Hebrew law had to be reinforced again and again with respect to forbidding any contact with the goddess-worshippers under threat of the most severe punishment for any Hebrew who would dare to approach the high places where the goddesses held forth. To survive as a people, the Hebrews needed to remain a tightly bonded community of believers and followers of a father-god who would protect them from contamination or conquest by their neighbors.

By the time the canon, the officially recognized version of the Hebrew Bible, was closed around 300 B.C., nearly all references to goddess worship had been expunged. Those that remained were subtly concealed so that one has to search for them. One example might be Rachel, who, when she was ready to leave her father's household to live with her husband Jacob, took with her the teraphim (graven images of the sort condemned by the second commandment) and hid them under her skirt. When her father discovered that the images were missing, she refused to get up from where she was sitting to be searched, pretending that she was menstruating so that no man could touch her (according to Hebraic law). This tale suggests that the idols (goddesses) were present among the Hebrews, but concealed. Although this event supposedly preceded the giving of the law, the decision to include it in the Bible came much later. Later still, the New Testament was compiled as the record of the life and times of Jesus; this canon, too, was closed at a certain time so that nothing more could be added to it.

While these "official" documents were being written, a large body of other sacred literature was also being produced by both Jews and Christians of many diverse schools of thought, all the way from the valley of the Tigris to the banks of the Nile. It has been conjectured that the closing of the Old and New Testaments came in part as the result of efforts to crystallize the intent of those sacred works at a certain stage.

Why was it necessary, one might ask, to limit the scope of the authoritative body of religious literature rather than allow it to expand and incorporate many different viewpoints? Scholars have suggested that some of the extracanonical literature contained reformist tendencies that threatened the authority of the orthodox factions and so had to be excluded from what was to be the acceptable body of doctrine. Others suggested that polytheistic Hellenic ideas and practices from various regions of the Near East, including goddess worship, should not be allowed to contaminate the minds of the strictly monotheistic Jews or Christians. But a certain amount of this material did survive in various forms, mostly through legend and myth. Many differing versions have been found, often in fragments that are difficult to assemble, translate, and understand. This extracanonical literature contains, among other things, symbolic "histories" of the origin of the lost Feminine in the Judeo-Christian tradition.

THE EXCLUDED FEMININE

I must of necessity select only a few bits and pieces of this material to review at this time, for its scope is far too vast to attempt anything like a com-

prehensive survey here. I will draw my examples from the recently discovered literature of the first and second centuries preceding and following
the birth of Jesus, namely the Jewish Dead Sea Scrolls found at Qumran in
the Judean hills around 1945–47, and the Nag Hammadi Library, a collection
of Gnostic Christian texts found in Upper Egypt in 1945.

The Essenes took flight from what they saw as profane practices in
Jerusalem that were at odds with their own ideas of piety and strict adherence
to Mosaic law. They epitomized the separation of the Masculine from the
Feminine when they formed an ascetic community in the Judean desert
(today's West Bank) of men who renounced sexuality as an interference
with the spiritual life. Sexual intercourse was permitted only for a small
number of priests in order to make possible the continuation of the priestly
lineage.

On the other hand, the Gnostics of Upper Egypt gave an important
role to the Feminine; indeed, she is seen in some Gnostic texts as a partner
of God, an emanation of the same substance as that of the Most High and
consequently equal with it. When the God of the biblical creation story
says, "Let us make man in our image, after our likeness," there is the
implication that he is speaking to the feminine aspect of himself or to a
feminine co-creator, for the biblical text follows with, "Male and female
created he them." The Feminine, whether a goddess or a part of God, is
described in Gnostic works as "heavenly light" or "the light of wisdom."
From the beginning, she is a wisdom figure. Traces of this aspect of the
Feminine are still to be found in the Bible, as, for example, in Proverbs
8:1, "Does not wisdom call, does not understanding raise her voice?" and
in the Song of Songs: "Who is this that looks forth like the dawn, fair as
the moon, bright as the sun, terrible as an army with banners?"

In another Gnostic myth the Feminine is seen also as a reflection of an
utterly alien, transcendent God. This God is static, coexistent with the
Fullness, which is not limited to the visible world but rather exists in
Heaven, which is to say, in the formless world of infinity. He is all-knowing,
so he contains the attribute of logos, which gives rise to mind, intellect,
and the word. The complementary Feminine is active; she has the capacity
to move between the heavens and the lower regions. This can be interpreted
to mean that she represents relatedness, an attribute of eros, the great binder
and loosener. In psychological terms this Gnostic dualistic god-image may
be a result of the repression of the Masculine affinity to the earth (the lower
worlds) and the projection of this earth-wisdom onto the Feminine. Consequently, the Feminine has tended to be associated with earth, with that
which is base and lowly.

A myth ascribed to the Gnostic school of Valentinus relates that in the
timeless time before creation, the Feminine appears as the "thought" of
God; hence she is given the title Sophia, from the Greek word for wisdom.
Being thought, she has a certain autonomy; she is free to look below and
to contemplate what she sees. Her gaze takes in all the negative aspects of
the lower places, and she is filled with compassion. Her thought is not pure

"splitting" rather than wholeness, integrity

intellect but something else—a yearning to relate and a yearning for something to which she can relate, namely a creation. Being of the essence of eros, she is impassioned with her desire and so, without the concurrence of the Divine Masculine principle, also called logos, the shadow of her thought assumes an independent existence. The consequence of this rupture in the primordial unity is the conception of a creator-god, who then is responsible for creating the visible world. This creator-god, called Yaldabaoth and many other names in Gnostic mythology, bears a strong resemblance to the creator-god of Genesis, or surely to his dark side or shadowy aspect.

Yaldabaoth is far from an ideal god, having been conceived through the error of Sophia, when she dared to form a thought even though her divine consort had not participated or concurred with her. As a result of the alienation of the Feminine from the Masculine, Yaldabaoth is imperfect: he suffers from jealousy and hubris. He announces that he is a jealous god and will have no other gods before him. By this very statement, he recognizes that there *are* other gods (and goddesses) and demands that he have dominion over them. He creates a whole panoply of malevolent spirits, devils, and demons to serve him and gives an important place to evil in the lower worlds where he reigns. The evils become reified as "archons" or powers of the lower worlds. They rule in the world of form. Psychologically, we would experience the archons as powers such as jealousy, envy, greed, lust, ambition, self-aggrandizement, cruelty, and deceit.

The myth continues. Sophia, gazing down from above, sees evil abroad and multiplying in the world. She is moved to descend, of her own free will or out of compassion, and the archons, seeing her, become desirous of her. They fall upon her and render her blind. She then suffers greatly in darkness and pain. Estranged from her heavenly home, she is distraught and helpless. She repents her error, that of acting without the concurrence of her consort and thereby sinning against Wholeness. She cries out to heaven for help.

Her prayer is heard and the logos sends forth an emanation, which is also logos, being of the same substance. The logos (in some versions of the myth he is Jesus, also called Anthropos, or the First Adam, because he was the supernal model after which the biblical Adam would be fashioned) descends to the lower regions and, with a touch, restores Sophia's sight. So logos is reconnected with eros, and the enlightened Sophia can once more embody the feminine or wisdom figure.

In this creation narrative, the archons cast their seed into the earth and bring forth a creature in the shape of a man. Or, in some versions, Yaldabaoth fashions the first man out of the dust of the earth. This "second" Adam (from *Adamah*, the Hebrew word for earth) is weak and impotent and cannot get up from the ground, because he was created through error. Seeing this, the ever-watchful Sophia sends forth an emanation in the form of the First Eve, a Heavenly Eve who is the prototype of the biblical Eve. She has with her a physical counterpart who, when she finds this supine

Adam, breathes (spirit) into him and thereby endows him with the gift of life.

When the Sophia/Heavenly Eve has raised Adam by inspiring him with the essence of the true God—of which she is a part—he lives. It is the female potency that is the creative agent in this myth, which has been excluded from the canonical literature of the Judeo-Christian tradition. But this very potency arouses once more the jealousy of the archons. They set upon Eve in order to cast their seed into her so that they, rather than Adam, may have a claim upon her offspring. But the feminine spirit removes herself from the body of Eve and flies upward into the Tree of Knowledge, that is, the Tree of Gnosis, and there she looks on while the archons mistakenly defile her likeness.

Failing to accomplish their ends and fearing the power of the earthly couple, the archons try another approach. They manage to persuade Adam that Eve came forth from his rib while he was sleeping, and that because she was second to him he should be lord over her and she should obey him.

The couple lives in the Garden, a metaphor for a state of unconsciousness that is close to nature. Here all the animals dwell, including the serpent, whom the Gnostics call "the Wise Instructor." He is also known as the Adversary because he alone is bold enough to oppose the creator-god who attempts to withhold knowledge from Adam and Eve. What kind of knowledge would this god withhold? It is not intellect, for Adam already has that, having been able to correctly identify and name all the animals in the Garden. The fruit of this tree is the knowledge of the heart. When the serpent says to Eve, "Eat, you will not die," he is instructing her in the wisdom of relationship, because after she has eaten and given the fruit to her husband they will know each other in a different way from before, and they will be able to procreate.

Therefore, in a certain sense it could be said that Adam and Eve are of a higher order than the angels, for the angels, being immortal, could not procreate or they would have filled the earth to overflowing. The price of immortality was that the angels had to remain as they were, passive and uncreative, in an unchanging form of suspended consciousness. But to Eve, and through her to Adam, the twin gifts of generation and death were given. Instead of remaining unconscious, they could grow in wisdom through experiencing the pains and passions of mortality, and pass on their wisdom to their offspring. The gift of life meant that one generation could learn from its predecessors, so that wisdom could increase. The gift of death meant that each new generation could replace the less conscious generation that came before it.

The Feminine principle here stands for the conjunction of the two aspects of eros: generativity and wisdom. Generativity is associated with passion, relationship, and life. Wisdom is associated with physical death, because only when one lets go of the physical body, the vessel in which ego-consciousness is held, can wisdom be freed from the shackles of the flesh. Then one may become aware of the totality in which we participate—the Fullness, the sacred marriage of heaven and earth.

We can see in these myths an interesting element of Gnosticism, the presence of the archetype of twinship, the idea that there are twin worlds: the invisible, eternal, and formless world; and the visible world of time, space, and form. Likewise, there exist the many gods of the peoples of the visible world, each belonging to a particular race, tribe, or religion. And there is the Highest God, whose realm contains all that is visible but is not limited to the visible world. We who are created in the image of the Highest God also partake of this twinship archetype. We have our physical bodies that are born in and die in the visible world, but also our spiritual essence that preceded our appearance here and returns to the Fullness when we have completed our span on earth.

What, then, can we deduce from Gnostic mythology concerning the meaning of true wisdom? Does wisdom, or gnosis, inform that level of consciousness which reaches outside the confines of the personal ego and all the tribal gods and goddesses, enabling the individual to recognize the true and eternal God? One can take this proposition as a metaphor for a perspective of life which says that beyond everything personal lie values that are concerned with the common good, the common effort, and the common goals of humankind. What are some of these values? How do these relate to the problems we face today, the long-postponed consequence of the alienation of a patriarchal culture from the Feminine principle? Let us consider the five problem areas which, as I suggested earlier, have contributed to the formation of those contemporary values that have led to an imbalance in some mainstream cultural attitudes of our time.

First, on the archetypal level, we can see fundamental patterns that result in attitudes, images, and behavior that are judged as gender-appropriate in every society. In the past we regarded these archetypal patterns as fixed and immutable. But over the years we have learned about the wide variety of cultural norms, all the way from goddess worship in the distant past, to all kinds of patriarchal societies, to flashes of androgynous ideation in more recent times. In every part of the world, different groups established their own norms, assumed that these were correct, and indoctrinated their children with them. It is only since foreign cultures have been investigated that variations in gender attitudes have come to be appreciated.

Today we recognize that much of what we had accepted in the past as being archetypal is far more fluid than we had thought. What is considered natural behavior varies not only from place to place, but from time to time. Consequently we need not be locked into so-called archetypal differences between males and females. We are able, at last, to throw away our archaic lenses and see our own sex and the opposite sex as *members of a species of individuals*, each with his or her unique characteristics and capacities. All patterns of thought and behavior are indeed flexible and changeable, as the study of the history of gender relationships clearly demonstrates. As we take personal responsibility for changing ourselves and our institutions, newer archetypal images are giving expression to the basic underlying archetypal principle of gender differentiation.

Second, on the interpersonal level, we need to heal the breach between men and women. Here the myth of Sophia has relevance for us. The Feminine principle represented by Sophia experiences herself as being overlooked by an all-knowing Masculine principle, who is not particularly interested in anything but dwelling in the Fullness. Sophia is curious, thoughtful, and perhaps even weary of having been disregarded by her consort for endless ages. She has little experience in thinking, and even less in exercising her creative powers, but nevertheless she determines to extend her efforts in these directions. Clumsily, she errs and has to live with the resulting frustration.

Women who have lived through the beginnings of the women's movement will find resonance here. It is not until the Feminine recognizes that it has allowed itself to be alienated from the Masculine that it can ask for and receive help. Perhaps this myth can serve to remind us that women and men need to consider the needs and special qualities of each other in order for a creative relationship to take place between them. Even before this, each gender must let its needs be known by the other. As long as one or the other, male or female, insists on autonomy or dominance, interpersonal relationships will be destructive in nature. Each person must be willing to give up something to the other so that each can receive something of value from the other.

Third, social issues reflect changing images of the Masculine and the Feminine. We are beginning to see radical alterations in our social institutions as a result of the mass entry of women into the work force at every level. With more and more women rising to important and influential positions in such fields as medicine, law, education, and business, gender differences are being recognized and sensible allowances are being made for them. Flexible working hours, parental leaves, health insurance, day care for children, and low-cost housing are a few examples of areas where beginnings have already been made.

What yet needs to be done staggers the imagination, yet the changing attitudes are already evident. Men and women are discovering that they need to cooperate with each other both in the work place and in the home if they are to preserve the values. Sophia, the personification of wisdom, teaches us that neither the Masculine principle nor the Feminine principle can create a harmonious order alone. They are most effective when they work together.

Fourth, none of this will be of any use unless we turn our attention to the state of the visible world in which we live. Logos, which has been traditionally associated with the Masculine principle, has to do with planning, organizing, and expediting. Eros, traditionally associated with the Feminine principle, has to do with nurturing, conserving, and offering compassion. When logos alone is in the ascendancy, people plan how best to extract from the earth all her riches and utilize them, with insufficient concern for conservation, preservation, and equitable distribution. When eros alone is in the ascendancy, sentimental considerations can take the place of good, hard planning for the general welfare.

For example, millions of dollars may be spent in providing food and shelter for homeless people, while the much tougher job of providing training and work opportunities that would enable these people to become economically self-sufficient and to enrich the environment receives a lower priority. When eros and logos *together* turn their attention to the world we live in, there can be sensitivity to the needs and values of individuals, as well as planning to make a reality out of the ideal. When men and women, with their special interests and shared concerns, work together to shape a better environment, there is hope for the future of our planet.

Finally, first and last, the spiritual domain requires our attention. While we are saving our lives and the life of the earth, we must also heal "the rift in heaven." For too long modern men and women have strayed from the search for the soul, the imperishable aspect of ourselves that provides meaning for the temporal aspect. The lost Feminine in the Judeo-Christian tradition looks down again in sorrow upon the world below. It is more than fortuitous that books of Gnostic myths, including those of Sophia, have been rediscovered in the second half of our century. Hidden from the light for nearly two thousand years, Sophia, the embodiment of the Feminine principle, returns at a time when her message is sorely needed. She reminds us of the importance of understanding that everything we think or do takes place in a larger context.

Translated into contemporary terms, the message may well be that to be locked into the concerns of only everyday matters means that we isolate ourselves from the profound energy of the universe that carries us when our puny egos fail us. The wisdom transmitted by the Feminine reminds us that the father-god is not the only god. The Highest God symbolizes the concurrence of the Feminine and the Masculine. This conjunction of opposites is an ideal well worth striving for.

20 · DESCENT TO THE DARK GODDESS

· · · · · · ·

SYLVIA BRINTON PERERA

In Descent to the Goddess, *New York Jungian analyst Sylvia Brinton Perera retells the ancient myth of Inanna, Sumerian goddess of heaven and earth, to present a model of initiation for women today who seek to reconnect with the depths of feminine instincts. This is a story of opposites, split apart by the patriarchy, forever separate yet forever joined: the upper and lower worlds, the sky gods and the two goddesses, the light Queen of Heaven and the dark Queen of the Netherworld.*

Inanna journeys to the underworld to meet her shadow counterpart, Ereshkigal. With a female lookout left behind in the world above, Inanna descends, down and down. She is stripped of her adornments, her persona, her gods, even her caring nature. She faces the cold, depressed, ruthless side of the Feminine and learns to "incorporate the mother's dark powers rather than destroying or escaping them." She releases her masculine ideals, absorbed from a culture that devalues anything feminine. Ultimately, she is killed and her corpse is left hanging on a peg to rot.

The story of Inanna is the story of a sacrifice of self to gain a deeper wisdom. As Perera says, "She descends, submits, and dies. This openness to being acted upon is the essence of the experience of the human soul faced with the transpersonal."

Eventually, Inanna is rescued and her life renewed; she returns to the world above and must find a scapegoat to fill her niche below.

Unlike the hero's journey of meeting an exterior challenge and defeating a foe, this feminine journey moves downward and inward, and demands sitting, waiting, and rotting in order to find something real, something that does not serve the patriarchy. During this process, her connection to the old way of life, the old sense of self, must die. This confrontation with the loss of ego-ideals can be paralyzing; the reality of our oppression truly is a depressing one.

Perera's intricate dissection of the myth, her attention to its detail and to its relevance today, are striking. For her, facing the shadow side of the Feminine is an essential step toward developing a Conscious Feminine principle. If the darkness is not made conscious but remains underground, it can erupt in full destructive force. But if the shadow side of the Feminine is faced and given room to breathe; if the shadow side of the patriarchy is named and put in its place; and if one's entrenched identification with the Masculine principle can be sacrificed, then a more fully conscious sense of the Feminine can emerge in a woman.

I have chosen to excerpt that portion of Perera's commentary on the myth that centers around the divorce of the father's daughter from the dark aspects of the Feminine. The "return," or reconnection with the Self, refers to re-finding our sacred feminine nature following the long and often-arduous journey within. I have placed the piece in this section on the divine because, as Perera points out, Inanna is a Christ-like figure whose dark and light aspects join in the sacred marriage.

This piece is reprinted from Descent to the Goddess *(1981) with permission from Inner City Books.*

Sylvia Brinton Perera is a Jungian analyst in private practice in New York and Connecticut and is on the faculty of the C. G. Jung Institute in New York. She is the author of Descent to the Goddess: A Way of Initiation for Women; The Scapegoat Complex: Toward a Mythology of Shadow and Guilt; *and, with Edward C. Whitmont,* Dreams: A Portal to the Source. *She is currently researching Celtic mythology and its relation to psychotherapy and is working on a forthcoming book,* Mythic Rites in Modern Therapy.

The return to the Goddess, for renewal in a feminine source-ground and spirit, is a vitally important aspect of modern woman's quest for wholeness. We women who have succeeded in the world are usually "daughters of the father"—that is, well adapted to a masculine-oriented society—and have repudiated our own full feminine instincts and energy patterns, just as the culture has maimed or derogated most of them. We need to return to and redeem what the patriarchy has often seen only as a dangerous threat and called terrible mother, dragon, or witch.[1]

The patriarchal ego of both men and women, to earn its instinct-disciplining, striving, progressive, and heroic stance, has fled from the full-scale awe of the Goddess. Or it has tried to slay her, or at least to dismember and thus depotentiate her. But it is toward her—and especially toward her culturally repressed aspects, those chaotic, ineluctable depths—that the new individuating balanced ego must return to find its matrix and the embodied, flexible strength to be active and vulnerable, to stand its own ground and still be empathetically related to others.

This return is often seen as part of the developmental pattern of women—what Erich Neumann calls a reconnection to the Self (the arche-type of wholeness and regulating center of the personality). [It follows] the wrenching away from the mother by the patriarchal uroboros [the mythical snake that eats its own tail, signifying self-containment], and the patriarchal marriage partner.[2]

But Adrienne Rich speaks for many of us when she writes, "The woman I needed to call my mother was silenced before I was born."[3] Unfortunately, all too many modern women have not been nurtured by the mother in the first place. Instead, they have grown up in the difficult home of abstract, collective authority—"cut off at the ankles from earth," as one woman put it—full of superego shoulds and oughts. Or they have identified with the father and their patriarchal culture, thus alienating them-selves from their own feminine ground and the personal mother, whom they have often seen as weak or irrelevant.[4] Such women have all the more necessity to meet the Goddess in her primal reality.

This inner connection is an initiation essential for most modern women in the Western world; without it we are not whole. The process requires both a sacrifice of our identity as spiritual daughters of the patriarchy and a descent into the spirit of the Goddess, because so much of the power and passion of the Feminine has been dormant in the underworld—in exile for five thousand years.

It is precisely the woman who has a poor relation to the mother, the one through whom the Self archetype first constellates, who tends to find her fulfillment through the father or the male beloved. She may have an intense experience in the contrasexual sphere [a highly developed animus], but she lacks the ballast of a solid ego-Self connection.

The problem is that we who are badly wounded in our relation to the Feminine usually have a fairly successful persona, a good public image. We have grown up as docile, often intellectual daughters of the patriarchy, with what I call "animus-egos." We strive to uphold the virtues and aesthetic ideals which the patriarchal superego has presented to us. But we are filled with self-loathing and a deep sense of personal ugliness and failure when we can neither meet nor mitigate the superego's standards of perfection.

For what has been valued in the West in women has too often been defined only in relation to the Masculine: the good, nurturant mother and wife; the sweet, docile, agreeable daughter; the gently supportive or bright achieving partner. As many feminist writers have stated, this collective model (and the behavior it leads to) is inadequate for life; we mutilate, depotentiate, silence, and enrage ourselves trying to compress our souls into it, just as surely as our grandmothers deformed their fully breathing bodies with corsets for the sake of an ideal.[5]

We also feel unseen because there are no images alive to reflect our wholeness and variety. But where shall we look for symbols to suggest the full mystery and potency of the Feminine and to provide images as models for personal life?

Most of the qualities held by the upper-world goddess [Inanna] have been desacralized in the West or taken over by masculine divinities, and/ or they have been overly compressed or overly idealized by the patriarchal moral and aesthetic codes. Most of the Greek goddesses were swallowed up by their fathers; the Hebrew goddess was depotentiated. We are left with particularized or minimized goddesses. And most of the powers once held by the Goddess have lost their connection to a woman's life: the embodied, playful, passionately erotic Feminine; the powerful, independent, self-willed Feminine; the ambitious, regal, many-sided Feminine.

Constricted, the joy of the Feminine has been denigrated as mere frivolity; her joyful lust demeaned as whorishness, or sentimentalized and maternalized; her vitality bound into duty and obedience. This devaluation produced ungrounded daughters of the patriarchy, their feminine strength and passion split off, their dreams and ideals in the unobtainable heavens, maintained grandly with a spirit false to the instinctual patterns symbolized by the queen of heaven and earth. It also produced frustrated furies. For as Inanna lives unconsciously in women under the patriarchy's repression, she is too often demonic.

On the other hand, lived consciously, the goddess Inanna in her role as suffering, exiled Feminine provides an image of the deity who can, perhaps, carry the suffering and redemption of modern women. Closer to many of us than the Church's Christ, she suggests an archetypal pattern which can give meaning to women's quest,[6] one which may supplant the Christian myth for those unable to relate to a masculine God. Inanna's suffering, disrobing, humiliation, flagellation and death, the stations of her descent, her "crucifixion" on the underworld peg, and her resurrection, all prefigure Christ's passion and represent perhaps the first known archetypal image of the dying divinity whose sacrifice redeems the wasteland earth. Not for humankind's sins did Inanna sacrifice herself, but for earth's need for life and renewal. She is concerned more with life than with good and evil. Nonetheless, her descent and return provide a model for our own psychological-spiritual journeys.

I first came to the myth of Inanna's descent through a woman's initial dream: "I go under the water to the bottom of the sea to find my sister. She is hanging there on a meathook." This image suggested her necessity to search for qualities of the multifaceted, passionate and strong Feminine suspended deep in the unconscious, and to return them to conscious life, for her sister is analogous here to Inanna and her own capacity for fruitful, trusting relatedness. She had lived with a sense of being alien and exiled as if in hell, and felt closer to Ereshkigal's dark realm than to the energies symbolized by the image of Inanna.

This woman had been identified with the values of the patriarchy. She was in graduate school, trying to be heroic and smart and charming. But she was full of anger and fear, and could only relate to men if they were homosexual. Her dream, as does the myth itself, suggests the necessity of connecting the upper-world Feminine, whether pathologically compressed or healthy, with the underworld shadow. For before a woman can dis-identify from the cycle, to reverence its wholeness pattern as transpersonal, she must suffer the death of her ego-ideal within it. Maintenance of this ideal is connected to repression of part of the Feminine wholeness pattern in the underworld.

The implication [of the myth] for modern women is that only after the full, even demonic range of affects and objectivity of the dark Feminine is felt and claimed can a true, soul-met, passionate and individual com-radeship be possible between woman and man as equals. Inanna is joined to and separated from her dark ancestress-sister, the repressed Feminine. And that brings forth Geshtinanna—a model of one who can take her stand, hold her own value, and be lovingly related to the Masculine as well as directly to her own depths; a model of one who is willing to suffer humanly, personally, the full spectrum that is the Goddess.

. . . .

PART 6

RENEWING THE WORLD: THE FEMININE AND THE FUTURE

When the Feminine emerges, life is
honored.

JEANNE ACHTERBERG

Consciousness is trying to move from
power to love.

MARION WOODMAN

In this last section, our contributors envision the manifestation of the Conscious Feminine as a source of renewal in individuals and society. As Edward
C. Whitmont says, the qualities of the Feminine stand in contrast to the
qualities of the extroverted, materialistic, highly structured patriarchal tradition. She is the "priestess of the fullness of life."

While the Masculine is exclusive, the Feminine is inclusive; while the
first is objective, the second is subjective; while the first is dominated by
thinking, the second is dominated by feeling. While the Masculine seeks
perfection, the Feminine seeks completion.

When these new-old values are reintegrated within us and between us,
life changes meaning and direction. The outward struggle of the hero's
journey toward the heights takes an inward turn toward the depths. This
initiates a new relationship to Self, to Other, and to the Divine.

With this shift in priorities comes a qualitative shift in our relationship
to matter, to our bodies, and to the earth. Several contributors noted the
etymological link between "mother" and "matter," which has led to both
unconscious mothering and unconsciousness of matter. Marion Woodman
has pointed out that the world has never known Conscious Mother, let
alone Conscious Mature Woman. But the Feminine principle can act as a
counterpoint to the hunger for power that underlies the patriarchy.

Woodman says: "We have to connect to her because the power that
drives the patriarchy, the power that is raping the earth, the power drive

behind addictions, has to be transformed. There has to be a counterbalance to all that frenzy, annihilation, ambition, competition, and materialism."

As the Feminine becomes more conscious, its allied archetype changes as well. We have never known the Conscious Masculine either. Woodman points out that we have confused the patriarchal power principle, which controls and shapes nature at any cost, with the Masculine. It, too, suffers from imbalance due to the loss of the Feminine, and it, too, will become renewed, clarified, and eventually more conscious.

Ann Belford Ulanov concurs with this idea in her book *The Feminine in Jungian Psychology and in Christian Theology*:

> We are as familiar with the Masculine as it is possible to be familiar with something that is as truncated as the Masculine must be without the Feminine. We have dealt long and thoroughly with the rhetoric, the imagery, and the special vocabulary of the Masculine. . . . We still do not really know the Masculine and will not until we see it in its full complementarity with the Feminine. The Feminine is the missing link in our chain of connections to the knowledge and deepened experience of [our] psychic life.
>
> There is no access to full conscious and unconscious life without the feminine modality. The Feminine must be worked on, probed, examined, meditated upon, conjectured about, and contemplated, for the Feminine is the completing element in every effort we can make to become a fully human person.

With a growing balance between these two forces, a woman's ability to respond with her whole being will be enhanced. While the neglect of the Feminine has stunted our capacity for spiritual experience, its development will increase our capacity for growth. For women, the goal of the spiritual quest becomes the wholeness of self *as a woman*—in relationship to men and the Masculine, but not defined by them.

In her article in this section, Genia Pauli Haddon claims that it is our developmental task to receive and integrate the Conscious Feminine into daily life. Haddon dubs this "yang-femininity," that portion of the Feminine that is exertive and birth-giving, rather than receptive and gestating.

She echoes Emily Hancock when she describes young girls whose natural femininity is yang-style before cultural restrictions are imposed on them. And, like other critical supporters of feminism, she points out that many members of the women's movement have confused yang energy with phallic energy, rejecting altogether the Feminine principle.

Haddon's piece is particularly post-Jungian, in that it warns against defining the animus as the sole carrier of yang energy in a woman. This limiting belief, she maintains, can lead to overidentification with the Masculine, as well as a feeling of shame about a style that may appear pushy, aggressive, and therefore unattractive to others.

In his book *Return of the Goddess*, Edward C. Whitmont also expands on the changing meanings of animus and anima since Jung's time. He points out that reserving the animus for women and the anima for men has severe limitations: "Men can be as animus-ridden, dogmatic, belligerent, busy-bodying and power hungry as women; women as anima-possessed, moody, seductive, unrelated and depressed as men."

Especially today, certain women can be ruled in their conscious outlook by logos and out of touch with their feelings, while certain men can be sensitive to instinct and feelings, or eros, and out of touch with logos. Therefore, Whitmont, like Haddon, calls for releasing the terms *animus* and *anima* (or *yang* and *yin*) from their gender-bound meanings.

In the same way, the Conscious Feminine is alive in every one of us. She is not reserved for women. But it is extremely difficult to write about the Feminine without defaulting to the archetype's connection with women from time to time. The mind seems drawn back by some strange attraction to make this link again and again.

When this book was originally conceived it was not to be solely about women but about the Feminine in both women and men. Sadly, the men who were invited to participate in writing about the anima all declined. So the psychological picture here is incomplete.

But just as men had a special and primary role in ushering in the masculine reign of the patriarchy, so women have a special role today. In his article, Whitmont begins to clarify this task for women to bring the Feminine to the forefront.

In closing, Robert A. Johnson, author of the immensely popular books *He, She*, and *We*, tells a story about the reintegration and renewal of the lost Feminine.

21 · THE PERSONAL
AND CULTURAL
EMERGENCE
OF YANG-
FEMININITY

• • • • • • •

GENIA PAULI HADDON

By dividing the Masculine/Feminine pie differently—into quarters rather than halves—Genia Pauli Haddon, minsiter and depth psychologist and author of Body Metaphors, *dramatically alters our definitions of gender and archetype. Besides the usual association of masculine with yang and feminine with yin, she further refines our categories, shedding light on two new possibilities: feminine yang and masculine yin. Her highly developed abilities to discriminate among these qualities result, for us, in greater choice: these four modes of experience are not exclusive but live within each of us as available resources to be used in daily life.*

Haddon draws on body metaphors: the yang-masculine is tied to the penis/ phallus; yin-masculine is tied to the testicles; yin-feminine is tied to the gestating womb; yang-feminine is tied to the exertive or birth-giving womb. In this way, her ideas move out of the hypothetical realm and into our bodily reality.

When seen from this perspective, it becomes clear that our culture has promoted only half the story: phallic masculinity and yin femininity. Although the near-total repression of yang-femininity has permitted the full development of yang-masculinity, the costs of this imbalance have been great. And for those women who are naturally prone to express themselves in a yang style, the pain and confusion have led to a chronic identity crisis.

Haddon recounts the fairy tale to illustrate the development of the Feminine today. She also draws on genetics to make a further biological/psychological parallel.

Finally, she links three eras in the development of human society to her four styles: the Matriarchal Age emphasized the yin-feminine; the Patriarchal Age emphasized the yang-masculine; and the Emergent Age is currently bringing forth the yang-feminine. She paints a clear picture of our task, to be achieved both individually and together: to bring into consciousness a new style of the Feminine that is at once powerful and nurturing, active and receptive, related and autonomous. With this

achievement, she says, the Masculine will be renewed, because these dancing op-
posites will bring one another into harmony and balance.

Genia Pauli Haddon, Ph.D., D. Min., is an ordained minister, United
Church of Christ, who specializes in depth psychotherapy, Kripalu yoga, and
shamanic counseling techniques in Scotland, Connecticut. She is the author of
Body Metaphors: Releasing God-Feminine In Us All.

Femininity customarily is said to be receptive and nurturing, as exemplified
by the receiving and gestating function of vagina and womb. It follows
that to be feminine is to be like a vessel: receiving, encompassing, enclosing,
welcoming, sustaining, protecting, nourishing, embracing, containing,
holding together—in other words, *yin*. However, this receptive and gestating function of vagina and womb is only half of their story. The womb
is also the organ that pushes forth mightily in birthing. Our understanding
of the nature of femininity needs to be revised to take into account the
birth-pushing *yang* function of the womb.

One woman told me she came to this realization during the birth of
her first child. Fully conscious throughout delivery, she experienced herself
as participating in an act of ejaculation: the culmination of a nine-month
erection. The fact that she resorted to describing this most womanly of
experiences in terms of male physiology is a commentary on how little our
culture appreciates this dimension of the Feminine in its own terms.

If we were to define femininity solely in accordance with the womb's
birthing power, we would speak of it as the great opener of what has been
sealed, the initiator of all going forth, the out-thrusting yang power at the
heart of being. As the birthing womb brings forth new life, so yang-
femininity is concerned with transformative processes and the experience
of self-transcendence.

The word *ejaculate* comes from roots meaning "out" and "to throw."
Womb power might better be described as *exertive* ("out" and "to join
together"). An old meaning of the word *exert* is "to thrust forth, to reveal."
To name this mode of the womb's functioning as exertive brings to mind
also that the birthing process is commonly called labor, signifying great
exerting.

If our ideas about femininity were based on the birth-pushing function
of the womb rather than solely on its containing function, women would
be expected to be initiators and movers; then, to call a woman "pushy"
would be to compliment her on her femininity.

Although existing stereotypes assign yang qualities exclusively to men
(and Jungians would say also to the woman's animus) and yin qualities
exclusively to women (and the man's anima), there is nothing to indicate
such an equation in the original meaning of the words *yin* and *yang*. In its
primary meaning yin is "the cloudy," "the overcast," and yang actually
means "banners waving in the sun," that is, something "shone upon" or
bright.[1]

The fact that these primal opposites are qualities that can color aspects of both Masculine and Feminine is suggested by the classic Taoist analogy in which yang is associated with the bright side of both mountain and river, yin with the shaded side of both. In a landscape where the south side of the mountain receives sunlight, it is the north bank of the river that is illuminated and warmed. Both yang and yin are manifested in both river and mountain, although differently in each. In terms of this analogy, we might say that the Masculine is like the mountain, having both yang and yin sides; the Feminine like the river, also both yang and yin. These four modes of human experience correspond metaphorically to the penis/phallus (yang-masculine), testicles (yin-masculine), gestating womb (yin-feminine), and exertive womb (yang-feminine).

Traditionally, Masculine and Feminine have been pictured as a simple complementarity. This further differentiation of two sorts of femininity and two sorts of masculinity reveals that what is called the Masculine in the classical Jungian model really is only the phallic half of masculinity. Western-style ego development entails differentiating and greatly developing this phallic half of the Masculine totality. The way is cleared for such refined development of the phallic half by projecting the testicular (yin) half onto the Feminine, which is defined so as to encompass the intermixed gestative-yin and testicular-yin qualities. For the same reason, the exertive half of femininity falls out of the picture entirely. Whether in individual development, culturally, or in psychological theory, yang-femininity generally has remained unnamed, repressed, banished, relegated to the shadow.

This repression of yang-femininity has allowed full cultural expression of yang-masculinity, with many benefits. For example, the phallic emphasis in Western culture underlies the development of allopathic medicine and surgery, objective-scientific methodology and technology, and religious and legal systems that clearly codify and spell out distinctions among things. Penis power is visible as the rocket probing outer space, the scalpel dissecting the body, the electron microscope differentiating the component parts at subcellular levels, the electron accelerator splitting the atom.

If it has been of value to the species for yang-femininity to have been repressed for a time, it is just as essential now that we develop these very attributes. It seems to be the task of many women and men today to undertake the integration of the long-exiled feminine-yang side of the psyche—both for their own development and for the further evolution of human consciousness. It is no longer sufficient for a woman to be assertive solely through the good graces of her animus. She must come to know that sometimes being assertive is feminine.

Forcefulness from a woman typically is given nasty names. We say she is bitchy, witchy, wearing the pants, a ball-buster, animus-ridden. It is not surprising that many women are at first completely unaware of this force, having learned early to repress and fear it as "unfeminine." For example, when she began depth psychotherapy with me, forty-two-year-old Marcia[2] did not consciously notice when she was being "a bitch" and could have imagined nothing more discrediting than being proved one. As she grew in self-awareness, she developed the ability to recognize when she "acted like a ball-busting bitch." This was a difficult admission, and at first she wanted to be cured of such behavior. Traditional Jungian theory would have said that Marcia's animus had taken over and that her task was to disidentify from the yang energies in order to become nurturing (yin-feminine) again.

Different meanings emerge, however, if we ask what *birthing value* Marcia's bitchiness might serve. The man at whom she tended to bitch was stuck in procrastination, a negative expression of poorly integrated testicular masculinity. At its best, testicular masculinity gives one the capacity to "hang in there," hence steadfastness, patience, and stability. In exaggerated form, this becomes stagnation. In this context, the image of busting open the balls suggests not castration but opening the way for the seeds of creativity to come forth. Marcia came to see that her task was not to eliminate her feminine force but to become more and more conscious in exercising its birthing function.

Even women who are uncomfortable with feminine assertiveness nevertheless are able to describe childhood experiences of their yang-femininity. With gusto, Tess tells the women in her support group her experience as a ten-year-old when she stopped a big fourteen-year-old bully who was picking on younger children. As she describes the incident, her face is radiant. "I felt so whole!" Then, with a trace of regret in her voice, "I guess that was the last time I did something like that." Jenny, fifty, describes the intensity of her experience of self-birthing when, as a five-year-old, she undertook to pedal her little red tricycle over forbidding terrain. The motive was not to get to the other side of the field or to be the first to do it. She was simply responding to an inner urge to exercise untried strengths and abilities. This was energetic action in harmony with the context of the moment, rather than for the purpose of reaching a goal or winning a contest.

These are yang experiences of girls before they banished that side of themselves as "masculine." A woman's readiness to reconnect with those banished energies may be signaled by a dream of a vigorous little girl of the age at which this aspect of femininity was lost. At such a turning point, Jenny dreamed of a five-year-old "with springs in her legs" running exuberantly and freely to get on the school bus for kindergarten. She weeps as she tells this seemingly unimportant dream, so moved is she by this image of her long-dormant yang-femininity announcing its readiness to come forth again in her life.

The woman (or anima) whose exertive yang-feminine side develops wholesomely will know how to push herself and others toward new life in harmony with organic processes of transformation. Her style will be to *move with* the birthing process in ongoing affirmation of herself and others through the throes of change. Like a womb at full term, she responds to the intrinsic timing of birth labor with contextually harmonious initiative —whether she is a psychotherapist nonjudgmentally reflecting back to someone a clear picture of behavior patterns that are no longer adaptive; or a mother encouraging her five-year-old going off to kindergarten or nudging adult children from the nest; or an artist or writer working through the night, not because of an extrinsic deadline, but in order to catch the wave of creativity. She bears down, demands, pushes, and thrusts forth creatively.

A distinction worth noting is that whereas the thrust of phallic yang energy acts *toward* a focused goal, feminine-yang initiative acts *from* a field of reference.[3] This contrast between goal-oriented and contextual yang energy is illustrated by the experience of Beth, the only woman on the five-person board of directors of a large nonprofit organization. Each year the board draws up a five-year plan, allocating funds and setting priorities accordingly. Beth has noticed, however, that emergencies play a large role in determining how resources are actually applied. Phallic energy goes into planning long-range goals and strategies for reaching them. Exertive energy expresses itself in the emergencies, through which a sense of direction emerges out of the needs and gifts of the moment. When we are heavily invested in the phallic style, emergencies are frightening, distressing, taken as signs of poor planning. If we are comfortable with the ways of the exertive womb, we recognize such emergencies as *emergences*. If we greet them as welcome input urging us to make a timely course adjustment, then the transformational energy they represent need not escalate to full emergency proportions in order to express itself. So Beth continues to make careful five-year plans, but she now values emergencies as well, trusting both ways to move the work of the agency forward.

If yang-femininity becomes overcharged (either directly or through compensatory buildup), a woman's style becomes "forced." She pushes prematurely, demanding untimely changes of herself and others, rejecting old patterns without respect for the purposes they may serve, often abandoning tender new potentialities before they are mature enough to survive. Figuratively speaking, this is the kind of person who repeatedly opens the oven door while the cake is baking, prematurely exposing what should be left covered, meddling where such "help" is not needed.

In a culture where femininity is defined as yin, women are conditioned to neglect their yang side. When little libido flows in the yang-feminine mode, the woman or anima hangs back, perpetually "in neutral," afraid of initiating, never throwing her weight into what is developing, afraid to push. Long after another person would have "had a bellyful," she continues on the same track, failing to give birth to what might be. The young woman in the fairy tale "The Frog-King, or Iron Henry"[4] is like this. Closer examination of this story reveals a solution, both for individual women and for our culture, which is collectively characterized by the same lack of yang-femininity. As we shall see, at the behest of her father, the king, who represents the wisdom of the patriarchal system, she responds affirmatively to every demand for nurturance, expressing her feminine nature exclusively in the gestative mode, as prescribed for women within patriarchy.

The tale begins when the princess drops the ball that she has been endlessly tossing in the air and catching. This might be taken as an early sign that her seemingly perfect receptivity as nurturing womb no longer suffices. The ball rolls into a deep well, from which a male frog retrieves it. That evening, the frog comes to the castle to claim his reward. The princess would refuse him entry, but her father insists that she invite him in. When the frog wants to sit near her at the table and eat her food, her father insists that she provide nurture from her own plate. When the frog wants to crawl in bed with her—perhaps more like a little child than a suitor—again, the father insists; it is her duty to be receptive. In all of this, the maiden exemplifies the qualities of the idealized gestating womb.

Finally, she has had enough. She becomes furious, snatches the frog from her bed, and throws him with all her strength against the wall. At first glance this seems a destructive act and perhaps reminds us of the dark side of such goddesses as Lilith and Hecate, or the bitchiness of Marcia. However, it also can be understood as a dramatic emergence of the young woman's assertive femininity. In powerfully ejecting the frog, she is pushing-to-birth: the frog is not destroyed after all, but transformed into a youthful king.

One would think that would be the end of the tale, and in some popularized modern versions it is. However, in the original story there is an odd addendum about the simultaneous deliverance of the young king's faithful servant, Henry, who arrives with the king's fine gold carriage drawn by eight white horses to take the couple back to the kingdom. Faithful Henry helps them in, then resumes his place behind the carriage. He had been so unhappy while his master was a frog that he had caused three iron bands to be laid around his heart, lest it should burst with grief. Now he is so full of joy because of this deliverance that the bands spring from his heart one after another with great cracking sounds, which the young king at first interprets as the carriage breaking apart.

Iron Henry typifies the testicular quality of steadfast faithfulness. Like the testicles, he literally "stands behind" the flashy, up-front horsepower of the phallic king. He rejoices that the maiden exercises yang energy, for in connecting with her exertive womb she delivers both sides of the Masculine from deformity and constriction. As has often been pointed out by proponents of the women's movement, men suffer as well as women when femininity is not allowed full expression.

It is important to recognize that a woman who accomplishes this sort of initiative is coming into a new relationship not simply with masculinity but with the assertiveness of her own feminine womb nature, by actively delivering a lost side of herself. Notice that the transformation comes not through kissing the frog but through forcefully ejecting him; not through nurturing warmth but through fiery feminine thrust. If a woman at this stage of development shrinks from her own exertive womb power and reverts to kissing the frog, she may end up with nothing more to show for it than warts.

This tale casts a revealing light on contemporary cultural changes. We could say that, like the princess, cultural femininity has been slow to assert its values against those of the patriarchy. From this perspective, the women's movement is long overdue. A woman's awakening to feminist values commonly is marked by a period of outrage and anger: "We're mad as hell, and we're not gonna take it anymore!" Ideally, this energy should express *exertively*, along the lines modeled by the maiden in the story and with equally transforming effects. However, as long as yang and phallic are equated, women's only access to yang energy is to adopt phallic rather than exertive values. Figuratively speaking, some women graft on a phallus but find it doesn't work right for them. Chronic impotent anger is the result.

There *is* a place in the economy of a woman's psyche for all four gender modes. In some circumstances, phallic energy is just what is needed—but never as an unconscious substitute for yang-femininity. Both for individuals and for the collective culture at large, the solution is for women to differentiate between phallic-yang and exertive-yang styles, claim their exertive feminine birthright, and push the entire culture into rebirth.

In the story, we see that phallic masculinity is dually depicted. On the one hand, it is the king, the patriarch, the ruler of the culture. At the same time, it is an odious frog hidden deep in a well. Despite the great development of phallic consciousness in the human species, there are ways in which phallic masculinity remains very primitive. As the feminine yang values begin to emerge with vehemence and power, we can expect even the seemingly well-developed patriarchal consciousness to be tranformed. At the time when I was writing *Body Metaphors*, I had not fully recognized this. Recently I have noted that with the emergence of yang-femininity in a woman's consciousness, yang-masculinity begins to function in new ways in her own personality and in the world around her.

One hallmark of yang-masculine consciousness is the ability to cut through irrelevancies and get straight to the goal. Commonly this gift is exercised with an attitude of mastering and overpowering obstacles. With the emergence of yang-femininity, this phallic talent is found to operate with humor, lightness, and laughter rather than aggressiveness. Ann, a naturally gestative woman, was just emerging from her patriarchally prescribed role as exclusively nurturing and maternal. She sought a new way to engage with an everyday situation in which phallic energy had been expressing itself in a manner she described as "guerrilla warfare." As she said the word *guerrilla*, we were reminded of her recent dream of a gorilla menacing a nun who intended to stab him. Through active imagination[5] culminating in physical enactment, Ann had a vivid experience of Gorilla. As she enacted Gorilla, jumping, scratching, flaring her nostrils, snorting and snuffing, I was repeatedly dissolved in thoroughly unprofessional laughter. She *was* Gorilla; and she was very funny as she danced around the scissors-wielding nun. The hostile nun was disarmed by the laughter that bubbled up, and the two happily embraced instead of either dominating the other.

Afterward, Ann said she had especially noticed the male organs swinging between her thighs as she danced around. When she subsequently considered the "guerrilla warfare" situation from the perspective of the laughing Gorilla, suddenly she could envision responding a different way: cutting through the bullshit with humor rather than aggression, disarming the situation rather than overpowering the seeming menace. This is not the derogatory, cutting, stabbing sort of humor often seen in both men and women who are expressing yang-masculinity in its more usual mode. It is a joyful and contagious invitation to shared delight in "getting on with it."

Gail visualized the transformed role of phallic energy in another manner. During intense active imagination she saw a beautiful, round stained-glass window in the center of her body break up into its constituent pieces. These shifted around and came back together in an equally beautiful pattern, leaving out one elongated triangular piece. This piece was then released through the crown of her head "to return to the far distances." Through working with her associations, we recognized that this triangular piece had to do with Gail's customarily experiencing phallic energy in both the men and the institutions around her as a thorn in her side. Having at one time identified with yang-masculinity, then subsequently having transferred her allegiance to the exertive feminine style, she was frequently irritated and upset by the predominantly phallic tone of our culture.

Immediately following this vision, Gail developed a significant friendship bearing out its implications. Her new friend, Karl, was a decidedly yang-masculine man seriously engaged in personal growth work, who envisioned his spiritual path in typical phallic manner as a straight and narrow, ever-upward way, requiring heroic exercise of firm will. What struck her most about Karl, however, was the humor and good will with which he homed in on obstacles to growth. She found his low-key laughter a gracious and contagious catalyst to her own continued transformation, pictured from her exertive-womb perspective as a circular, perpetually spiraling process. No longer in danger of falsely identifying with yang-masculine ways or experiencing them as a thorn in her side, Gail found it natural to stay true to her own exertive process without denigrating Karl's phallic approach to spiritual work. And she experienced Karl doing the same vis-à-vis her, respecting her way though unable to comprehend it fully.

All women have both gestative and exertive sides; in each personality, one or the other seems naturally dominant. If, like Gail, a woman's authentic nature is characterized by a preponderance of feminine-yang energy, she faces the difficult predicament of living in a culture that equates yang with masculine and overvalues both. If she eschews her own considerable assertiveness (projecting it onto inner and outer men) in order to be completely "feminine" by cultural standards, her individual femininity is sabotaged. Having a good relationship to a yang-animus does not suffice. She has an intrinsic need and responsibility to fulfill her feminine-yang proclivities. Furthermore, cultural values tell her that the yang mode is "better," so if she values herself, she has that added incentive to develop her "more valuable" yang qualities.

However, if she does begin to fulfill her femininity in the yang mode, she (or others around her) may name as masculine this authentically feminine development.[6] Partly because of this cultural predisposition to call her yang-feminine gifts both "more valuable" and "masculine," she is particularly vulnerable to inauthentic identification with masculinity. If she is familiar with Jung's description of the animus, she may picture her inner man as the exclusive personification of all yang energy. She may feel that in order to develop the yang aspect of her own feminine consciousness, she must wrest it from the animus or become masculinized herself.

Terry, a woman in her early thirties struggling with this dilemma, dreamed that she needed to keep her blouse buttoned up high so that no one would see she had hair on her chest. Her discomfort with the very qualities most central to her natural personality arises in part from not knowing that there are womanly yang expressions as well as masculine ones. She feels both covetous of yang energy and ashamed of owning it. This inner conflict is lived out in her relationships with men. On the one hand, she values the company of males more than that of females. At the same time, she is likely to feel hostilely competitive and resentful toward men. She projects her own yang power on men, then seeks to reclaim it first by affiliation, then by force. Such a woman may feel admiration for strong men of accomplishment, yet choose as a mate an ineffectual man, as though for reassurance that all the yang resources have not been preempted by the male.

Women with natural tendencies toward yang-femininity are especially affronted by the old feminine stereotypes. In their urgency to demonstrate their freedom from those false ideals, they may take on another false identity, expressing their bountiful yang energy in phallic patterns. When this happens yang-femininity remains repressed, and the overburdened phallic channel no longer functions wholesomely. It lends a driving and driven intensity to the personality, a brittle hardness, an acidic sharpness. In a caricature of phallic effectivity, these misplaced yang energies generate a powerful canon of "shoulds" and "oughts," which the woman applies without compassion to both herself and others.

When functioning wholesomely in either a man or a woman, phallic energy generates goals and fuels purposeful activity toward those goals. When substituted for the woman's exertive-womb energy, the phallic animus instead fixates an abstract, unreachable goal that, although irrelevant to the real concerns of the woman's life, become her taskmaster. She is as though possessed by a frantic energy that operates in the services of this inhuman goal.

In contrast, if her yang-femininity develops, she pushes *from within* her actual life context. Forward movement is oriented toward the flowering of what has been gestating within the situation, rather than toward an extrinsic goal. Preoccupation with authoritarian "oughts" is replaced by a compassionate demand for authenticity rooted in the actual context of each situation. Womb power, in the service of bringing forth newness by the fullness of time, tends to push with what is being birthed rather than insisting that things should be different in accordance with an extrinsic idea.

Culturally, we stand at the brink of a definitive shift in dominant archetype as foundational and radical as the transition from matriarchy to patriarchy. The Matriarchal Age brought to cultural expression qualities associated specifically with the gestative womb: yin-feminine nurturant containment. The Patriarchal Age has brought to cultural expression qualities associated with the penis or phallus: yang-masculine, goal-oriented objectivity, differentiation, and mastery.[7] As we move out of the Patriarchal Age, there are signs that the next age will bring to primary cultural expression the long-dormant yang half of the Feminine, as seen in the exertive womb.

To say that each age brings to cultural expression one of the four sexual modes does not mean that the other three have no function within that age. It means that the key cultural features of an age correspond to the characteristic qualities of a particular gender mode. Within the frame of reference defined by the dominant gender mode, each of the four then plays some role.

Elsewhere I have provided a detailed analysis and comparison of the Matriarchal, Patriarchal, and Emergent ages in terms of dominant body metaphor.[8] Consciousness itself can be seen as evolving in accordance with this schema. The participational style of consciousness[9] that is characteristic of the Matriarchal Age correlates with figurative containment in the nurturing womb. In matriarchal culture, the fundamental human unit is not the person but the encompassing clan or group. Identity is via immersion in the collective matrix (from *mater* = "mother"). Here, the ego has not yet condensed out of the unconscious matrix of the psyche.

With the coming of the Patriarchal Age, participational consciousness was displaced by differentiating objectivity as the predominant style of consciousness. This means that the key psychological feature for both men and women is the development of an ego clearly distinct from the unconscious matrix. The fundamental human unit is no longer the group but the individual subject, differentiated from all others as objects. Reality is experienced in terms of mutually exclusive opposites: subject and object; male and female; good and evil.

Extending the metaphorical analysis of gender differences to include the contrasting XY and XX sex chromosomes reveals a significant correlation between chromosomal gender differences and the various styles of consciousness characterizing the Matriarchal, Patriarchal, and Emergent Ages. Chromosomes in all the cells of the body are paired, one coming from the father's sperm, the other from the mother's ovum. Typically, the members of each pair are as alike as two matching strings of hand-crafted beads. Figuratively speaking, they have the same numbers of "beads" (genes), arranged in the same order, but with subtle differences between paired "beads" reflecting their individual origins. To produce new body cells for growth and maintenance, the chromosomes in a cell duplicate themselves and the cell then divides into equal halves, one set of chromosomes going to each. Thus the "daughter" cells each have a complete set of genetic material identical with the "mother" cell. In simple life forms, such as the amoeba, all offspring are produced by the direct duplication of the parent in this manner: generation after generation, all "mothers" and "daughters." Culturally, this pattern repeats in the matriarchal system, where the male role in reproduction is not noticed and human lineage is pictured as coming through the womb, traceable ultimately to the Divine Mother as Original Parent of us all.

Schematically, the twenty-three pairs of human chromosomes can be represented alphabetically, with superscript *p* designating "paternal," superscript *m* showing "maternal" origin:

$$A^m A^p, \ B^m B^p, \ C^m C^p \ \ldots \ V^m V^p, \ W^m W^p, \ X^m X^p.$$

The final pair in this series represents the sex chromosomes, carrying genes that orchestrate the development of feminine or masculine traits. In females, this final pair is a matched set, on the same order as the rest of the series. In the same way, matriarchal consciousness is participational rather than differentiational.

In males, however, this pair of chromosomes departs from the pattern applying to all other chromosome pairs. In males, one of this pair is so unlike the other[10] that it is conventionally designated by a different letter: $X^m Y^p$. In other words, this is a pair of opposites, correlating with the phallic style of consciousness that emphasizes differentiation and discrimination of pairs of opposites. Moreover, genes on the Y chromosome assert their dominance over those on the X, triggering the production of masculinizing hormones in the early stages of embryo development.[11] Without this dose of hormone, every embryo develops into female form. Thus, the XX or female sex is the neutral state on which maleness is superimposed. Biological development of human maleness consistently entails imposing a pattern that is contrary to the natural course of events. The Y chromosome and the testosterone-producing male gonad function at the cellular and organ level in a style analogous to that of the proverbial patriarch at the sociocultural level: asserting themselves counter to the underlying world of nature; prevailing over the Feminine; introducing and maintaining differentiation of unlike pairs, with all that goes along with such distinctions. In other words, the patriarchal style may reflect patterns literally programmed into the man's being at the level of his genes, gonads, and hormones.

We might say the patriarchal system is uniquely the male's contribution to the psychocultural evolution of the species. Through it, human culture enacts the primordial masculine impulse of the Y chromosome. Patriarchy's emphasis on differentiation, discriminating consciousness, objectivity, male dominance, subordination of the female, and development "contrary to nature" all aptly express at the cultural level the masculine contribution to biological evolution. Through this cultural incarnation of the Masculine, the entire species, both males and females, has been brought to a new degree of psychocultural development. It was a matter of course that men catalyzed it, out of the depths of their biological nature; but once the biologically founded pattern is brought into being at the level of psyche, culture, and spirit, conscious engagement by both men and woman becomes possible.

The obvious next questions are: What pattern is programmed into the woman's being at the level of her genes, gonads, and hormones? And what benefits might cultural incarnation of this Feminine principle bring to humankind, perhaps to be catalyzed at first out of the depths of woman's biological nature, and then to become available for conscious engagement by women and men alike?

One answer, which looks backward from the perspective of male-initiated differentiation, notes that the female way is simpler, less developed, more primitive, closer to nature, lacking in discriminating consciousness. The matriarchal stage of human development may be thought of as expressing in the psychological and social realm what the AA . . . XX pattern of mother-and-daughter replication typifies: identity by inclusion rather than by differentiation; self-evident lineage through the mother; primacy of mothers and daughters. Although the body cells of both men and women replicate in accordance with this design, it is a feminine pattern in that this matched-pair format encompasses the female (XX) but not the male (YY) chromosome pattern.

However, the XX formulation also has a second set of meanings, which may indicate features to be expected in the Emergent Age. The XX pair functions in a way fundamentally unlike any other chromosome pair. During embryological development, at some sites the X^m genes turn themselves off. At other sites the reverse takes place, creating an intricate mosaic.[12] Instead of dominance of one over the other, both X^m and X^p are given expression. They retain their distinct identities in a mosaic of creative co-existence. Herein lies the message encoded at the level of genes and chromosomes, which may in time be manifested in a psychocultural system, in the same sense as the underlying pattern of masculine differentiation has found expression in the Patriarchal Age. In the age to come, not only masculine and feminine but *any* pair of opposites differentiated by patriarchal consciousness will be discovered to have equal value and stature. Metaphorically speaking, this exemplifies the sort of both-and quality characteristic of yang-feminine consciousness. It illustrates an egalitarian rather than hierarchical relationship between opposites.

As the Patriarchal Age draws to a close, a new sort of consciousness, reflecting the exertive womb and the X^mX^p chromosome pattern, is beginning to emerge. It overcomes the subject-object split not by reimmersing ego-consciousness in the matrix, but by transcending ego-consciousness through a both-and perspective. The ego and the unconscious psyche come into dialogue as equally important components of the total psychological field. The new consciousness is no longer identified with the ego or with any single perspective. It operates flexibly across shifting psychological contexts. Opposites that are mutually exclusive as seen by differentiating consciousness are no longer contradictory when seen from consciousness that is simultaneously at home in multiple contexts. Ego and unconscious might be pictured as mutually midwifing the delivery of self-transcendence, back and forth between themselves. Although uncommon in the Patriarchal Age, this style of consciousness has been attained by the great mystics of every religion and the great shamans of every century. In the Emergent Age, such multivalent consciousness will likely become commonplace.

The belief that patriarchy must be rejected outright in order to move into a new age is itself an expression of the patriarchal proclivity for either-or choices and for the ranking of alternatives as good or bad, rather than as simply unlike. From the phallic perspective, transcending this either-or duality entails building bridges between opposites. Such configurations as truces and treaties, even the gesture of shaking hands, express the motif of bridging between alien opposites. In patriarchal terms, the route to the next age is a bridge connecting the old worldview to the new one. From the perspective of the exertive womb, what is needed is not a bridge but a more comprehensive context that transcends and embraces both ways.

22 · THE FUTURE OF
THE FEMININE

· · · · · · ·

EDWARD C. WHITMONT

In his seminal work, Return of the Goddess, *New York Jungian analyst Edward C. Whitmont, M.D., elegantly lays out compelling evidence for the reemergence of feminine "ego values" in both individuals and society at large. He believes that these values, denied and suppressed for thousands of years of masculine domination, come at a time of dire need: the end of the patriarchy and the beginning of a critical impasse into a new era.*

Whitmont proposes that the heroic tradition—which relies upon pushing, strength, will, reason, honor, responsibility, and the myth of objectivity—is now being replaced by the Goddess tradition, which values inwardness, feeling, acceptance, paradox, uncertainty, and living in the moment. In this new context, the reality of our subjectivity, dubbed by Whitmont "the old enemy," becomes an honored source of wisdom. And women, who often have easier access to the feeling-subjective realm, become the guides for men and culture and the "guardians of interiority."

As we increasingly turn away from an extroverted, materialistic orientation and toward the deep unconscious, more of us will come face-to-face with the dark, long-buried Feminine. Whitmont points out that women have been as guilty as men of disowning "improper," uncaring, enraged, or depressed qualities; we have all colluded in devaluing the forbidden Feminine. And because women are by and large more feminine than men, he says, we have been socially and politically declared inferior by mutual consent. Like Robert M. Stein, who calls for liberating the Feminine rather than liberating women, Whitmont endorses the goals of feminism while insisting on honoring archetypal differences between the Masculine and the Feminine.

Whitmont uses the word return *in referring to the arrival in our midst of the Feminine or the Goddess; however, he is aware that the historical sacrifice of this principle was needed for the evolutionary development of the patriarchy and the psychological development of separate, individual egos. So this phenomenon is not a return to the old form of the Goddess; she has evolved along with humanity and emerges now more fully conscious than ever before.*

This piece is reprinted from Return of the Goddess *(1982) with permission from Crossroad.*

Edward C. Whitmont, M.D., is chairman emeritus of the C. G. Jung Institute of New York. His books include The Symbolic Quest; Psyche and Substance; *and, with Sylvia Brinton Perera,* Dreams: A Portal to the Source.

Femininity can no longer be limited to responsiveness, passivity, and mothering. It will discover and express its active, initiating, creative and transformative capacity. This expresses itself in the readiness to demand and challenge: for example, to demand subjective affirmation and acceptance of one's being as it is, to affirm readiness to play and to be played with. It includes whatever is given, whether deemed poor or bad, and it leads to acceptance of empathy, "suffering with." Such new stirring is also bound to affect men, in the form of inevitable new demands from women, as well as from the anima, the feminine aspect of their own psyches.

For women and for the anima [the Feminine in men], the new femininity requires self-affirmation if they are to be able to give adequate affirmation to the uniqueness of others. We cannot really give what we do not have ourselves. We treat others as we treat ourselves, regardless of conscious attempts to the contrary.

Self-affirmation for women means, first and foremost, acceptance of their differentness from men, rather than identification, imitation, and competitiveness with them. Only by first finding this basic feminine stance can they also claim their Yang element and give expression to their masculine drives and capacities, in their own ways, as women. Then they can call upon the rousing, ordering, and creative impulses to enter, fill, and impregnate them. They can allow themselves to contain and suffer these urges in their conflicting, nourishing as well as destructive, natures until they are assimilable into a human relationship.

The raw impulses—to hurt, to possess, to make something or someone conform to one's expectation—can be destructive when vented as they occur. This is true for men no less than women. We have been trained by our culture, therefore, to deal with these impulses by means of control or disguise, by will and discipline only, or to reason them away. The male psyche, attuned as it is to repressive discipline, may partially get away with this way of dealing with impulses. Such evasion is felt as hurtful by the woman's psyche. It amounts to a repression of the transformative Yin, the Medusa aspect that needs to generate new forms and make them rise out of the depth in its own way and timing. Equally, it thwarts those who manifest this generative process: Lila, the play experimenter, and Athena-Pallas, the civilizer.

While men may wait for a strategically feasible moment, women's timing is determined by the inner experiencing of cycles and events that "fit" together because they are felt as one. The instinctual impulses need to be affirmed within until they ripen into what, on the personal level, is mutually bearable and acceptable. Then they are to be issued as the challenge of inner fact, not as manipulation by guilt or threat. Thereby woman takes on the role of an initiator and leader into a new experience of subjectivity.

She initiates by arousing and yearning, by clearly stating her needs and affirming her standpoint, both to herself and to her partner.

For men and the animus [the Masculine in women], the new demands of the Yin require the courage to let go of their firm ego position of control over self and others. They have to learn to affirm what is *not* I—the reality of the other—and to respect power and needs that are beyond their control or competence. Instead of putting all of their efforts into the attempt to achieve their superego ideal, they will have to learn a measure of "letting be." This is essential if they are to become capable of genuinely affirming what they really are, rather than what they wish to be. This requires a new type of courage: namely, to live not only with strength but also with vulnerability.

One will suffer the conflict between opposing drives and callings, living between the "ought to" and the "want to," without attempting a premature decision. A *tour de force* of will in favor of one or the other side will no longer do. One will need to live in uncertainty while abstaining from seemingly rational decisions until reason, wish and "gut" feelings can agree.

That means mustering the courage to enter the abyss by allowing oneself to be enveloped, temporarily, by the chaos of subjectivity, the old enemy. It means to lose oneself in order to find oneself eventually. In so doing, men and women will be called upon to try and give tentative expression to their "foolish" or "absurd" feeling urges and personally toned reactions, without losing the integrity of ethical responsibility. They will need to practice "letting go" without betraying or throwing overboard honor, self-respect or respect for the rights of others. The ethical precept "Thou shalt not inflict harm" must still be primary.

The change we are speaking of means to learn to affirm one's psychological pregnancy and sensitivity and thereby reclaim one's own femininity, the personalizing and civilizing force arising out of subjective chaos. In this way, men too can discover their relative passivity, or rather, responsiveness, to the initiating challenge of the Feminine without and within.

These new ego values necessitate a radical change in the masculine value system of both sexes. The heroic striving for dominance, conquest and power, the topdog-underdog order of things, the rule of authority and rank, of right and wrong, my way or your way, will have to be modified by the capacity to endure simultaneous, seemingly mutually exclusive opposites. We must learn to appreciate shadings and a spectrum of colors rather than black-and-white systems; to enjoy intertwining polyphony rather than a single dominant melody to which the rest of the ensemble merely adds harmonizing voices. The new masculine values must respect a variety of different gods or ideals, rather than only one dominant God who is lord and king. Parliamentary cooperation is called for rather than monarchical or even majority rule. Such a value system, far from being chaotic, would initiate a new integrative, moving, and balancing order rather than the static version we are used to.

The former masculine ideal of conquering hero or king is now modified by the role of the seeker or discoverer. The new aspect of the Feminine appears as revealer, guardian, and challenger; the mediator to herself and to the masculine way of being as it is, the priestess of life's values and mysteries. Women, too, need to find the seeker in themselves. Men need to respond to the guardian revealer and challenger of personal value—within, no less than without.

What is the value which the new Feminine finds itself called upon to reassert in the face of the patriarchal trends within and without? It is the very one which is the goal of the masculine search for the Grail, the vessel or magical cauldron of life's play and renewal. It is the self-experience of soul through subjective and personal feeling and intuiting in relation to the concrete here and now. What is valued is the feel of this moment in joy and pain, not the abstract ideas or remote heavens of unending, peaceful perfection to which the patriarchy was wont to aspire.

Patriarchy repressed the magical stratum, the fairy world. In this global awareness, life and death were the peak and valley of one wave. Emotional oneness was experienced with group, clan, nature and blood. Life was known through instinctual tides and rhythms, ESP communication, and yielding openness to whatever came along.

In their archaic form, these tendencies are overly passive, fatalistic and hence regressive relative to our present level of consciousness. Integrated, however, with the best achievements of the mental phase and of patriarchal ethics, and reality-tested in the here and now of self-experience and inter-personal relationships, they are to contribute a new step in the evolution of consciousness.

The new femininity is to establish the value of inwardness, and of affirmation (but also conscious clarification and differentiation) of whatever *is*. It is open to—and able to integrate—woundedness, pain, and ugliness, as well as joy and beauty. The sensuous is to be valued no less than the spiritual; the intangible no less than the concrete. Finally, the patriarchal achievements of the past must not be overthrown, but integrated into this new outlook.

The archetypal role of the new femininity is to stand as a priestess of the fullness of life as it is, with its unpredictable pitfalls and unfathomable depths, richness and deprivation, risks and errors, joys and pains. She insists on personal experiencing and personal response to the needs of the human situation.

She may play and dance as Artemis, allure as Aphrodite, domesticate as Vesta, or be maternal as Demeter. She may function as Athena by furthering civilization and skills, or be concerned with comfort and the relief of misery as Mary. These are but a few of the many faces of the Great Goddess. They all aim at transforming the chaotic power of the abysmal Yin, the Medusa, into the play of life. They mediate the terrifying face of the Gorgon into the helpful one of Athena. Life is to be lived and savored for its own sake, in sensitive interplay with earth and cosmos as living organisms, rather than as dead objects of exploitation for the sake of economic or technological "progress."

Tomorrow's woman, if she is to meet as well as issue this challenge, will need to be open and attuned to her own tides and instinctual directives. The awareness that hurts can heal us. The wound is inevitable. Awareness of this allows her to risk involvement rather than opt for avoidance. Particularly in subjective and personal encounters she will be open to and accepting of facts, impulses and feelings—even though they may seem ugly, destructive, and forbidden by traditional (as well as her own) standards of aesthetics and morality. This means nothing less than receiving into consciousness and clarifying feelings, fantasies, and desires regardless of their moral or aesthetic implications.

It also means separating emotion and motivation from action. Traditionally we have held that guilt lies in thought and feeling, no less than in action. We have held ourselves responsible for asocial or unconventional desires, impulses, or fantasies because we have the sense that feeling is equivalent to action. In the good world created and regulated by the good King-God, any impulse or feeling contrary to his law must be an expression of Satan, or of our own evil. Hence, we have learned to repress our "improper" wishes, feelings, and fantasies. We do not allow ourselves to admit, for example, that in a rage we might feel like breaking the neck of our own child. Such a feeling is too horrible for words, or even thoughts.

Yet even such an impulse is an expression of the life force. It shows us what feeling is actually there at this moment—regardless of what we may wish. Later we may feel differently again. The fantasy, if it can be contained, waited with, nourished, meditated on and listened to as a symbolic statement—no matter how awful or repellent the thought—may eventually reveal a hidden wisdom and open new avenues of energy. The urge to wring the child's neck may alert an all too lovingly sweet and cloying mother to the desirability of a different outlook. Symbolically, she may need to turn or twist the neck into a different direction, or break a too-rigid, stiff-necked stereotype in her indulgent attitude toward herself or to the child. It is a challenge to think and feel through everything that may present itself, and wait for its hidden symbolic message, rather than to act out or sweep things under the rug.

The new woman (or the anima in a man) will have to champion and protect the need to live through and experience everything that (lest it threaten established order with chaos) has been repressed by the patriarchy. She stands not for abstract oughts but for emotional facts, however these may affect people in a given situation and moment of time.

It is important to realize that when the woman (or the anima) allows this "night phase" of forbidden impulses to touch her, she enters the realm of Medusa, the underworld of the dark Yin. It is like the Sumerian Inanna's descent into the underworld of death and terror to meet her sister, the black Ereshkigal. During this phase she is as though lost to the daily world of the living. Hence she must wait and refrain from acting upon her impulses. What she beholds is not yet fit for this life. For while in this phase she is related only to her own as yet unknown, puzzling, and even threatening depth, not to any person, as dear or close as they may be to her otherwise. She may feel utterly detached, indifferent, and devoid of warmth—even hateful—toward anyone who makes demands upon her. Like Inanna, in the legend, she is naked, impaled, and dead in the presence of Ereshkigal; devoid of external relatedness.

This state can be extremely frightening to her and to those around her, needless to say. The temptation is great, therefore, to deny and repress the experience and do something instead. But whatever is done while in that state is likely to be the wrong, if not outrightly destructive, thing to do. On the other hand, the descent into the underworld presages a renewal of life, if consciously suffered through. Through waiting, and through listening to the images of the deep as to a child to be guarded and raised, a new phase of personal life can be gained. Risking the descent into "incubation" by the dark Yin for the sake of such a transformation and renewal necessitates a disregard, temporarily at least, for all oughts or shoulds and abstract notions. Only in the light of the raw personal experiences can new values be found and reality-tested.

If she can sustain the tension of this phase, a woman functions as a challenger in the service of unfolding life. She brings forth new patterns out of the depth of chaos, and demands that they be accepted and somehow integrated and valued, not only in their nurturing, but also in their potentially destructive implications. For a need can be life-sustaining yet, at the same time, shatter an already existing state. Change and transformation must do away with the established old. Hence the affirmation of the new is first for the sake of confrontation and internal gestation. Temporarily at least, it requires a renunciation of "I want" no less than of "I should."

For the time being, the question of enactment of the fantasies or impulses is disregarded. Psychological acceptance, contemplation, and meditation come first. Then I often suggest that the images be woven into a semblance of a mythological play or ritual that could be enacted by mutual consent, for the sake of experiencing the emotional charge and symbolic significance. Now the wringing of the neck of the formerly mentioned fantasy may be transformed into a pantomime of clawing or tearing to pieces, or forcefully turning in a new direction; into an ecstatic dance or Dionysian frolic, for instance. A new life-myth can thus be found. It may be experienced, totally or in part, in ritual or psychodramatic enactment, and then be reality-tested in terms of what is possible or mutually acceptable in relationship. Only through this gestation period will new insights and a new conscience be born which, with the full consent of the "deep," can risk defying conventional rules of morality, should this be necessary. Prior to this process, all action carries the risk of acting out.

Such acceptance and protection of the urges of newly emerging life impulses require an attitude comparable to dealing with a little child. It involves a readiness to play and experiment, while ever concerned with relative safety, with whatever happens to be, for the sake of gentle disciplining, rather than repressing. This attitude is like dancing an attentive and sensitive moving with the tides of being and happening, regardless of whether or not they fit in with what should be.

In thus gestating her feelings, impulses, and fantasies, the woman becomes a revealer, both of herself to herself and of others to themselves. For our motivations to action flow from our emotions and feelings, not only from our thoughts. Only through mobilizing feeling do thoughts motivate action. All too often, they merely rationalize feeling and emotional bias. We cannot understand ourselves fully without understanding our feelings and feeling-toned urges.

Like the moon, this gestating affirmation reflects; it has a mirroring and gently revealing effect. Not only does it reflect one's own being, it can help others experience their subjective reality as it emerges in a particular encounter. This kind of learning—far better than abstract explanations or precepts of how it should be—occurs through gradual revelation and experiencing.

It is a significant parallel that in our time also the new physics has discovered that all reality is subjective in so far as it grows out of the encounter between the observer and his interaction with and orientation toward a "you," the reacting object of the observation. What we have formerly considered objective reality we are now discovering to be subjective experience of encounter and relationships.

Such affirmative revealing contrasts with, but also complements, the masculine questioning, doubting, and criticizing that characterizes our intellectual tradition. The goal of the quest is a discovery of "faith." This means trust in the "river," the flow of life. This cannot be seen and touched in space, but can be discovered only through time and through experiencing its significance and value in one's own emotional self. For that reason, the feminine self has a greater difficulty than the male in feeling her a *separate* self. Hers is rather a *feeling with* selfness.

The feminine ego is more like an open channel, a flow in herself of emotions, feelings and perceptions. She is not as rigidly will-and-conviction-determined as the male, but more open to finding natural order in what at first seems like chaos; namely, the flow of unstructured and unordered, nonrational dynamics and events. By empathizing with and nurturing, the feminine ego reveals and affirms the subjective experience of the moment as a new dimension of reality which extends not only in space, but also in the moving dimension of time. While opening a new capacity for psychological sensitivity through empathy, this relative ego plasticity, however, can also pose difficulties. This undifferentiated flow—not sufficiently sustained by her own Yang clarity, differentiation and assurance—can spell confusion, self-doubt, and dependency. The result is a need for affirmation, for being told by others, particularly men, that she really exists and that her revelations and subjective experiences are of value for others, not just for herself. That sensual and sensuous connectedness to whatever is, the sense of beauty, pleasure, enjoyment, and play also has tended to bring upon women the reproach of frivolousness (if not being the tool of Satan) by the patriarchy.

The above by no means invalidates, but rather extends, the maternal and nurturing role, which is deeply and fundamentally an inseparable part of the feminine character. In some form or other, some tendency to mothering or being the daughter makes itself inevitably felt in every relationship encounter. A feeling for the other as a child, and of union with that child, is an intrinsic part of the nonseparative way of experiencing existence. The Feminine, consequently, implies also a sense of conceiving and nursing, of caring for life, and of being in touch with one's roots in nature. It is important for a woman to be able to relate consciously to this dimension, lest it get out of hand in the form of suffocating or overbearing mothering, and also in case its conventional channels seem closed.

When pulling away from one's children or projects, and when the ego position feels threatened by the pressure of abstract oughts and shoulds which can make one feel childish, the necessity for self-mothering arises in men as much as in women. Then one's own weakness and neediness call for support from oneself, for tender comforting and protecting until one can rally oneself. When this need for nurturing is not satisfied, emptiness and depression are likely to set in. This applies as much if not more to self-mothering as to caring for others. Acceptance of this necessity is again in contrast with, as well as complementary to, the predominantly extroverted patriarchal tradition of the West, which one-sidedly stresses outgoing activity and "doing for others" in disregard of one's own needs and desires.

Caring for and respecting others in their true otherness is an indispensable first step of individuation. The next step fills and deepens this through the emergence of the new Feminine as the embodiment of inwardness, which stands maternally in defense of inner values and of one's own uncertainties resulting from the untrustworthiness of outer rule and law. It expresses the need to gestate, patiently to listen into the time dimension, to let the tides rise and ebb until time brings forth the moment of birth.

Lastly, the intrinsic inward directedness of the Feminine ushers in a new form of relationship to—and experience of—the divine and of one's life as a transpersonally given individual pattern of destiny. With the exception of its mystical undercurrents, the stress of Western patriarchal religiosity has been extroverted. God is depicted as a grim, self-righteous, and humorless male patriarch, in spite of all the protestations that "God is love." He has his abode somewhere "up there." Heaven and hell have been represented as localities in space. A religious life is taught in behavioral terms of omission and commission of certain acts regardless of individual needs and differences in obedience to God's law, as certified by church and state.

This extroverted religiousness taught us social consciousness. But in our time, it has reached its saturation point. It has degenerated into moralistic preaching and into a worldview that can see only material and economic dynamics, devoid of any relevance to the mystery of existence. The resurgence of the Feminine, however, reopens the possibility of access to this mystery by revalidating the inward subjective dimension.

In the world of the Goddess, materiality is seen as a manifestation of spirit, rather than as something separate from it. Matter is but one form in which the ever-creative pulse of life, meaning and evolving consciousness is perceived. It is the palpability and visibility of soul and spirit, as are our bodies. Hence the experience of the mystery of the "ultimate" is to be sought in the subjective, here-and-now experiencing of our problems, pains, and joys, including those of our bodies. The unfolding of daily life—its personal and relationship conflicts, difficulties and discoveries—can become transparent with a meaning that aims to incarnate through the time dimension. Personal experience takes precedence over abstract reasoning and dogma. Joy and pain, beauty and ugliness, spirituality and sensuality are to be accepted and recognized as manifestations of transcendent power, hence as sacred and sacramental. They are the ways in which we experience the webs of our life's destiny, inner as well as outer. In accepting and embracing them we submit ourselves to the tests of growth and transformation. Through asking "What do they serve?" [the question asked of the Grail], we can discover a dimension of meaning in our lives that points beyond ego limitations. Asking "What ails you?" and "What pleases you?" helps us toward awareness of feeling, toward becoming conscious of the depth and richness of our subjective emotional being.

Feeling now takes on a new orienting and validating function. In its subjective circular way (unlike the "objective" linear path of reason), it nevertheless contains its own objectivity in the sense of providing reliable intelligence. It is a new informational guide, largely undifferentiated and awkward as yet, to be refined and developed into a skill, in a way that is not unlike the way thinking evolved during the patriarchal epoch.

A new, inwardly oriented depth psychology is discovering in feeling new avenues to life decisions and existential orientations. Feeling qualities or attitudes are seen to be inherent in the web of life and cosmos, and need to be related to as objectively given and many-faceted, rather than just good or bad.

An example illustrates this new experiential attitude. A middle-aged analysand was wrestling with the problems posed by her traditional black/white morality. She had a hypnagogic vision or dream. In it she beheld a divine, creatorlike being holding the earth globe in its hands and, with amused detachment, watching and playing with conflagrations, wars, catastrophes and destruction on earth. Upon being questioned by the horrified dreamer, "Why do you let such things happen?" it answered: "Because it pleases me."

The shocked dreamer was confronted here with that aspect of the creative force which we have previously described as the transformative. In the West, this aspect has been sundered from the patriarchal God image of absolute goodness and justice. In the older Goddess representations, such as the Egyptian Sekhmet or the Indian Kali, we still find the complementary aspects of engendering life, love, and joy as well as revelling in suffering, destruction, and death. This duality of function emotionally encompasses the actual fullness of existence, the *no* phase which we have repressed.

It is this very *no* phase that is to be revalidated in the new experience of the Feminine. The feeling function as a guide includes this *no* phase in the form of not caring, detachment, and even affirming destruction as a necessity, when the nourishing and supportive phase has run out and is no longer relevant to the given situation. For, in order to affirm, one must also be able to reject; in order to support, one must also be able to allow failure. The feminine instinct refuses to have to give, to be told how it should feel, that it should love and support when the actual feeling says *no* and calls for detachment and even rejection. This is a new lesson to be learned in the relationship between people and in one's way of being in the world.

Relationships, of necessity, contain varying degrees and timings of distance, noncommunication, and even rejection and dislike. These need to be acknowledged, tolerated, and affirmatively worked with if the connection between participants is to be kept alive. The negative can give background to whatever attracts and holds the participants together. In the same way, a two-dimensional flatness is avoided in a painting by allowing dark/light contrasts. Likewise, dissonances in music intensify the emotional impact of their resolution in consonance. Without them, the result would be boredom. At other times, renewal of life which has run its course can occur only through death and destruction. This also calls for emotional affirmation.

Seemingly difficult and painful *no* phases, when everything seems to go against us, are not just frustrating waste periods. They express a purposeful, if negative, inward-turning phase. They manifest a special feeling aspect unfolding in the time dimension. They are just as vital in their messages and perceptions as the affirmative ones.

Over and over again, the psyche seeks inner changes which need to be mediated through psychological understanding if acting out is to be avoided. Destruction is always the ending of a cycle, and is the indicator of a new beginning. It calls for creation rather than mere repression or paralyzing despair.

The Feminine is attuned to moving about more naturally than the Masculine in the ups and downs of this dimension, in not expecting (indeed distrusting) perfection and semblance of permanent stability. Thereby it remains in touch with the mystery of becoming; of birth which equals death, of both the allure and the threat of the world-play as an unending process. It is in touch with the destiny aspect of the Goddess.

23 · FEMININITY
REGAINED

· · · · · · · ·

R O B E R T   A .   J O H N S O N

Eminent Jungian storyteller Robert A. Johnson retells this legend about King Arthur's search to answer the perennial question: "What does woman really want?" It offers us clues about how to awaken and redeem the interior Feminine.

As Johnson always reminds his listeners, we need to interpret the story in the inner realm, in the realm of the psyche. The wise old woman, in her guise as ugly witch, represents the rejected and despised aspect of the Feminine. She claims that she wants one thing only. And when Gawain marries her and treats her in a special way, she receives it—and is alchemically transformed into a beautiful young maiden.

The story urges us to invite in and to honor the abandoned Feminine within ourselves and within society, so that she will hold her rightful place in the scheme of life.

This piece is reprinted from Femininity Lost and Regained *(1990) by Robert A. Johnson with permission from Harper & Row.*

Robert A. Johnson is a noted Jungian lecturer and writer in San Diego, California. He is the author of He: Understanding Masculine Psychology; She: Understanding Feminine Psychology; We: Understanding the Psychology of Romantic Love; Ecstasy: Understanding the Psychology of Joy; Inner Work: Using Dreams *and* Active Imagination for Personal Growth; *and* Femininity Lost and Regained. *He studied with C. G. Jung in Switzerland and at the Sri Aurobindo Ashram in India.*

Femininity is so basic and fundamental a part of human personality that it cannot be disregarded for long. It may be set aside for a period of time so that masculinity might have center stage to solidify the partriarchal values of law, order, form and science. It is unlikely that these values could be established and rooted unless they were given exclusive rights to the center stage of evolution, as they have had for the last three thousand years.

But the Feminine will return and take its rightful place as soon as the masculine evolution is secure. Some wonderfully bright and warm examples of this return are to be seen in our age. Probably humanity has never been in so rich a position as now; a golden age of mechanical power is available, and a new age of feminine values is possible. To establish the basis of leisure which the modern world offers for great numbers of people has been a noble accomplishment. To add the feminine insights of a conscious mentality is our next step. As truly modern people we are at the crest of a wave where we can have the best of both worlds, if we are wise enough to escape the modern prejudice of one-sidedness. To fail this is to invite the worst of both worlds, which would set us back into a dark age.

A profound lesson about the way that feminine energy can be returned to modern life is illustrated in one of the stories of King Arthur. We return to the mythic dimension of life to learn about our interior psychological dynamics. In general, the Arthurian stories are the appearance of a new idea of chivalry and nobility, but they recount only a partial delivery of femininity from its bondage. But one story is far in advance of its time (or are we far behind in our comprehension?), and tells the noble story of a transformation of darkness into light. It is the story of Arthur and the puzzling question, "What does woman really want?"

King Arthur, in his youth, was caught poaching in the forests of the neighboring kingdom and was caught by that King. He might well have been killed immediately, for that was the punishment for transgressing the laws of property and ownership. But the neighboring King was touched by Arthur's youth and winsome character. He offered Arthur freedom if he could find the answer to a very difficult question within one year. The question: What does woman really want? This would stagger the wisest of men and seemed insurmountable for the youth. It was better than hanging, so Arthur returned home and began questioning everyone he could find. Harlot and nun, princess and queen, wiseman and court fool—all were questioned, but none could give a convincing answer. Each advised, however, that there was one who would know, the old witch. The cost would be high, for it was proverbial in the realm that the old witch charged ruinous prices for her services.

The last day of the year arrived and Arthur finally was driven to consult the old hag. She agreed to provide an answer, which would satisfy the accusing King, but the price had to be discussed first. The price? Marriage of the old witch to Gawain, the noblest knight of the Round Table and Arthur's lifelong and closest friend. Arthur looked at the old witch in horror; she was ugly, had only one tooth, gave forth a stench that would sicken a goat, made obscene sounds and was humpbacked. Never was there a more loathsome sight! Arthur quailed at the prospect of asking his lifelong friend to assume this terrible burden for him. But Gawain, when he heard of the bargain, agreed that this was not too much to give his companion and for the preservation of the Round Table.

The wedding was announced and the old hag gave of her infernal wisdom: What does woman really want? She wants sovereignty over her own life. Everyone knew on the instant of hearing this that great feminine wisdom had been spoken, and Arthur would be safe. The accusing King did, indeed, give Arthur his freedom when he heard the answer.

But the wedding! All the court was there, and none more torn between relief and distress than Arthur himself. Gawain was courteous, gentle and respectful; the old witch brought forth her worst manners, wolfed the food from her plate without aid of utensils, made hideous noises and smells. Never before or since had the court of Arthur been subject to such a strain. But courtesy prevailed and the wedding was accomplished.

The wedding night was worse, according to the tale, and we shall draw a curtain of circumspection over the proceedings, except for one wonderful moment. When Gawain was prepared for the wedding bed and waiting for his bride to join him, she appeared as the loveliest maiden a man could ever wish to see! Gawain, in his astonishment, asked what had happened. The maiden replied that because Gawain *had been courteous to her*, she would show him her hideous side half of the time, and her gracious side the other half of the time. Which of the two did he choose for the day and which for the night? This is a cruel question to put before a man, and Gawain did rapid calculation. Did he want a lovely maiden to show forth during the day where all of his friends could see, and a hideous hag at night in the privacy of their chamber; or did he want a hideous hag during the day and a lovely maiden in the intimate moments of their life? Noble man that he was, Gawain replied that he would let the maiden choose for herself. At this, the maiden announced that she would be a fair damsel to him both day and night, since he *had given her respect and sovereignty over her own life*.

If femininity has been driven into its hideous mode, the best that a man can do is maintain respect and courtesy. This is the magic of transformation which will restore femininity-gone-dark more quickly to its true beauty than any other way. This story about the dynamic of interior feminine energy is as important for men attempting to relate to their feminine side as it is for women trying to live out of their core identity. And it is a principle that should not be lost on external male-female relationships.

We are only beginning the task of restoring the precious feminine quality of humanity which is so infinitely valuable to us. Our discontent and subtle suffering spring from the loss of the feminine values, and we face formidable obstacles in restoring this value. At present, we make feeble attempts at gender equality—getting equal remuneration for equal work, respect and dignity for specifically feminine things such as name, title, ownership. But a much more subtle task remains: gaining equal time and dignity for those feeling values which are the subtle dimensions of femininity. Leisure, spontaneity, and artistry ask for dignity and respect equal to the time-honored pursuits of money and security. These tasks remain to be done and await our attention.

EPILOGUE

. . . .

Two violent contrary winds, one masculine and the other feminine, met and
clashed at a crossroads. For a moment they
counterbalanced each other, thickened, and
became visible.

This crossroads is the Universe. This
crossroads is my heart.

This dance of the gigantic erotic collision
is transmitted from the darkest particle of
matter to the most spacious thought.

NIKOS KAZANTZAKIS

After an intense conversation in which the ideas in this book came truly
alive for us, my dear friend Marian Rose, a dance ceremonialist in San
Francisco, wrote this Ode to the Feminine:

This is what I know: The Feminine has been wounded and devalued. The
Feminine is not about women, even though traditionally women have been
the guardians of the Feminine. But we have abdicated that power—no
blame—it has been a way of survival to do so.

But the Feminine is the feeling function, the relation function, eros and
sexuality, nurturing, supporting and honoring the earth and her life forms.
The Feminine is not about women! It is not about men; it is not about the
battle of the sexes or the battle of power between the matriarchy and the
patriarchy.

The Feminine is not about how to manipulate a man to get commitment,
security, and power; it is not about how to fight the system to achieve equality;
it isn't about women's art and our silenced voices; it's not about biology as
destiny when we define ourselves as our bodies, as the givers of life, as vessels.

The Feminine is cross-cultural, cross-sexual. The Feminine is the voice
of rebirth.

The Feminine is the voice of the hag, the voice of the victim, the voice
of the adulteress, the voice of the Vietnam veterans, the voices of the devas
and spirits. The Feminine is not to be defined and limited for the sake of this
book because to define it is to limit and categorize, and the Feminine is not
ready for that animus function now.

The Feminine has not been silenced really; it is just speaking another
language. It is not invited inside certain places. It has been collectively devalued,

and yet it is not a victim, it is not wounded; it is strong, it is present. It is dark *and* light. It is one with the patriarchy. It is the alienation and the women's movement, and the arms buildup, and the wife-beater. It is neither the great victim nor the great savior.

The task that is being asked of us is that we make a quantum leap out of the duality of matriarchy and patriarchy. When women are released from being holders of the relating function, we will have more creative energy to go forth. When men are released from being bullies and heroes in reaction against the powerful mother figure, they will have more energy to go forth.

So the task of transformation is not to be left on women's shoulders just because it is our voice that has seemingly been repressed. The voice of the Masculine also has been repressed, and it too needs to be reborn.

Today it is the voice of rebirth that is reaching out to make itself heard among the clamor—the rebirth of matter *and* spirit, the rebirth of power *and* love, the rebirth of the Masculine *and* the Feminine, each sovereign in its domain, each whole in relation to its counterpart.

If the nature of this world is duality, then unity can arise only from a conscious duality. A premature transcendence, an alliance of opposites that have not yet become themselves, can only collapse like a three-legged chair.

So our task is to clarify, to differentiate the archetypes. Although this sounds like a straightforward mandate, it is not so, for the Feminine can be known only symbolically. This is the reason for our struggle and, inevitably, for our failure to attach to the Feminine a specific set of traits. For this reason, each of us must seek and find our own way to the images, feelings, and actions that arise from within and that express the Feminine for us.

For me, the conception, labor, and birth of this book have paralleled the ongoing birth of the Conscious Feminine within. Toward the end of the writing, I had the following dream: *I'm swimming in a large natural pond and come to a rope, where Hispanic people are stopped. I take them across, explaining that they are now in the United States, "Los Estados Unidos." People cry and hug. I swim back to a large woman, a colorful contemporary Goddess and hug her. She says she thinks she will be destroyed. But I say, "No, I will take you across."*

To me this dream is hopeful: I am swimming in deep waters, facing a border crossing, bringing with me my instincts and my femininity. The Goddess expresses her fear of destruction, her awareness of her vulnerability as we approach a new world, perhaps the technological patriarchal society. I pledge to protect her, to carry the consciousness of the Goddess and her plight into this new environment.

I see this integration in women everywhere. A deep healing is taking place in all the domains described in this book: the Mother World, the Father World, the body, the divine, and the collective. Our intimate relationships with men, especially, need our careful attention as we navigate the waves of change, giving up our victim status, our co-dependence, our anger and blame, and our myths of romantic perfection.

In the 1960s, we used to say "the personal is political." Today, with a new understanding of archetypal psychology, I would say "the personal is collective." That is, in our individual psyches we participate in something larger. We cannot do the personal work of making the unconscious conscious without affecting the collective unconscious. For this reason, inner work is not selfish.

It also is not simple or easy. The quest for self-knowledge is a lifelong quest, and there are many pitfalls on the path. In our case, to choose the Feminine in a culture that devalues it is a difficult and courageous task.

But in our era, for the first time in human history, small numbers of people have the opportunity to do the psychological and spiritual work of the Self, which Jung called individuation and teachers of the East call self-realization. This evolutionary opportunity arises because our basic survival needs are met and some of our basic ego needs are met.

The cultural wave is beneath us, supporting our efforts, buoying us to shore. The paradox of the patriarchy has peaked: an underdeveloped sense of self coupled with an overdeveloped technology has created the crisis we face. In response, the Feminine has appeared in many forms: a renewed respect for the earth, for relationship, for children; a surge of interest in healing, compassion, and altruism. Ecology itself implies action in the context of relationship, a quintessentially feminine kind of action.

As the feminine voice is reinstated, another kind of masculinity is beginning to appear. Poet Robert Bly calls it "the deep masculine." Marion Woodman calls it Conscious Masculinity. With its emergence we have the very real opportunity to do spiritual alchemy, to meet the mystery of the Other in the sacred marriage.

Dream the myth onwards. . . .

C. G. JUNG

NOTES

. . . .

CHAPTER 3/STEIN

1. Genia Pauli Haddon, "On Delivering Yang-Femininity," *Spring* 1987, 133.

2. Walter F. Otto, *The Homeric Gods: The Spiritual Significance of Greek Religion* (London: Thames & Hudson, 1954), 203.

3. This notion that "the behavior of man depends on reason, whereas all animals are governed by instinct" (Saint Thomas Aquinas), which has such deep roots in Western tradition, is absolutely foreign to the Eastern mind and Oriental religions.

4. Frank Thilly, *A History of Philosophy* (New York: Henry Holt, 1927), 272f.

5. Otto, *The Homeric Gods*, 161.

6. Ibid., 53.

7. Ibid., 55. In this and other quotations from Otto, let me suggest that "Feminine" and "Masculine" be substituted when he uses "woman" and "man."

8. Ibid., 56.

9. Ibid., 161.

10. Robert Stein, *Incest and Human Love: The Betrayal of the Soul in Psychotherapy* (Baltimore: Penguin Books, 1974).

11. Ibid. For a more detailed discussion of this issue, see the section on Phallos.

CHAPTER 4/HANCOCK

1. Emily Hancock, "Women's Development in Adult Life" (Ph.D. diss., Harvard University, 1981).

2. D. W. Winnicott identified this as a zone of the psyche.

3. This phenomenon, noted by Piaget, is called the great cognitive shift by Sheldon White of Harvard University's Department of Psychology and Social Relations. See White's "Some General Outlines of the Matrix of Developmental Changes Between Five and Seven Years," *Bulletin of the Orton Society*, 20: 41–57.

4. Robert Kegan uses this term in a beautiful description of the features of this stage in *The Evolving Self* (Cambridge: Harvard University Press, 1982).

5. H. S. Sullivan named competition and compromise the two hallmarks of the juvenile era.

6. The effect of competence, noted decades ago by Margaret Mead, appears still to operate as it did then. A 1987 cover on *Savvy* magazine proclaims that success makes a woman sexy, but the article concludes that in women, competence and power deflate a man. The author, a psychologist who specializes in human sexuality, advises

a woman to do her best to hide her abilities and feign "submission" if she wants a fulfilling sexual relationship.

CHAPTER 5/HUNT

1. Marion Woodman, lecture delivered at Esalen, Calif., March 1989.

2. Jean Shinoda Bolen, *Goddesses in Everywoman* (New York: Harper & Row, 1985), 100.

3. Carl Gustav Jung, "Psychological Aspects of the Mother Archetype," *The Archetypes of the Collective Unconscious* (New York: Pantheon Bolingen Series, 1959), 90–91.

4. See Adrienne Rich, *Of Woman Born* (New York: W. W. Norton, 1976), Foreword.

5. Marion Woodman, *Addiction to Perfection* (Toronto: Inner City Books) 128–129. The drawing is in the National Gallery, London.

6. John Broadus Watson, *Psychological Care of Infant and Child* [1928] (New York: W. W. Norton, Arno Press, 1972), 5.

7. Ibid., 47 and 81.

8. Alice Miller, *For Your Own Good: Hidden Cruelty in Child-Rearing and the Roots of Violence* (New York: Farrar, Straus & Giroux, 1983), 30.

9. Karen Payne, ed., *Between OurSelves: Letters Between Mothers and Daughters* (New York: Houghton Mifflin, 1984), 189. Includes letters between author Hunt and her daughter Diana.

10. "Dark and Bright Fires," *Bachy* 12, 13 (1978, 1979): 85–93, 107–111. Performed at The Woman's Building, Los Angeles, 1976.

11. Nor Hall, *Mothers and Daughters* (Minneapolis: Rusoff Books, 1976), 36–37.

CHAPTER 7/LOWINSKY

1. Carol Gordon, "Calling Out the Names," in *Women and Aging, an Anthology, Calyx* 9, no. 2 and no. 3 (Winter 1986): 120.

2. Irene Claremont de Castillejo, *Knowing Woman* (New York: Harper Colophon Books, 1973), 174.

3. C. G. Jung, "The Psychological Aspects of the Kore," in Jung and Kerenyi, *Essays on a Science of Mythology* (Princeton, N.J.: Bollingen Series XXII, Princeton University Press, 1959), 162.

4. Barbara Walker, *The Woman's Encyclopedia of Myths and Secrets* (San Francisco: Harper & Row, 1983), 1018.

5. This concept became clear to me in correspondence with Joseph Henderson.

6. Nor Hall, *The Moon and the Virgin* (New York: Harper & Row, 1980).

7. Paula Gunn Allen, "Who Is Your Mother? Red Roots of White Feminism," in *The Sacred Hoop* (Boston: Beacon Press, 1986), 209–210.

8. This term was suggested to me in a personal communication by Leah Shelleda Fulton.

CHAPTER 8/WOODMAN

1. C. G. Jung, "The Personal and the Collective Unconscious," in *Two Essays on Analytical Psychology*, trans. R. F. C. Hull (New York: Meridian Books, 1956), 79–80.

2. Shakespeare, *Macbeth*, act 1, sc. 5, lines 44–45.

3. William Blake, *The Marriage of Heaven and Hell*, in *Selected Poetry and Prose of William Blake* (New York: The Modern Library, Random House, 1953), 123.

4. Shakespeare, *Macbeth*, act 5, sc. 5, lines 19–26.

5. Emily Dickinson, *The Complete Poems of Emily Dickinson*, ed. Thomas H. Johnson (Boston: Little Brown and Co., 1960), poem no. 761.

6. See Susan Cady, Marian Ronan, and Hal Taussig, *Sophia: The Future of Feminist Spirituality* (New York: Harper & Row, 1986).

CHAPTER 13/YOUNG-EISENDRATH

1. R. T. Hare-Mustin and J. Marecek, "The Meaning of Difference: Gender Theory, Postmodernism, and Psychology," *American Psychologist*, 43 (1988) 6: 455.

2. Polly Young-Eisendrath, "The Female Person and How We Talk About Her," in *Feminist Thought and the Structure of Knowledge*, ed. Mary Gergen (New York: New York University Press, 1987); Polly Young-Eisendrath and Demaris Wehr, "The Fallacy of Individualism and Reasonable Violence Against Women," in *Christianity, Patriarchy and Abuse: A Feminist Critique*, ed. Joanne Carlson Brown and Carole R. Bohn (New York: Pilgrim Press, 1989); Polly Young-Eisendrath and Florence Wiedemann, *Female Authority: Empowering Women Through Psychotherapy* (New York: Guilford, 1987).

3. C. G. Heilbrun, *Writing a Woman's Life* (New York: Norton, 1988), 42.

4. Ellen Moers, as quoted in Heilbrun, 35.

5. Polly Young-Eisendrath, "The Absence of Black Americans as Jungian Analysts," *Quadrant*, Fall 1987, 47.

6. Demaris Wehr, *Jung and Feminism: Liberating Archetypes* (Boston: Beacon Press, 1987) and Andrew Samuels, *The Plural Psyche: Personality, Morality, and the Father* (London: Routledge, 1989).

7. Wehr, *Jung and Feminism*.

8. Luce Irigaray, *Speculum of the Other Woman*, trans. Gillian Gill (Ithaca, N.Y.: Cornell University Press, 1985).

9. Riane Eisler, *The Chalice and the Blade: Our History, Our Future* (San Francisco: Harper & Row, 1987).

10. Jean Lipman-Blumen, *Gender Roles and Power* (Englewood Cliffs, N.J.: Prentice-Hall, 1984).

11. M. Daly, *Gyn/ecology: The Metaethics of Radical Feminism* (Boston: Beacon Press, 1978), R. Reuther, *Sexism and God-Talk* (Boston: Beacon Press, 1983), and N. Goldenberg, *Changing the Gods: Feminism and the End of Traditional Religions* (Boston: Beacon Press, 1979).

12. M. F. Belenky, B. M. Clinchy, N. R. Goldberger, and J. M. Tarule, *Women's*

Ways of Knowing: The Development of Self, Voice and Mind (New York: Basic Books, 1986); Carol Gilligan, *In a Different Voice: Psychological Theory and Women's Development* (Cambridge: Harvard University Press, 1982); and R. T. Hare-Mustin, "An Appraisal of the Relationship Between Women and Psychotherapy: 80 Years After the Case of Dora," *American Psychologist* 38 (1983): 593–601.

13. T. S. Kuhn, *The Structure of Scientific Revolutions* (Chicago: University of Chicago Press, 1962).

CHAPTER 16/STRAHAN

1. Lillian Rubin, *Women of a Certain Age: The Midlife Search for Self* (New York: Harper & Row, 1981).

2. Barbara Walker, ed., *The Women's Encyclopedia of Myths and Secrets* (San Francisco: Harper & Row, 1983), 633–648.

3. Mircea Eliade, *Rites and Symbols of Initiation* (New York: Harper & Row, 1965), 128.

4. C. G. Jung, "The Structure of Dynamics of the Psyche," vol. 8, *Collected Works* (Princeton, N.J.: Princeton University Press, 1969), 387–403.

5. Walter F. Otto, *Dionysus: Myth and Cult* (Bloomington, Ind., and London: Indiana University Press, 1965).

6. Murray Stein, *In Midlife* (Dallas: Spring Publications, 1983), 46–61.

CHAPTER 17/STONE

1. The Shekhina is not actually a goddess but is portrayed in Hebrew literature as a cosmic and sacred figure.

CHAPTER 20/PERERA

1. Erich Neumann, "On the Moon and Matriarchal Consciousness," *Fathers and Mothers* (Zurich: Spring Publications for the Analytical Psychology Club of New York, 1973), 59.

2. Erich Neumann, "Psychological Stages of Feminine Development," *Spring* (1959): 96.

3. Adrienne Rich, "Reforming the Crystal," *The Fact of a Doorframe: Poems Selected and New: 1950–1984* (New York: Norton, 1984), 228.

4. Carolyn G. Heilbrun, *Reinventing Womanhood* (New York: Norton, 1979), 37–50.

5. See Tillie Olsen, *Silences* (New York: Dell, 1989); Adrienne Rich, *Of Woman Born* (New York: Norton, 1986) and *On Lies, Secrets, and Silence* (New York: Norton, 1979); Carolyn Heilbrun, *Reinventing Womanhood* (New York: Norton, 1979); and Dorothy Dinnerstein, *The Mermaid and the Minotaur* (New York: Harper & Row, 1977).

6. See C. G. Jung, "The Symbolic Life," vol. 18, *Collected Works* (Princeton, N.J.: Princeton University Press, 1969), paragraphs 630ff.

CHAPTER 21/HADDON

1. Richard Wilhelm, in his introduction to the *I Ching or Book of Changes* (Princeton, N.J.: Princeton University Press, 1967), lvi.

2. Names and identities of all persons are disguised.

3. Carol Gilligan's research on the distinct moral perspectives of males and females corroborates this image. *In a Different Voice* (Cambridge: Harvard University Press, 1982).

4. This is tale no. 1 in the classical Grimm's collection.

5. Active imagination involves allowing a fantasy to unfold to the mind's eye. It differs from daydreaming in two ways. First, an active effort is exerted to suspend censoring and receive "whatever comes," even if it is nonsensical or disturbing by ego standards. Second, the conscious mind enters into active dialogue with the fantasy, perhaps asking questions and then seeing how the fantasy responds.

6. "If she pursues the [yang] virtues . . . she is to be avoided with fear and loathing as a mutant, a denier of [her feminine] destiny. If she fails to take up these values and pursues others [exclusively yin]—she is weak, vacuous, and superficial." Linda Singer, "Nietzschean Mythologies: The Inversion of Value and the War Against Women," *Soundings* 66/3 (Fall 1983), 283.

7. Such hallmarks of patriarchal culture as these reflect the experience of the individual male, for whom the question "Who am I?" is first answered with the awareness, "I am different from the mother who gave me birth." To assert that difference entails a struggle to overcome the original state of oneness with the maternal source. From this experience derive such patriarchal motifs as separation of subject from object, differentiation, the mutual exclusivity of opposites, competition, and dominance. Such traits as linearity, goal-orientation, and an "upward and onward" mind-set are metaphorically like the penis.

8. See Genia Pauli Haddon, *Body Metaphors: Releasing God-Feminine In Us All* (New York: Crossroad, 1988).

9. Commonly known as *participation mystique*.

10. The Y chromosome is very small compared to the X with which it is paired. It is thought that early in the course of mammalian evolution most of the length of one member of the primordial pair of sex chromosomes broke off and reattached to its mate, resulting in the creation of Y and X chromosomes of very different sizes. This is strikingly parallel to the biblical account of the rib being taken from Adam to form Eve.

11. A single gene on the Y chromosome causes any cell containing it to produce a certain protein on its surface, which functions as a histocompatibility antigen (H-Y antigen)—a substance that rejects grafts of incompatible (that is, "non-Y," or female) tissue. The factor was first discovered in tissue-transplant experiments with mice. It was later found that the same cell-surface protein, H-Y antigen, is responsible for causing the neutral gonad of the embryo to develop into a testicle. It is remarkable that "this single gene locus contributes to two of the most powerful differentiating attributes of individuals: male versus female and self versus other." Paul Saenger, "Abnormal Sex Differentiation," *Journal of Pediatrics* 2 (Jan. 1982), 31.

12. This phenomenon is called *lyonization* after its discoverer, genetic researcher Mary S. Lyon of Great Britain. See T. C. Hsu, *Human and Mammalian Cytogenetics: An Historical Perspective* (New York: Springer-Verlag, 1979), 77.

ABOUT
THE EDITOR

· · · · · · ·

Connie Zweig is a freelance writer and book editor living on a ridgetop in Topanga Canyon, California. She is the former executive editor of *Brain/ Mind Bulletin*, a former columnist for *Esquire*, a regular contributor to the Los Angeles *Times*, and currently senior editor for Jeremy P. Tarcher, Inc. She has a long-standing interest in developmental and transpersonal psychology and, as a meditation student and teacher, has been devoted to the spiritual journey.